A NOT-SO-ELEMENTARY CHRISTIAN METAPHYSICS:

Written in the Hope of Ending the Centuries-old Separation between Philosophy and Science and Science and Wisdom

VOLUME ONE

Re-establishing an Initial Union among Philosophy, Science, and Wisdom by Recovering Our Understanding of Philosophy, Science: How Philosophy, Science, is, and Always has been, Chiefly a Study of the Problem of the One and the Many

To Fr, Patrick Farley,

A courageous young priest.

Best wishes,
Peter
P A Redpath

ADLER-AQUINAS INSTITUTE SPECIAL SERIES

Volume 1

A Not-So-Elementary Christian Metaphysics:

Written in the Hope of Ending the Centuries-old Separation between Philosophy and Science and Science and Wisdom

VOLUME ONE

Peter A. Redpath

Socratic Press

Manitou Springs, Colorado, USA 2012

ISBN: 978-0-9792380-8-6 (paper)

DEDICATED

to

Pope Benedict XVI, Blessed Pope John Paul the Great, and the People of Poland, who have suffered so much and for so long under the cruel yoke of utopian socialism

While I silently pondered these things, and decided to write down my wretched complaint, there appeared standing above me a woman of majestic countenance whose flashing eyes seemed wise beyond the ordinary wisdom of men. Her color was bright, suggesting boundless vigor, and yet she seemed so old that she could not be thought of as belonging to our age. Her height seemed to vary: sometimes she seemed of ordinary human stature, then again her head seemed to touch the top of the heavens. And when she raised herself to her full height she penetrated heaven itself, beyond the vision of human eyes. Her clothing was made of the most delicate threads, and by the most exquisite workmanship; it had—as she afterwards told me—been woven by her own hands into an everlasting fabric. Her clothes had been darkened in color somewhat by neglect and the passage of time, as happens to pictures exposed to smoke. At the lower edge of her robe was woven a Greek Π, at the top the letter Θ, and between them were seen clearly marked stages, like stairs, ascending from the lowest level to the highest. This robe had been torn, however, by the hands of violent men, who had ripped away what they could. In her right hand, the woman held certain books; in her left hand a scepter

When she saw the Muses of poetry standing beside my bed and consoling me with their words, she was momentarily upset and glared at them with burning eyes. "Who let these whores from the theater come to the bedside of this sick man?" she said. "They cannot offer medicine for his sorrows; they will nourish him only with their sweet poison. They kill the fruitful harvest of reason with the sterile thorns of the passions; they do not liberate the minds of men from disease, but merely accustom them to it. I would find it easier to bear if your flattery had, as it usually does, seduced some ordinary dull-witted man. But this man has been educated in the philosophical schools of the Eleatics and the Academy. Get out, you Sirens; your sweetness leads to death. Leave him to be cured and made strong by my Muses.[1]

Anicius Manlius Severinus Boethius (b. 480; d. 524/525)

The Consolation of Philosophy, trans. with an intro. and notes, Richard Green (Indianapolis and New York: The Bobbs-Merrrill Company, Inc., 1962), Bk. 1, Prose 1, pp. 3–5.

CONTENTS

FOREWORD

Those who dare to enter here, beware! *This book should come with a warning label.* It is not for the faint-hearted, nor for those who rest comfortably in the conviction that they actually understand the nature and history of philosophy, science, and, especially, Thomism. Peter A. Redpath's unconventional interpretation of these topics could (probably will) get some readers severely upset. Likely, some will have to rethink virtually everything they had previously thought they knew about these subjects.

Reading this book essentially altered my understanding of the nature and history of philosophy, science, and Thomism (subjects I have been studying for decades and thought I knew fairly well). If you are not up to changing the way you think, do not read this book. Put it down, and rest comfortably in your ignorance.

If you enjoy living dangerously, read on; even buy the book, if you have not already done so. You will be happy you did. It is a boon to philosophy, science, and just the elixir the Catholic Church and Western civilization need at this precarious moment in history.

The task Redpath undertakes in this monograph is monumental, something many tntelligentsia today would consider impossible, absurd: to re-establish in an intial way the essential connection between philosophy and science, and science and wisdom, that started to become severed centuries ago around the time of the birth of "modern science." As impossible and absurd as this goal might appear to some intellectuals today, by the end of this book, Redpath claims, beyond reasonable doubt, to have effected this reunion; and I agree with him.

In making this claim, Redpath does not pretend to show in precise detail how all the specific principles of different divisions of essentially-nominalistic, modern science are specific philosophical principles that explain the division and methods of what, borrowing a phrase from philosopher John N. Deely, Redpath calls science "falsely-so called." Instead, he has written this book as the first volume of a wider project that he hopes, with the help of others, will be able to achieve this longer-term, specific goal.

Because the main goal of his volume entails *reuniting in an initial way* what most contemporary intellectuals claim are two really distinct natures, within the context of this monograph, Redpath understands that he must precisely explain what is this single nature of philosophy and science, how what appear to be two distinct natures are actually one. To do this he has to re-examine the general history of philosophy and science from the ancient Greeks up to the present day.

As he engages in this study, Redpath radically reinterprets the natures of philosophy, science, universals, and analogy. He challenges commonly-received scholarly opinions about the origin and nature of (1) the problems of the one and the many and universals, and (2) nominalism. Following Aristotle and St. Thomas, he maintains that logical and philosophical universals, genera, are not identical; and that, strictly speaking, philosophy, science, is an intellectual habit, not a body of knowledge. He denies that anyone can be a philosopher, scientist, without simultaneously, accepting theism, the existence of God, the human soul, habits, virtues, and the essential connection between science and wisdom. He completely overturns the prevailing interpretation of Descartes's and Rousseau's roles in Western intellectual history (especially in connection with the rise of modern, utopian socialism, upon which he claims, modern science is dependent as a substitute for a real, metaphysical first principle). He even goes so far as to claim that Rousseau is a neo-Averroist and that Rousseau's political thought and contemporary, utopian socialism are rooted in analogous transpositions of teachings that, knowingly or not, Rousseau borrowed from Averroes.

Again, this work is not for the faint-hearted. *Verbum sat sapientiae.*

Curtis L. Hancock
President, The Gilson Society

AUTHOR'S INTRODUCTION

Ever since the start of the twentieth century, and especially toward the rise and end of World War II, some Western intellectuals started to recognize that something was radically wrong with modern Western civilization and culture, that these appeared to be in their twilight years. Starting in the 1930s, these thinkers began to diagnose the problem in some detail. In doing so, in one way or another, they tended to arrive at the same conclusion: outside of the intellectual order of what, even today, Westerners call "science" or "physical science," the West had largely lost its conviction that any truth or wisdom existed. Outside this narrow intellectual sphere, most Westerners had largely turned into skeptics and sophists.

While many contemporary Westerners tend to view the West's present decline to be due to a loss of faith, these intellectuals disagreed. They attributed this decay to a loss of *logos*, of reason, especially of wisdom.

Belief has not been something in decline in the modern West, or world in general. It has existed, is, everywhere. Even "science" is supposed to be simply one more "belief system," or "feeling," supposedly superior to other forms of belief or feeling because it is an "Enlightened," not a backward, "religious belief system" or feeling. The problem with the modern world is not that we believe in nothing. It is that we believe in everything except religion. We have lost our understanding of the range of reason and have largely turned into skeptics and sophists: secularized fundamentalists.

Hence, the peculiar mental extremism that Westerners tend to exhibit. On the one hand, like all skeptics, we pretend to shy away from being judgmental. Since the whole of truth and wisdom supposedly reside in "physical science," and since all truth and wisdom essentially involve being judgmental, not making judgments outside the area of physical science is supposed to be a self-evident principle of the modern Western creed. Anyone who does not unquestioningly follow this creed is supposed to be, evidently, intellectually backward, not a true believer, a rube, unsophisticated, and (worst of all), intolerant. Within the modern West's Enlightened belief system, the only sin (except for the Enlightened) is for a person to behave inconsistently with his or her belief system: to be a hypocrite.

Of course, as skeptics, Westerners cannot, with any intellectual consistency, rationally justify making any of the above skeptical judgments. Skeptical judgment is an oxymoron. Skeptics are not supposed to be judgmental. Skeptics, however, do not worry about being logically consistent. They know *with absolute certainty* that all knowledge is a kind of belief. Hence, modern Western skeptics do what skeptics always do within this situation: they use sophistry to defend their hubristic and imperious intellectual claims.

Anyone familiar with Western intellectual history knows that (1) metaphysical principles found civilizations and that, based upon these principles, civilizations generate cultures of different kinds; and (2) once cultures lose their conviction about the truth of their founding metaphysical principles, they decay from within. Hence, the existence of strong metaphysical convictions generates civilizations, and skepticism and doubt about them kill civilizations.

Realizing these truths about civilzational and cultural experience, some Western thinkers of the last century recognized that the West needed a renaissance of metaphysical reason to bridge the gap between wisdom and science that appeared to be the root cause of the skeptical and sophistic mindset that, for centuries, has been causing the West progressively to rot from within. Unhappily, having spent most of their lives diagnosing the problem, these scholars did not have time to do what, with their help, I have tried to do in this book: write the full story they had sought to tell.

Peter A. Redpath
Rector, Adler-Aquinas Institute
Tutor, Harrison Middleton University

ACKNOWLEDGMENTS

While I started composing this work in early June 2011 and completed the first draft of it at the end of July of the same year, the research that went into the book took me decades. During that time, I have been blessed to have had the counsel and encouragement of my colleague and friend Curtis L. Hancock who, since the 1980s, has helped me clarify my thinking about many of the issues I discuss in this monograph. Had it not been for his prodding, and that of our mutual friend and colleague, Piotr Jaroszyński, Chair of the Philosophy of Culture at the Pope John Paul II Catholic Univeristy of Lublin, a good likelihood exists that I would have postponed starting this project for years, or never have begun it.

In addition to these two colleagues and friends, I have several others without whose help this book would not have been possible to complete: Patrick S. J. Carmack, John N. Deely, Jude P. Dougherty, Jorge J. E. Gracia, Robert Ginsberg, David Curd, Max Weismann, and my wife Lorraine.

Other than Hancock and Jaroszyński, Deely is one of the few contemporary intellectuals and students of St. Thomas that I trust to understand what I write and, pulling no punches, to tell me when he thinks I am wrong and precisely why I am wrong. He kindly took time to read much of the typescript of this book and gave me many suggestions about how to improve it.

I thank Pat Carmack for publishing the book through his Socratic Press; Jorge Gracia, for showing me how to do research; Robert Ginsberg, for showing me how to write; David Curd and Max Weismann for providing me with readings that helped me tie together much of my final thinking about the topics I discuss within this monograph; Jude Dougherty, for the many acts of encouragement that, for decades, he has given me in my work; and my long-suffering wife Lorraine for patiently enduring the long hours I had to spend completing this part of my project.

One

WHY CARE ABOUT METAPHYSICS, CHRISTIAN METAPHYSICS AND ENDING THE SEPARATION BETWEEN PHILOSOPHY AND SCIENCE?

1. Some reasons why philosophical metaphysics is essential to the existence and nature of philosophy, science

For centuries after the development of modern physical "science," Western "philosophers" largely avoided the study of metaphysics. As I will show in this book, a chief reason they did so was because, long before the modern age had come to be, the West had largely lost its understanding of the nature of philosophy and science, and the crucial role that metaphysics plays in relation to the existence and nature of philosophy and science. As a result, currently metaphysics has largely become the "Cinderella of the Sciences," and the West has largely lost its understanding of the nature of philosophy and science.

If asked about the nature of metaphysics, many people today, including many professional intellectuals, "philosophers" falsely-so-called, would answer in a way that would identify the study with something akin to "news from the spirit world." If asked about the nature of philosophy and science, most contemporary "philosophers" could not precisely explain the nature of either and most "scientists," also falsely-so-called, would likely conflate science with mathematical physics, but could give no rational explanation for so doing.

From a practical standpoint, educationally and culturally for the contemporary world, and the West especially, the results of this neglect of metaphysics and lack of understanding of its relation to philosophy, science, have been devastating. In ancient Greek and later medieval times, metaphysics had been largely equivalent to what professional "philosophers" today call "philosophy of science." During the high points of ancient Greek culture and the high middle ages of Christendom, metaphysics was viewed as "first philosophy." It was recognized to be the only discipline that existed capable of judging the nature, divisions, and methods of the different arts and sciences, the only human science that could rationally judge the other sciences and rationally explain how they relate to each other and justify their existence in relationship to human life as a whole.

In the architectonically-arranged hierarchy of classical science, metaphysics tended to be viewed as the final cause of all the other arts and sciences: the one science that all the other sciences were ordered toward generating as the highest intellectual achievement of the human mind and chief explanation for the nature and existence of the arts and sciences, human culture, and civilization. One reason for this is that some influential ancients, like Aristotle, recognized that the principles of metaphysics were common to all the arts and sciences, and that devoid of integrated arts and sciences no culture can exist. Because all the arts and sciences borrow and use these principles as their chief measures, criteria, of truth, in a way, metaphysics provided for classical philosophical antiquity, classical culture, the chief means for fulfilling the Delphic Oracle's admonition to every human being that the key to achieving science is to "know thyself."

By, in some way, containing all the knowing principles borrowed from it and used in all the arts sciences, classical metaphysics contained for the arts and sciences the means of self-knowledge, of rationally explaining to practitioners of each and every science the origin and rational justification behind the assumptions they used as their starting points for judging truth within their respective disciplines. By so doing, it rationally justified the claims of all the arts and sciences to be arts or sciences at all, and not to be simple matters of belief or arbitrary dogmatism.

In a way, as the final cause of all the other arts and sciences, some ancients, like Aristotle, recognized that all the other arts and sciences were borrowing, analogously transferring to their own disciplines, principles, rules, for measuring truth that chiefly belong to metaphysics. As a result, strictly speaking, metaphysics alone was worthy of the name "philosophy" or "science." Even though the science of metaphysics had not existed in a fully-developed form prior to the philosophies, sciences, of physics and mathematics, the terms "philosophy," "science," had been analogously transferred to other divisions of human knowing (in a way had been given to them on loan, inasmuch as these divisions of knowing maintained an essential connection to the gradually-emerging science of metaphysics).

For this reason, absent philosophical metaphysics, strictly speaking, no coherent philosophy of education can exist; and no rational means exists to explain how (1) *arts and sciences can integrate with each other to produce a common culture or civilization; or* (2) *how any art or science can exist at all. In fact, absent an essential connection to philosophical metaphysics, as I will show beyond reasonable doubt in this monograph, strictly speaking, no art or science can exist.*

What I say in the paragraph immediately above is so true that, within the twentieth century, the negative effects of the West's loss of understanding of the nature of metaphysics in relation to arts and sciences started to cause "philosophy" departments at colleges and universities, especially those dealing with classical philosophy, to become largely gutted. As a result, other disciplines, philosophical mimics, generally referred to by the oxymoronic title "social sciences" (oxymoronic because, by nature, they are not social or scientific) attempted to replace metaphysics as the queen of the sciences.

Since they could not fulfill this role, higher education became weakened to the point that many institutions of higher learning have had to close, or will have to close. And the cost of education in general has skyrocketed.

We cannot be wrong about the nature of science and expect not to suffer damage educationally, culturally, politically, and economically.

While, during the twentieth century, the hate-metaphysics attitude that had dominated the West for several centuries had started to abate somewhat, it had come too late to save many of the West's institutions of higher learning from their essential quest to self-destruct. Having lost with metaphysics what little sense of self-identity they had had, they could no longer even pretend intelligently to explain to others precisely what was their nature or chief aim.

During this time, some metaphysics texts appeared to try to stem the tide of Western educational and cultural decay, including ones written by students of St. Thomas Aquinas (b. 1224/25; d. 1274). Most, if not all, of these were composed specifically for use in academic programs. None was especially successful because none was able to show in adequate detail (1) how philosophical metaphysics is crucial to understanding the nature, divisions, and methods of the classical and contemporary sciences and (2) for solving the host of educational and cultural problems that we face today as necessary effects of the West's loss of understanding of the nature of philosophical metaphysics and the role it plays in integrating human culture and civilization.

I write this book, then, in part, to help reverse this trend: to provide a work in philosophical metaphysics that will serve as a philosophy of science that can show in an intelligible, general way, the nature, methods, and divisions of the sciences, how these arose historically, and why they are reasonable.

I also write it, however, as a Christian, Thomistic metaphysics, because I think that only this metaphysics has the intellectual resources to (1) bridge the gap between ancient and contemporary culture so as to end the centuries-old separation between philosophy and science and (2) thereby, help stem, and reverse, the tide of the West's cultural and civilizational decline.

2. How Descartes became the proximate, modern cause of the gradual separation of philosophy and science, science and wisdom

From the end of Greek antiquity up until the start of the twentieth century, the terms "philosophy" and "science" were largely used synonymously. For this reason, when he wrote his classic work in physics, Sir Issac Newton (b. 1642; d. 1727) understood himself to be working as a scientist/philosopher. Hence, he entitled his ground-breaking book in physics, *Principia mathematica philosophiae naturalis* (*The Mathematical Principles of Natural Philosophy*, not *Principia mathematica scientiae naturalis* [*The Mathematical Principles of Natural Science*]). Further evidence of the truth of the claim made in the first sentence of this paragraph above is that St. Thomas Aquinas, who is well-known to have been influenced by Aristotle (b. 384 BC; d. 323 BC) and neo-Platonism, used these terms synonymously.[1] Noting the radical difference between St. Thomas's understanding of "science" and the prevailing contemporary notion, Armand A. Maurer (b. 1915; d. 2008) remarks:

> Today, no one would think of equating philosophy and science, even though there is little agreement as to what the distinction between them is. Science in general is thought of as any reasoned knowledge that is universal and systematic. The ideal of scientific knowledge is an exact science such as mathematical physics, which uses precise mathematical calculations and a highly refined method involving experimentation, formation of hypotheses and their verification. Whatever philosophy may be, it obviously does not fit this description.[2]

The move in the West toward separating the two terms and have them designate different human activities came about gradually, over centuries, and had its proximate root in the work of the person often honorifically called, "The Father of Modern Philosophy": René Descartes (b. 1596; d. 1650). Descartes thought of himself as divinely elected to be the first true philosopher *and* scientist, as someone who had given birth to true philosophy after centuries of intellectual decadence in which, strictly speaking, philosophy, science, had not existed. Prior to him, he claimed no one had possessed "The Method" of science, philosophy, as a system of clear and distinct ideas whereby human beings could finally completely know truth and totally eradicate doubt from our minds.

Strictly speaking, as I have argued extensively in my book *Cartesian Nightmare: An Introduction to Transcendental Sophistry*, Descartes was no philosopher.[3] Like Italian renaissance humanists before him, strictly speaking, he was a sophist.[4] His sophistic method consisted of an elaborate reduction of philosophy to systematic logic (a logical system of supposedly clear and distinct ideas) as a means of separating mathematics and physics from the influence of metaphysics and revealed theology, while, simultaneously, identifying mathematics and physics with the whole of science, understood as rational, logically-systematic, knowledge of sense reality.

As I show in the above-mentioned work, among the many mistakes Descartes made in working out his project were to (1) conflate truth, science, and wisdom; (2) relocate truth, science, and wisdom from acts of intellect, or reason, to that of will; (3) replace the human soul with a "mind," which he confounded with a collection of ideas; and (4) separate philosophy, science, and wisdom from any essential connection to a human faculty, habit, or virtue whose first principle is the intellectual soul of an individually-existing human being, a soul/body composite.

For Descartes, to know, to possess truth, is identical with knowing scientifically. As Étienne Gilson (b. 1884; d. 1978) tells us, Descartes's grand project consisted in knowing everything by one method with the same amount of certainty or knowing nothing at all.[5] Descartes had reduced truth, all knowledge (including wisdom) to science and was condemned to possess the whole of science or no truth at all.

Further complicating his mistakes, Descartes reduced truth (and with it philosophy, science, and wisdom) to strength of will. According to him, truth is chiefly a relation between the human will and intellect, an act of will on the intellect, not of reason or intellect considered as such. For him, the power of the will to cause reason to attend to, or focus on, an idea, is the cause of all truth, is truth, just as weakness of will that causes reason (which is simply a collection of ideas) to wander under the influence of unrestrained imagination (again, simply a collection of ideas) is the cause of all error, is error.

By replacing the human soul with a collection of ideas he called a "mind" and eliminating from the individual knower any numerically-one and intrinsic principle, starting point, that generated many natural and acquired psychological powers, Descartes and his intellectual descendants became totally incapable of explaining how science, philosophy, can consist of many acts performed by numerically-one subject. In so doing, he (1) separated wisdom, science, philosophy, from the individual intellect of the individual knower; (2) transformed wisdom, science, philosophy, into will-power having no individual as its principle of origin; and (3) changed the formal object of wisdom, science, philosophy into a system, or nominalistic collection of ideas or facts (somewhat resembling Plato's World of Forms), clearly visible only to someone (like him) with a will supposedly strong enough to enable his mind to see it.

Regarding the physical world around us, Descartes maintained that only mathematical ideas viewed by an exceptionally strong will can stabilize reason to be able to apprehend truth about physical reality. Hence, long before Friedrich Nietzsche (b. 1884; d. 1900), in his founding principles, Descartes had made the egregious mistakes of alienating truth, philosophy, science, and wisdom from natural reason, human habituation, and intellectual virtue, and identifying all wisdom, science, and philosophy, including that about the

physical universe, with practical science and practical science with
will-power.

3. How, by reducing metaphysics to history, Rousseau and his progeny replaced metaphysics with modern utopian socialism and transformed Cartesian will-power into the utopian socialist will-to-power

Unhappily, in short, for subsequent generations, modern "philosophy's," "science's," birth with Descartes had been accompanied by,
founded upon, (1) a disordered understanding of the human person
as a pure spirit: (2) an imperious, rationally-unjustifiable, attempt to
reduce the whole of wisdom, philosophy, science, truth, and
knowledge to some blind urge to power; and (3) a similar attempt to
reduce all knowledge of the physical world around us to the order of
modern mathematical physics (often today called "empirical science" or "positivism") and its method of productive reason. As a
result, even if philosophy, science, had existed prior to him, anyone
coming after him who accepted his method and imitated it, could
not, strictly speaking, be a philosopher, scientist.

All of us are born into problems and difficulties that we in-
herit from others. For centuries the Western world has been beset by
a host of social problems that resulted from mistakes made over the
last several centuries by Descartes and those who accepted many of
the founding principles of their "philosophies," "science," upon disordered notions of human nature, human knowing, and metaphysics
that they, more or less, directly inherited from Descartes.

Consider some simple examples of such disordered ways of
thinking common to the contemporary Western mind. Today, virtually all, somewhat-educated, Westerners tend unquestioningly to accept that "science" and "positivistic science," or "mathematical
physics," are identical. Ask virtually any Western college student
today the question, "What is truth?" and the student will tend to reply: "A fact," or "What is factual." Follow with the question, "What

is a fact?", and the same student will tend to answer, "What can be proven." Ask, "What does the word 'proof' mean?", and the student will tend to say: "What can be scientifically, or experimentally, tested or demonstrated."

Among other things, evident about such replies is the tendency that contemporary Western college students have to rule out evident truths and many traditional subjects of scientific study (like metaphysics, ethics, politics) from possessing truth. The mind of the contemporary Western college student tends to reduce the whole of truth to positivism: the practical science of mathematical physics. Apart from accepting truth to exist in positivistic science, the contemporary Western college student, like most Western adults, tends to be an absolute skeptic.

This situation has become so pronounced in the contemporary West that, on 22 March 2011, the Vatican issued a declaration entitled "Decree on the Reform of Ecclesiastical Studies of Philosophy," regarding the crucial role of philosophy, especially metaphysics, in training priests. Commenting upon this declaration, Vatican Secretary of Education Cardinal Zenon Grocholewski said that the most fundamental aspects of life are under assault today: "[R]eason itself is menaced by utilitarianism, skepticism, relativism, and distrust of reason's ability to know the truth regarding the fundamental problems of life." He added that science and technology, those icons of what he called "materialist philosophies," cannot "satiate man's thirst in regard to the ultimate questions: What does happiness consist of? Who am I? Is the world the fruit of chance? What is my destiny? etc. Today, more than ever, the sciences are in need of wisdom."

Westerners today owe the tendency to think precisely the way we now do about science and philosophy chiefly to another Frenchman: Jean-Jacques Rousseau (b. 1712; d. 1778). Like many thinkers of his time, Rousseau admired the twofold attempt by Descartes to overcome the growing skepticism of his age and, simultaneously, to separate philosophy and science from the influence of theology and theologians. Like other admirers of parts of Descartes's project, Rousseau recognized that Descartes's attempt metaphysically to refound science and philosophy in terms of a system of clear and distinct ideas was overly ambitious. He realized that the success of Descartes's dream to join all our ideas into a unified scientific body of knowledge depended upon overcoming a chief weakness in Descartes's system: the ability of substances to communicate.

As is well known, Descartes had attempted metaphysically to construct his scientific system by maintaining that only two substances exist, mind and matter; and that these substances cannot communicate. Descartes considered matter to be totally inactive and mind, or spirit, to be the only thing that acts.

Rousseau recognized that, in the real world, matter and mind communicate. Since Descartes could not explain this communication between the substances of mind, or spirit, and matter, Rousseau resigned to overcome this failure by accepting a position that Descartes had rejected. He declared "modern philosophy's principles" to be "essentially dualistic, animistic, and obscure."[6] Hence, Rousseau maintained, "only spirits are substances." He thought that only spirits exist and even "apparently inanimate beings, like stones, are animate."[7]

While Rousseau accepted Descartes's claim that science is a system of clear and distinct ideas, he rejected Descartes's contention that God had given us this system simultaneously whole in a multitude of clear and distinct ideas buried in our mind waiting there to be uncovered. Instead, Rousseau constructed an elaborate fairy tale: *a utopian history about human nature and origin that replaced metaphysics with history as the means to explain the nature and development of true science, philosophy.*

Rousseau maintained that, under the influence of the "voice of conscience," or "tolerance," God has intended this system of science, metaphysics, to emerge from the history of the human race through progressive self-development (what Westerners, today, tend to call "progress"). In this process, in his classic work entitled *Émile or On Education*, Rousseau claimed that God intends humanity's true teacher to be a person of inspired, or Enlightened, faith, the singular person of strong feeling who has only nature as a teacher.[8]

Shortly prior to Rousseau, Newton had also rejected Descartes's metaphysical understanding of science as a system of clear and distinct ideas buried in his soul and had conceived of science, philosophy, metaphysics, as a prophetic history. Newton had conceived of this history to be deflated theology, historical truth about God's operation in creation.[9]

Metaphysically, historically, considered, Newton looked upon the whole universe and its parts as a riddle, a secret, that he could read by applying pure thought to the world around him, "certain mythic clues which God had left about the world to allow a sort of philosopher's treasure hunt to the esoteric brotherhood." He believed that a secret brotherhood had transmitted these truths, this hidden teaching, about the nature of universe in an unbroken chain back to the original cryptic revelation in Babylonia.[10]

Beyond these strange ideas, Newton thought that, "throughout history, God continuously raised up prophets to lead his people back to the original truth revealed to the first followers of Jesus."[11] He believed he was one of these prophets, a magi "descended from a long line of scientific prophets who had anticipated his discoveries in a prefigured and oracular fashion." Apparently, he saw his birth on 25 December 1642 as a sign of his special relation to the Magi.

In a fashion analogous to many Renaissance humanists and to the medieval Islamic thinker Averroes (ibn Rushd, b. 1126; d. 1198), Newton believed that Scripture hides a true teaching, philosophy, science, metaphysics. But, according to Newton, this teaching is about the history of creation, the original Christian religion, not a *mystical and esoteric* moral or metaphysical system (as many Renaissance humanists had thought) or a historically-emerging social system (as Rousseau had thought). In standard Renaissance humanist fashion, Newton maintained that the educational deficiency of their audience had caused Moses and other Biblical authors to describe this creation history poetically to make it comprehensible.[13] By so doing, these writers gave to these simple truths about the original Christian religion and physical creation a lofty moral and metaphysical appearance that a correct exegesis of Scripture would deflate.[12]

In *Cartesian Nightmare* I have argued extensively that, despite claims by Gilson to the contrary, precisely speaking, Descartes did not move the West from the skepticism of Michel de Montaigne to a new philosophy. Precisely speaking, Descartes moved the West from the predominance of one branch of the classical liberal arts, the *trivium* (the poetry and rhetoric of Italian renaissance humanism) to another, the *quadrivium*.

Strictly speaking, Descartes did not generate a new philosophy or a return to constructive philosophical thinking. He wedded together a new rhetoric and poetic view of the world in which mathematical abstraction united to a new logic of invention, not the rhetoric and poetic view of the world that had dominated Italian renaissance humanism, would prevail as the primary means by which Westerners would, from that point on, read the Book of Nature.[14]

In doing this, I maintain that Descartes (1) was doing little more than making an attempted correction in the more major political revolution initiated centuries before him by Francesco Petrarcha (Petrarch, b. 1304; d. 1374) and (2), under the rubric of the *quadrivium*, was involving himself in a poetic and rhetorical continuation of the age-old battle between poets and philosophers that Plato (b. 424/423 BC; d. 348/347 BC) had described in Book Ten of his famous *Republic*. Under the rubric of the "Battle of the Arts" this conflict had resurfaced during the twelfth century between faculty members of the cathedral school of Chartres and the monastery of St. Victor in Paris; in the thirteenth century between members of the faculties of arts and theology at the University of Paris; and during the Italian renaissance with Petrarch and his Renaissance humanist followers.[15]

Part of the thesis of this introductory chapter is that we get a more accurate understanding of Descartes's scientific project and its affect upon subsequent generations if we see it as a continuation of the Italian renaissance humanist movement, if we see Descartes and his progeny not as coming out of, or continuing, the Western philosophical tradition (which had died centuries before Descartes), but as coming out of and continuing the Italian renaissance humanist (poetic/rhetorical) tradition.

Once we do this we become better able to understand the modern and contemporary ages as a whole and to recognize the truth of a startling statement that Gilson makes in his classic, *Reason and Revelation in the Middle Ages*. There he tells any historian who might investigate the sources of "modern rationalism" that an uninterrupted chain of influence exists from the Averroistic tradition of the Masters of Arts of Paris to the European freethinkers of the seventeenth and eighteenth centuries.[16]

Clearly, this neo-Averroistic tendency is present within much of the Italian, and post-Italian, renaissance humanist movement. It is clearly present later in Newton. I maintain that it is equally present in Descartes's metaphysical claim that philosophy, or science, is a hidden system buried in his soul like in a book that only he, or someone who imitates his *Method*, can read.

During the twelfth century, Averroes had constructed a sophistic argument to safeguard the rights and freedom of philosophy against intrusion by theologians and others and to protect Islam against heresies that a weak understanding of philosophy is prone to generate. This sophistic argument consisted of distinguishing three categories of human minds and three corresponding degrees and limits of human understanding, learning, and teaching "of one single and same truth": (1) the most true and abstract scientific mind of the philosopher, which supposedly apprehends, learns, and teaches this truth in an absolute sense in its hidden, interior meaning, through demonstrative reasoning "from the necessary to the necessary by the necessary"; (2) the less true and symbolic unscientific mind of the logician, and theologian, which grasps this truth in its exterior, imaginative, symbolic meaning, through logical interpretation and probability; and (3) the simple religious and believing mind, which apprehends this one and same truth through the imagination, emotions, and oratorical arguments.

Gilson explained that, while Averroes claimed, "the Koran is truth itself," he maintained that the Koran "has an exterior and symbolic meaning for the uninstructed, an interior and hidden meaning for scholars." He considered revelation's true meaning to be its most lofty meaning. Its most lofty meaning was its philosophical, or scientific, meaning.

Averroes thought that philosophical truth is "the highest type of human truth." This means that, for Averroes: (1) human truth is the highest type of Koranic truth; (2) the highest type of human truth is philosophy, or science; (3) philosophical, or scientific, truth is present in a hidden fashion in the Koran, and (4) only philosophers can recognize it![17]

Unhappily for subsequent philosophical history, I maintain that (1) Petrarch took and adapted Averroes's division of human minds by designing his own program and method for *harmonizing religion and philosophy* and a new, fabricated interpretation of philosophy and its history to support it: (2) *mutatis mutandis*, Descartes unwittingly adopted Petrarch's program and method, and a new interpretation of philosophy and its history to support it; and (3) *mutatis mutandis*, to correct weaknesses in Descartes's system, by introducing his own trinitarian hierarchy of three categories of human minds and limits of human understanding, Rousseau accepted and modified the program and method of Descartes and Petrarch, and introduced a new interpretation of philosophy and its history to support it.

In Petrarch's program a new mind and profession replaced the trinitarian hierarchy of Averroes. In Petrarch's scheme, the highest form of human mind is that of theologizing poets (*poetae theologisantes*), not the mind of philosophers. As a complement of this new mind in the order of teaching and learning, Petrarch created a new profession of poetry that combines the techniques of rhetoric, poetry, and theology: *theologia poetica* (poetic theology).

In short, Petrarch appears simply to have attempted to use dialectical arguments and reductionism to defeat the claims of Averroes. He accepted the truth of Averroes's premise that the whole of truth is a hidden teaching, or body of knowledge; but he sought to drive Averroes's teaching into an opposite and an unwelcome conclusion by claiming that this truth is contained in the Book of Nature, which only the theologizing poet, not the philosopher, had the capacity to read.

From the standpoint of the prevailing, contemporary Western view of the relationship between philosophy and science, crucial to understand is that, in attempting to reform Descartes's view of systematic science, by using an analogous sort of dialectical argument against Descartes to that used by Petrarch against Averroes, Rousseau shakes hands across the centuries with Petrarch and Averroes. Descartes had reformed Petrarch's teaching by claiming that the whole of science exists completely within the human mind as a system of clear and distinct ideas; but only a person of exceptional ability, like Descartes, could recognize it. Recognizing that Descartes could not explain how mind and matter interact, Rousseau attempted to solve this problem by getting rid of Descartes's notion of matter and of Descartes's claims that, through application of simple Cartesian doubt, we find the system of science whole and complete in our minds and that only the Cartesian can read it.

To effect his goal, Rousseau (1) reduced matter to spirit and (2) conceived Descartes's scientific system of clear and distinct ideas as initially obscure but spiritually- and historically-emerging, in a neo-Averroistic mental trinity, through the ideas of tolerance, progress, and the voice of conscience. For Rousseau scientific truth historically evolves, is the evolution of historical consciousness, and only the Enlightened, tolerant mind can read this history.

While Rousseau accepted Descartes's claim that science is a system of clear and distinct ideas, Rousseau rejected Descartes's contention that God had buried this system in our minds simultaneously whole in the present, and that truth consists in simple will-power. Instead, Rousseau maintained that God has intended this system of science to emerge from the human race, under the influence of the voice of conscience, or tolerance, through progressive self-development, or "progress." In short, truth consists in the socialist will-to-power.

Rousseau contended that conscience is a way of speaking: an oracle, or voice, that moves us to project our emotions in increasingly unselfish, "tolerant" ways across three stages of development: from being a child of mechanical instinct, to being a moral agent, to becoming a fully social civic being. For Rousseau, knowledge, science, true communication between substances, are simply the long-term result of projected emotion, of an increasingly socialistic will to, and extension of, emotional power. As he saw it, the voice of conscience is God's voice, free speech, an act of increasing states of tolerance or compassion whereby human nature emotionally emerges, or evolves, beyond a more primitive mechanical system of selfish individualism to an imperfectly social and moral stage, to, finally, a perfectly political social system of true science.

Rousseau realized that conscience in the proper sense (scientific will) cannot exist prior to the existence of knowledge and reason, the civic stage of complete Enlightenment. Where no truth exists, strictly speaking, no real conscience, freedom, or human communication exists. Like Descartes, Rousseau conflated truth and science and, like Descartes and Nietzsche, he located truth in an act of strong will, or emotion. For him, prior to the existence of real human science, no human truth exists. Hence, before humanity reaches its final stage of total social inclusion, a kind of totalitarian or collectivist civil will, scientific Enlightenment, Rousseau held that what we call "conscience" is a primitive, mechanical-like groping toward the human good; and no real, *scientific* will or true freedom exists.

Only the Enlightened system of ideas (global socialism effected by the General Will) can make conscience (emotive, individual will) fully emerge. Because non-Enlightened ideas (1) are obscure and indistinct feelings and (2) cannot produce audible sound, they can produce no real communication, no real free speech. Rousseau maintained that such ideas generate the counterfeit noise of fanatics. Hence, prior to the new Enlightenment political world order, conscience and true freedom had no voice. No real free speech or human communication, existed. Strictly speaking, human beings were not scientific, not free; and no true, or social, justice could exist.

Rousseau maintained that the voice of conscience maturely develops as a result of a system of human emotions (sensations of the self as a body) feeling themselves together, emerging, into a system of other, self-disclosed, individual emotions (the idea of self as spirit). Union of these two systems of emotion generates the voice we call "conscience": a voice that moves us to transport ourselves from one system into another, from a child of mechanical instinct to a moral agent, to a civic being.

For Rousseau, the voice of conscience, God's voice, is the act of free speech, an act of disclosure whereby the system of nature transports itself (human nature), according to a neo-Averroistic mental trinity, beyond a more primitive mechanical system to a social and, finally, political system. Conscience does this by changing the way we talk (just as a male's voice changes as he enters adolescence) as we move from the lower stage to the higher.

At the mechanical stage of human instinct, which corresponds to Averroes's totally imaginative and emotional level of the ordinary believer, persuaded only by oratorical arguments, Rousseau thinks that God's voice (conscience) speaks through the mechanical voice of human instinct, human nature viewed as a dumb animal, or machine. At the moral stage of educational development, which corresponds to Averroes's second stage of symbolic mind of the logician and theologian, God's voice still speaks through the Book of

Nature. But the Book of Nature is humanity emerged toward the first, primitive stage of Enlightenment reason and Scientific will, not the book of mechanical human instinct. At this point, the system of Enlightened ideas enables God, for the first time in human history, to utter his voice, and make it heard by the human spirit, not just by the body. That is, human beings get a taste of spirit, of freedom!

Rousseau uses the idea of tolerance to conflate the disciplines of metaphysics and politics and reduce the moral and political principle of justice to an epistemological tool serving a political project: to effect a state of higher metaphysical and historical consciousness, a state of Enlightened socialist feeling and Enlightened reading of history which, in our time, in some quarters, appears to be increasingly becoming the chief end of science. *In short, in Rousseau's hands, the classical theoretical discipline of metaphysics becomes reduced to a hermeneutic for reading history serving as a handmaid for effecting a practical political agenda: global socialism.*[18]

Chiefly because of the work of Rousseau, Descartes's dream of the monopoly of the mathematician alone over the whole of science of the universe did not last long. Chiefly through the writings of Rousseau, Enlightenment thinkers started to realize that Descartes's project to ground science as a logical system of clear and distinct ideas buried in the mind was a failure.

Hence, following Rousseau, and under the influence Newton, Enlightenment intellectuals like Immanuel Kant (b. 1724; d. 1804) and Georg Hegel (b. 1770; d. 1831) started to view the attempt to establish science as a social system of clear and distinct ideas to be the human project, a chief end of human life, an essential part of the human spirit's call of conscience and practical reason to cause the human spirit to emerge from conditions of religious backwardness.

The modern and Enlightenment reduction of science and truth to the social system of mathematical physics politically justified by the hermeneutic of tolerance in service to the socialist state is without intellectual justification. Apart from universal feeling that some higher, more-inclusive social feeling, a kind of neo-Aver-roistic, socialist intellect shared by "tolerant" people collectively establishes truth, it has no criterion of truth. It is little more than Enlightenment intellectual relativism, neo-sophistry: a myth.

Rousseau looks to me as if he knew this. In his hands "tolerant" people occupy the analogous position of Averroes's philosopher (and the separated possible intellect that knows through him), Petrarch's theologizing poets, Descartes's extraordinary man of pure reason, Newton's magi and prophets, Kant's Enlightened intellectual, Hegel's World Historical person, Marx's proletariat, and the liberal arts as handmaidens to higher learning. In his hands, science, philosophy, and wisdom become reduced to being in the right historical state of mind, having the right feelings about accepting any and all differences that the new possible intellect of Enlightened intellectuals at any time collectively dictate.

In his famous *Social Contract*, Rousseau simply analogously transposes Averroes's teaching about the unity of the scientific soul (a single, separated intellect that knows whatever truth humans know) from the order of theoretical to practical reason, thereby transforming Averroes's single human intellect for the entire human race into the General Will of the political body: a social will. *By so doing Rousseau gave birth to modern utopian and scientific socialism and its tendency to deny the reality of individual freedom and individual intelligence just as Averroes had denied the existence of knowledge, science, and freedom to the individual mind and the existence of the individual soul after death.*[19]

Rousseau's influence on Kant is legendary. Kant considered Rousseau to be another Newton. He claimed that just as Newton had completed the science of external nature and laid bare the order and regularity of the external world, Rousseau had discovered the hidden nature of man.

Rousseau's teachings about tolerance heavily influenced Kant's political writings, especially his famous work, "An Answer to the Question 'What is Enlightenment?'." Kant's political writings, views about Enlightenment, in turn, heavily influenced Hegel, who heavily influenced Karl Marx (b. 1818; d. 1883).[20] In this way, I maintain Rousseau's teaching about human knowledge and science gradually became the chief influence for the emergence of a neo-Averroistic understanding of science and an essential union between science and utopian socialism in the West in our time.

Ultimately, today, the reduction of "science" to positivistic science is essentially wedded to, depends upon, utopian socialism as its imitation of a metaphysical foundation. Today, a neo-Averroism inherited from Rousseau and the disordered understanding of tolerance that this neo-Averroism essentially employs as its hermeneutic for reading history has gradually become in the West the only means for scientifically and philosophically understanding politics, ethics, and truth in general.

Henceforth, serious concern about traditional metaphysical and moral issues about who we are as human beings, how we originated, what life is all about, and what is our ultimate destiny are supposed to be left to Enlightened, utopian-socialist intellectuals, intellectuals schooled in the methods of modern mathematical physics. They are not to be left to speculation of untrained specialists, to petty, bourgeois, philistine, individualists as a Marxist might say.[21]

4. Why recovering a proper understanding of metaphysics is essential to restoring a proper understanding of philosophy, science, and their essential relation to wisdom

In my opinion, the disembodied reason of Descartes, the depersonalized, collectivist reason promoted by Rousseau, and the anti-contemplative reductionism of modern and contemporary physical "science" falsely-so-called are foundational elements of the murderous depersonalization promoted by modern utopian, and scientific, socialism like Nazism, Fascism, and Marxism. Having a view of human reason totally out of contact with reality, these thinkers and the Enlightenment socialists they spawned, had no way of properly understanding real, individual, human relationships: individual, free, rational, living, loving acts. They had no way of comprehending human beings as metaphysical, contemplative beings, or moral or political agents. According to all these thinkers, outside of mathematically-measurable data, or mechanistically- or socialistically-controlled events, no truth exists about the physical universe that real human beings inhabit and no real relations that exist in that world are comprehensible.

For the purpose of understanding the main arguments of this book, need exists to comprehend that the metaphysical principles that underlie the prevailing, contemporary, Western understanding of science and its development are not philosophical. They are sophistic principles of human nature, conscience, and natural law; chiefly ideological, propagandistic, principles derived from Rousseau's sophistic, utopian dream of human nature, science, and happiness. Strictly speaking, no rational justification exists to reduce the whole of philosophy, science, wisdom, and truth to the procedures of the contemporary social system of mathematical physics. Such a reduction is founded upon a rationally unjustified assumption, nothing else.

Hence, if we want to transcend this fundamentalistic, Enlightenment mindset, and the murderous, utopian socialism that exists chiefly to justify it, in place of the disordered understandings of human reason that Enlightenment intellectuals mistakenly claimed to be the metaphysical foundations of philosophy, science, wisdom, and truth, then the acting person (the sentient, embodied individual actively engaged in free, personal, living relationships) must once again become a founding, metaphysical principle of philosophy, science. In place of some collectivist mass, disembodied spirit, or collection of mechanistically-controlled individuals as the foundation of scientific understanding, to re-establish the proper union between wisdom and science, the West needs to re-establish primacy of the individual, sentient being engaged in personal action as a first principle of knowing, truth, science, philosophy, and wisdom.

Moreover, need exists to recognize that our contemporary Western educational institutions and the socialist political regimes that give birth to and support these gulags are necessary effects of the application to the practical order of Enlightenment sophistry about the nature of philosophy, science, wisdom, and truth: of the political attempt to reduce the whole of knowledge to a social-system-science of historically-emerging clear and distinct ideas.

In short, mainly under the influence of Descartes's and Rousseau's disordered metaphysical understandings of science, philosophy, wisdom, and truth, the Enlightenment project unwittingly gave birth to educational institutions that are institutes of sophistry, essentially socialistic forms of propaganda and secularized fundamentalism. These arose as the necessary means for engendering a poetic, metaphysical myth in the form of utopian history that the whole of science, philosophy, wisdom, and truth are contained in the story, "narrative," of the birth and development of the practical science of modern physics, which only the socialistically-minded, mathematical physicist, like a shaman, can supposedly comprehend.

Under the influence of Descartes, Rousseau, and their progeny, modern physics sought to be intellectually all-consuming, to be the only form of human learning, of human truth. No rational argument can justify this quixotic quest. So, the modern "scientific" spirit turned to poetic myth, sophistry, fairy-tale history, and fundamentalistic spirituality to create the metaphysical arguments it needed rationally to justify its all-consuming nature. In practical terms, this means that, if universities are primarily institutes of higher education, and metaphysics is the highest form of natural human education, the modern scientific spirit necessarily inclined Western intellectuals to create propaganda institutes, and political regimes that support the existence of such institutes, to justify modern mathematical physics's false claim that it is the only form of human knowledge, science, and wisdom about the universe.

Most critics of modernity today correctly call these neognostic, fundamentalistic, principles "secular humanism." Precisely speaking, they wrongly call them "philosophy," "science." Educationally, under the influence of Rousseau, these sophistic principles maintain that all learning is revelation, or disclosure, of the something that replaces the traditional Western creator-God, of something they call the "human spirit." By "human spirit" they mean a universal scientific spirit (the spirit of progress, true human freedom, the human project: the utopian-socialist will-to-power) that grows by first revealing itself in forms of backward Scriptural writings and organized religious practices: the same sort of universal, anti-Catholic, anti-Semitic spirit that was a main cause of the development of Fascism, Nazism, and Marxism.

For their adherents, metaphysics is the epic poetic story, an Enlightened, fairy-tale history, about the evolution, or emergence, of human consciousness, the universal human spirit ("true science") from backward states of selfishness and primitive religions like Judaism and Catholicism, to that of a new political world order dominated by Enlightened systematic science and the religion of love of humanity, "secular humanism." And tolerance is this mythical history's chief engine of progress, story-telling, and means of reading history.

The means of such emergence consists of a synthesis of what Rousseau calls the "voice of conscience" (which he conflates with natural law) and poetic enthusiasm, or, more simply, "tolerance," an increasingly inclusive socialist feeling for love of humanity, an increasing willingness to incorporate all human differences into a higher state of socialist, political consciousness as a means for achieving the political goal of world socialism: for everyone to think in the same neo-Averroistic way Enlightened intellectuals think.

Traditional Western universities, classical liberal arts, the classical understanding of philosophy, natural law, individual liberty, the dignity of the individual human being, and republican government, individual rights, and families are unsuitable handmaidens for generating, growing, and sustaining these myths. Needed are imperious, centralized bureaucracies.

To defeat these myths, Westerners need (1) a radically different approach to philosophy and science: one that insists on the existence of forms in physical things, including that of a soul within the human person; and (2) a return to an educational philosophy rooted in human beings possessing human faculties that become maturely developed through human habituation.

A necessary condition for the start of such a recovery program is that, like the utopian addicts we are, Westerners must bottom out and recognize that (1) what my friend and colleague John N. Deely rightly calls "postmodernism falsely-so-called" is simply modernism on steroids and essentially out of touch with reality; and (2) we cannot build, or recover, a culture based upon the conviction that no real communication exists between substances. As Deely well says in a recent monograph, *Semiotic Animal: A Postmodern Definition of 'Human Being' Transcending Patriarchy and Feminism*, "Just as in politics you cannot effect a revolution and at the same time preserve the *ancien régime*, so in intellectual culture you cannot develop what is new simply by repeating what is old."[22]

If we want to transcend depersonalization in contemporary science, we have to transcend the Babelism of modern thought that is essentially related to the denial of the existence of individually existing human beings naturally capable of communicating with each other independently of social science and the utopian, socialist state. We have to restore wisdom to science because, absent wisdom, strictly speaking, science cannot be science. In such a situation, scientific reason becomes displaced by sophistry, intellectual malpractice, propaganda, myth: utopian dreams.

Once we understand that we properly (most precisely) name things through their proximate causes, and that, in the case of arts and sciences, in a complete sense, we properly attribute art or science to someone because that person's actions are being performed through a habit or virtue that perfects a person and a person's operations, what passes as science from an observer's point of view can become a form of malpractice from a practitioner's point of view.

If a person with the knowledge of medicine misuses that knowledge intentionally to make patients sick, strictly speaking, that person is no scientist, no physician. The proximate principle of that person's actions is malevolence, intellectual bastardization, not art or science; moral vice, not intellectual virtue. If this is true of a physician falsely so-called, it is equally true of a mathematician falsely-so-called and physicist falsely-so-called. Hence, strictly speaking, many contemporary mathematicians and physicists, even leading ones, are not scientists. They are shamans.

To claim that the whole of truth is contained in the science of medicine is absurd. Equally absurd is to claim that the whole of truth is contained in mathematics, or mathematical physics.

The mere fact that a person has a facility to make right judgments about a subject does not, in and of itself, strictly speaking, qualify a person to merit the title "scientist," which, strictly speaking, is only merited by the possession of the habit of science. Knowledge that has become divorced from wisdom tends to degenerate into a tool of malevolence, tends to divorce itself from right relation to other forms of human knowledge and become despotic. To claim that mathematics or mathematical physics is the measure of all truth is simply a modern version of the intellectual imperialism of Protagoras (b. 490 BC; d. 420 BC). Its intellectual foundation is non-existent. The claim is a piece of pure sophistry.

No medical knowledge that conceived of itself as being the whole of human truth could rightly claim to understand the nature of medicine. Many human beings would rightly judge such a grandiose claim to border on delusion, madness. Should not the same be true of a mathematics or mathematical physics that made such a disingenuous, imperious claim?

As Aristotle and St. Thomas understood centuries ago, by nature, human reason tends to rule politically (that is, justly), not despotically, over those human faculties that are naturally inclined to follow its directions. But this is true only of human reason rightly conceived. When a subordinate science, like mathematics, or physics, attempts to displace a higher science and, beyond this, to reduce the whole of truth and wisdom to its subject-matter and methods, such a project cannot be effected through rational persuasion. Ultimately, it must seek to effect such rule through coercion, propaganda, despotism, the blind will (better, urge) to power.

The human intellectual faculties are naturally inclined to co-operate with each other, and other human faculties, to help human beings become happy. This is one reason that, by nature, the human soul generates an order of arts and sciences. To be complete as science knowledge must do more than facilitate right judgment about its specific subject matter. It must also, simultaneously, contribute to the perfection of a human being as a whole. If one human science/philosophy becomes incapable of co-existing with other forms of human science/philosophy, even seeks to destroy them, something is rotten in the kingdom of science, philosophy, and needs to be corrected. Such a "science," "philosophy," is no science, philosophy, at all.

If, correctly understood, science, philosophy, is chiefly a habit, virtue, of the human intellect (which is a faculty of the human soul), any science, philosophy, that denies the existence of the human soul and intellectual habits and virtues cannot correctly understand its own nature and be what it claims to be. Moreover, if intellectual habits and virtues are psychological qualities that relate different intellectual faculties to each other and to the world around us, destruction of the notion of science, philosophy, as a human habit, virtue, of the human soul must completely disorder the real relation of human faculties to each other and of human beings to the physical world around us. The cumulative effect of this disorder will ultimately be total inability of a human being rightly to relate to anything.

5. How my present critique of contemporary "science," "philosophy" largely repeats and synthesizes criticisms made by several twentieth- and twenty-first-century intellectuals

Unhappily, the complaint I have lodged against the imperious nature of contemporary "science," "philosophy," is, in large part, nothing new. Most of what I have said above I have gathered from twentieth-century intellectuals like Mortimer J. Adler (b. 1902; d. 2001), Jacques Maritain (b. 1882; d. 1973), Étienne Gilson, and Pope Benedict XVI. In fact, knowingly or not (I suspect knowingly), the Vatican's recent admonition about the dangers of scientific positivism largely repeat critiques made by these intellectuals during the 1930s and 1940s.

Chief examples of such critiques are Adler's articles "This Prewar Generation," and "God and the Professors" in which Adler criticized American university professors, educators, and Deweyan "pragmatic-liberals" for producing a generation of American youth incapable of intellectually defending the principles of American democracy against Adolf Hitler's (b. 1889; d. 1945) program of Nazi socialism.[23]

In "This Prewar Generation," published in *Harper's Magazine* in October 1940, Adler described American youth of the 1930s and early 1940s as (1) appearing to have "grown up with no allegiances, no "moral philosophy to renounce"; (2) people who talk like "calloused realists"; (3) "having a distrust of any cause which spoke the language of principles"; (4) lacking a faith in democracy equal to that of Hitler's Nazi youth's faith in Fascism.[24]

Adler observed how, concerned about preparedness for war, commencement speakers in June 1940 "all spoke with amazing uniformity" about the dangers of the moral and political disaffection of American youth. "In their impatience, however sincere," Adler noted, these speakers "committed a basic error in rhetoric. They did not even ask themselves why all their words would fall upon deaf ears, why stirring words would not stir, why even the loftiest visions would not inspire."[25]

Adler claimed the reason such words fell upon deaf ears was that the speakers had forgotten that we can only control effects by altering causes. Based upon his then fifteen years of teaching experience, he proposed the thesis that the reason why American college students and recent graduates did not take any moral, economic, or political problem seriously was chiefly because "they are sophists in the most invidious sense of the term, which connotes an unqualified skepticism about all moral judgments."[26] Adler maintained that "their only principle is that there are no moral principles at all, their only slogan that all statements of policy, all appeals to standards, are nothing but slogans, and hence frauds and deceptions."[27]

In the political arena, Adler said that such skepticism reduces to the mindset of the ancient sophist Thrasymachos that justice is the advantage of the stronger, might makes right; with the exception that American students could not make, or defend, the case as intelligently and as could old Thrasymachos.

Adler laid the blame for immunization of American youth against the ability to defend democracy as a form of government intrinsically superior to Fascism clearly on the "scientistic" mindset that dominated American higher education, on the shoulders of American college and university professors who had reduced the whole of truth to positivistic science.

He maintained, further, that this mindset had not arisen overnight, was not the peculiar creation of the preceding generation. He claimed,"What has been happening in American education since 1900, what has finally achieved its full effect in the present generation, flows with tragic inevitability from the seeds of modem culture as they have developed in the past three hundred years. The very things which constituted the cultural departure that we call modern times have eventuated, not only in the perverted education of American youth today, but also in the crises they are unprepared to face."[28]

What Adler saw arising in American education since 1900 was a form of utopian socialism that Lewis Mumford (b. 1895; d. 1990) had labeled "pragmatic liberalism."[29] Adler considered as a "historical accident" the ascendancy of this mindset in the U. S. simultaneously with the rise of Fascism in Europe. But, he added,

"Only the timing is a coincidence" because "the European and the American maladies arise from the same causes" are "the last fruitions of modern man's exclusive trust in science and his gradual disavowal of whatever lies beyond the field of science as irrational prejudice, as opinion emotionally held."[30]

In making this claim, Adler was careful not to make "science" his essay's "villain." The villain, he claimed, was the intellectual and practical misuse of science. He said:

> We do not blame science for the murderous tools it has enabled men to make; neither should we blame science, or for that matter scientists, for the destructive doctrines men have made in its name, men who are for the most part philosophers and educators, not scientists. All these doctrines have a common center—positively, the exclusive adoration of science; negatively, the denial that philosophy or theology can have any independent authority. We can regard this intellectual misuse of science as another one of the false modern religions—the religion of science, closely related to the religion of the state. We can group all these doctrines together and call them by names which have become current: positivism and scientism. And again we can see a deep irony in the historic coincidence that just when the practical misuse of science has armed men for wholesale slaughter, scientism—the intellectual misuse of science—has all but disarmed them morally.[31]

While Adler was right not to blame "science" for being the villain of his essay, I maintain he was wrong to call "misuse of science" the culprit because, as he recognized when describing American college students as invidious "sophists," the proper proximate cause of their behavior was "sophistry," not "science." Science could not have been misused by them because science did not exist in them. If science is a psychological virtue, a virtue of the human soul present in the human intellect, divorcing science from any moral standards and philosophical metaphysics, wisdom (as these students had done), essentially disorders the human intellect and makes the practice of science impossible.

Science, philosophy, started to rise with the ancient Greeks when the ancient physicists, like philosophy's Father, Thales (fl. 585 BC) began to recognize (1) the existence of secondary causes, natures, in physical things; (2) that knowledge and wisdom were not the sole property of the gods, but were natural achievements of the human mind; (3) mystery exists that can cause sense wonder; and (4) that this natural wonder can be put to rest through thoroughly-natural, virtuous, reflection of the human intellect made in conjunction with the human sense faculties of the human soul.

Modern "science," "philosophy," is rooted in the Rousseauan conviction that (1) no natures, secondary causes (forms, including souls) exist in physical things; (2) no mysteries exist in physical reality; (3) strictly speaking, no physical reality exists: only *spirit* exists and is active; (4) the human spirit is God; (5) all human knowledge is an act of revelation; (6) science is a necessary condition of virtue and ethics; virtue and ethics are not necessary conditions of science; and (7) no human soul exists in which habits or virtues could exist.

In a way, in his "This Prewar Generation," Adler recognized that sophistry, not misuse of science, was the villain of his story when he said what he called the misuse of science was "another one of the false modern religions—the religion of science, closely related to the religion of the state."[32] Confounding science with religion, state religion, is not to misuse science; it is to misunderstand science, to mistake science for something it is not: an act of revelation; which is precisely what Rousseau and his progeny in "social science" have done. In so doing, a person does not misuse science in the sense of putting science to wrong use. A person displaces science and virtue with propaganda.

Moreover, since modernity has essentially displaced science, transformed what had been science into a kind of state religion, Adler is somewhat wrong to see the simultaneous existence of Fascism and pragmatic liberalism as a historical accident. If I am right, and the contemporary understanding of science is rooted in Rousseauean, utopian socialism, the rise of contemporary "science" in American education presupposed the existence of a socialistic mindset among American educators as a necessary condition for the existence of contemporary "science." While the fact that American socialism was pragmatic liberalism and not full-blown Fascism might have been a historical accident, that this mindset was socialistic was no accident. As Adler well knew, John Dewey (b. 1854; d. 1952) was the chief source of this way of thinking; and Dewey was largely recycling the socialism of Rousseau.

In his article Adler made other mistakes. For example, he claimed (1) "We do not blame science for the murderous tools it has enabled men to make"; and (2) "neither should we blame science, or for that matter scientists, for the destructive doctrines men have made in its name, men who are for the most part philosophers and educators, not scientists."[33]

Science did not enable men to make murderous tools. Lack of science, divorce of science from wisdom, morality, intellectual and moral virtue, did so. Science presupposes the existence of a moral culture rooted in minimum levels of professional honesty and justice as a necessary condition for its existence. A medical doctor who uses knowledge of medicine to murder is practicing murder, not the art of medicine; is using knowledge (not the science) of medicine to carry out his crime. Moreover, science can only be science if it derives its first principles from the being of intellectually-independent beings and virtues of the intellectual soul, if science is an act of this individual knower using as first principles natural knowledge of the being of things, not myth, superstition, or propaganda (even Enlightenment propaganda).

Hence, Adler was right to complain about "the exclusive adoration of" what he misnamed "science," as "one of the false modern religions." He was wrong, however, to call this false modern religion the religion of "science."

The mere fact that a person possesses knowledge, arrives at right conclusions, does not mean a person has done so by means of art or science. The person could just as well have done so through fraud, deceit, experience, cleverness, guessing, or knowledge. A student who arrives at right answers by cheating is no artist or scientist. Neither is a prophet; and, despite what Descartes mistakenly claimed, not every act of knowing is an act of science.

The contemporary reduction of the whole of knowledge and science to mathematical physics (to what Adler and many others call "positivism," "scientism") is a myth, chiefly the effect of a moral disorder, a political project: a moral refusal to admit that true science must have its initial foundation in intellectual virtue and evident, *per se nota*, principles that only a philosophical metaphysics (not utopian socialism or propaganda) can rationally justify. Divorcing itself from a rational foundation in intellectual virtue and philosophical metaphysics, and an essential connection to the generic end of all science to promote human happiness, destroys the claim of any intellectual activity to be "scientific" or "philosophical."

As Aristotle maintained and Plato recognized, science is more than knowledge of the fact: knowledge of the reasoned fact.[34] Science involves the habitual ability to explain why something is what it is, what chiefly causes this or that. This is true even in the case of answers to "how" questions, which, when considered precisely, necessarily involve "what" questions (for example, when I ask how to do something, I am asking what to do). Absent such habitual ability to give a reasoned explanation of why something is what it is, what we misname "science" is no more science than the epic poetry of the ancient Greeks.

If the ultimate reason that mathematical physics is supposedly the whole of science and measure of all truth is that Zeus says it is so, mathematical physics has no rational foundation. Why, then, should it have a rational foundation when the ultimate reason given for its imperious nature is that the utopian, socialist state, the collectivist human spirit, the law courts, or that contemporary "scientific experts" declare it is so?

No matter how precisely a person could predict the future using numbers, if that person were to say that the reason he was so good with his predictions was that numbers are revelations, bits of news from the spirit world, no rational human being would conclude that this person's exceptional intellectual ability was an act of science. If such be the case, why should any of us conclude that the mode or reasoning that Enlightenment intellectuals inherited from Rousseau and have tried to pass off to modernity as "science" merits the name "science"? According to Rousseau, all human knowledge is news from the spirit world, projections of irrational feelings, blind emotions, which have magically grown into science through conflict with other, supposedly backward, religious emotions.

As Adler noted, one net effect of such sophistry is that, like the youth of America's pre-World War II generation, human beings start to develop a "distrust of all language."[35] Hence, just as I noted above about the mindset of most contemporary Western college students and Westerners in general, in the first part of the twenty-first century, Adler said students were convinced that (1) only the methods of experimentation or empirical research generate valid knowledge of the nature of the universe and human beings; (2) questions we cannot answer by the methods of the natural and social sciences we cannot answer in any trustworthy or convincing way (or answers to such questions are arbitrary, unfounded, opinions); (3) the great achievement of the modern age is more than the accumulation of scientific knowledge: recognition of the positivistic method of empirical research and experimentation as the only dependable way to solve problems (in consequence, modern times have seen human "emancipation from the superstitions of religion, the dogmatisms of theology, and the armchair speculations of philosophers"); (4) study of social phenomena became scientific when research divorced itself entirely from normative principles, "when economists and students of politics no longer asked about the justice of social arrangements, but only who gets what, when, and how."[36]

Following Socrates' critique of Thrasymachos' claim that justice is the advantage of the stronger, and following what Plato's brother Glaucon says to Socrates shortly after the start of Book Two of Plato's *Republic*, Adler reasoned that, confronted by repeated exposure to such invidious rhetoric, a bright college student will readily conclude that: (1) moral questions cannot be answered by the methods of natural or social science; (2) in the domains of individual behavior and politics, except as expressions of personal prejudice, we cannot make "value judgments"; (3) economics and politics have no essential connection to ethics.[37]

Following Thrasymachos' modern reincarnation, such a bright young student will become a disciple of Machiavelli, "as much a realist in politics as Hitler and Mussolini." And, "if, in addition to being bright," Adler added, "he is proud of his modernity, he will regard anyone who talks about standards of goodness, principles of justice, moral virtues as an unregenerate old fogey; and he will express his aversion for such outmoded opinions by the *ad hominem* use of epithets like 'medieval," or 'scholastic,' or 'mystic.'"[38]

Under the sheer weight of such indoctrination, Adler observed that college students of the 1930s and early 1940s came to dislike words like "truth," "goodness," because they sounded like "absolute values" so widely decried in social science departments at colleges and universities at the time.[39] (Quite understandable since modernity had essentially divorced science from any and all virtue and any and all human good.) He then lamented the fact that opposition "to the teaching pronounced in unison by the social scientists" was not opposed by philosophy departments at these same institutions.

Adler wrongly attributed this lack of opposition to what he considered to be the fact that the doctrine of scientism was "certainly the dominant dogma of American philosophy" at the time. He saw this dominance as part of "the degenerative tendency of modern philosophy to move in this direction that had reached its culmination in American pragmatism and all its sequelae—the numerous varieties of positivism." He maintained that all the varieties of modern philosophy "agree on one point: that only science gives us valid knowledge of reality."[40]

As a result, Adler concluded, "philosophy, at its best, can be nothing more than a sort of commentary on the findings of science; and at its worst, when it refuses to acknowledge the exclusive right of scientific method to marshal evidence and draw conclusions therefrom, philosophy is either mere opinion or nonsensical verbiage."[41] Within such a context, Adler rightly saw that, especially as recounting "primitive times before the scientific era" (that is, the seventeenth century), philosophy's history is told as a history of guesses, some bright, some wild, but all equally unworthy of modern credence."[42]

In short, instead of opposing the social scientists, members of "philosophy" departments falsely-so-called championed their moral relativism. In "philosophy" courses, Adler claimed "the student really learns how to argue like a sophist against all 'values' as subjective and relative. Far from being the last bulwark against the scientism professed or insinuated by every other part of the curriculum, the philosophy courses reinforce the negativism of this doctrine by inspiring disrespect for any philosophy which claims to be independent knowledge."[43]

To complete their job, Adler maintained that philosophy departments used semanticism (what his friend Jacques Maritain would later call "Babelism") to implement the ancient sophistries that they had revived. In these departments, Adler claimed students learned "to suspect all words, especially abstract words." They were told that "statements which cannot be scientifically verified are meaningless," that abstract words like "justice," "right," "liberty," "happiness," that enter into moral judgments "have only rhetorical meaning. Denuded of deceptive verbiage, all such judgments can be reduced to statements of what I like or what displeases me. There is no 'should' or 'ought.'"[44]

   While Adler clearly understood the sophistic nature of "philosophy" and social "science" departments during his time, I find unfortunate that he would call modern "philosophy" departments "philosophical" and modern "social science" departments "scientific." Most twentieth-century U.S. college and university "philosophy" departments were not examples of "the degenerative tendency of modern philosophy" any more than the "social science" departments of the twentieth century were examples of the degenerative effects of modern "social science." They were and are prime examples the modern lack of philosophy and social science, of the degenerative cultural effects of neo-sophistry fulfilling its nature in modern culture under the rubrics of "philosophy" and "science." Modern "philosophy" is no more "philosophy" than modern "social science" is science. Both are forms of neo-Protagorean sophisty. And their net effect tends to be "Babelism," the inability of human beings to communicate with each other.

6. Why the future of Western culture and civilization essentially depends upon ending the separation between philosophy and science

As Adler observed in his article "God and the Professors," like the health and disease of the body, cultural health consists in the harmonious functioning of its parts, and cultures die from lack of harmonious functioning of these same parts. He added that "science, philosophy, and religion are certainly major parts of European culture; their distinction from one another as quite separate parts is certainly the most characteristic cultural achievement of modern times. But if they have not been properly distinguished, they cannot be properly related; and unless they are properly related, properly ordered to one another, cultural disorder, such as that of modern times, inevitably results."[45]

In short, if we do not properly understand the natures of things, we cannot properly relate and unite them as parts of a coherent whole. This, however, is precisely the problem we have with solving the decline of Western culture and civilization in our time. We do not properly understand the nature of philosophy and science, the way metaphysics essentially relates to both, and how, through this relation, metaphysics uses arts, philosophy, science, to generate cultures and civilizations.

Many modern "scientists," "philosophers," in fact, tend to glory in maintaining that things have no natures. Failing to understand the natures of things, we cannot properly understand the nature of religion and unite philosophy and science to religion to produce a healthy culture and civilization. Moreover, if the activity through which we unite parts is a state-sanctioned activity that essentially involves state-sanctioned sophists defining the state-sanctioned natures of things, the unity we generate we acheive by propaganda, myth, not science.

The chief reason we do not understand the nature of science and philosophy today results, as Adler says, from defects of our intellectual leaders, teachers, savants. "The disorder of modern culture is a disorder in their minds, a disorder which manifests itself in the universities they have built, in the educational system they have devised, in the teaching they do, and which, through that teaching, perpetuates itself and spreads out in ever widening circles from generation to generation."[46]

Such being the case, if we want to stop the decline of Western culture and civilization, we need to do a "Hail Mary" pass over the contemporary intellectual hierarchy of the Enlightenment socialist state (of state-sanctioned sophists who dominate our colleges and universities) so that we can learn once again how to communicate with each other in properly scientific, philosophical, and religious ways.

As long ago as 1947, like Adler before him, in his Mexico City address to UNESCO, the great twentieth-century Catholic intellectual, Jacques Maritian, started to glimpse the need for the West to overcome the Babelism of modern culture, the inability of individual human beings naturally to be capable of communicating with each other independently of social science and the socialist state. At the time, he called for the Organization effectively to use education, science, and culture to contribute to international security and concrete work for peace among peoples.[47]

Maritain's address touched on solving five interrelated and historically-rooted problems that he considered necessary conditions to building a supranational community of peoples and the future work of peace: (1) absolute national sovereignty; (2) *Machiavellianism*; (3) *Realpolitik*; (4) transcending the Babelism of modern thought; and (5) reconciling wisdom and science, especially in modern technology.[48]

At the time, Maritain claimed that modern nation states absurdly presumed the right of absolute sovereignty trumps all other moral authority while, simultaneously, appealing to the contradictory doctrine of natural law to justify whatever they chose to do. He called the claim that politics should be indifferent to a real good and evil "a homicidal error" and such appeals to natural law intellectually incoherent.[49]

He added that only the right spiritual, the right moral and metaphysical, climate, one based upon a proper understanding of human nature and capable of affirming the existence of real heroes, can produce that power of authentic political justice that can conquer the principle and power of Machiavellianism. He maintained that we will never achieve a stable and enduring peace in this world so long as, in the structures of civilization and human awareness, we maintain Babelism in human thought (the divorce between wisdom and science that modern "philosophy's" father, Descartes, had initiated) and we fail to start rigorously submitting the applications of science to moral right and the true ends of human life.[50]

Maritain thought that, to transcend the depersonalization in contemporary science, UNESCO needed to help the world recover a correct understanding of the human person and cultural truths from our classical ethical, metaphysical, and religious wisdom that support it.[51]

Maritain reasoned that, given the contemporary world's widely differing theological and metaphysical traditions, on a practical level, appeal to the existence of a natural law would be the best way for peoples of the world today to come to some sort of common agreement about what we are as people, what is wisdom, and how we should go about reintegrating these notions into physical science. If a natural law truly exists, he reasoned, it would depend upon a common understanding of the human person, and we should reasonably expect to find evidence of its existence and the notion of the dignity of the person that supports it historically in the world body of common law.[52]

While Maritain was engaging in such musings his French friend and philosophical colleague Étienne Gilson was musing about how some Westerners tend to be slow learners, have needed some time to grasp the full implications of the late modern project. At the close of World War II, Gilson claimed we in the West made our most astounding, involuntary, discovery: late modern science is essentially Nietzschean. "The great secret that science has just wrested from matter," Gilson observed, "is the secret of its destruction. To know today is synonymous with to destroy."

Gilson considered Nietzsche's declaration of God's death to be "the capital discovery of modern times," bigger than the explosion at Hiroshima. While Maritain was musing about how to use recognition of natural law to form common practical agreements among the world's people, Gilson thought that Nietzsche's declaration of God's death signaled a metaphysical revolution of the highest, widest, and deepest order in the West. Nietzsche is metaphysical dynamite. He knew it, readily admitted it.[53]

While Enlightened Westerners had gotten out of the habit of talking about things like "divine law," some, like Maritain, apparently still held onto its vestige in Enlightened, secularized appeals to "the voice of conscience" to solve the world's problems. But what will happen to us, Gilson asked, when more of us start to realize that the modern voice of conscience (and, presumably, its principle: natural law) is the reflection of nothing, a convenient illusion we have created to maintain the intoxicating joy of our own poetic and sophistic project?[54]

Finding ourselves totally free to engage in the perpetual, Sisyphean task of endless self-creation, Gilson said, we resemble a soldier on a twenty-four hour leave with nothing to do: totally bored in the tragic loneliness of an idle freedom we cannot productively use.[55]

To Gilson's ears, the explosion of Hiroshima resounded a solemn metaphysical assertion of post-Nietzshean, late modern, man's statement that, while we no longer want to be God's image, we can still be God's caricature. While we cannot create anything, we now possess the intoxicating power to destroy everything. As a result, feeling totally empty and alone, late modern man offers, to anyone willing to take it, the futile freedom he does not know how to use. "He is ready for all the dictators, leaders of these human herds who follow them as guides and who are all finally conducted by them to the same place—the abbatoir" (the slaughterhouse).[56] Having freed ourselves from divine rule, the necessary political consequence for "postmodern man" falsely so-called is political enslavement by a totalitarian State. Having refused to serve God, we have no one left to judge the state, no arbiter between us and the state.[57]

As Gilson saw it, just after World War II, appeals to conscience helped some of us in the West, apparently Maritain included, to pretend not to understand the catastrophic consequences for the

West and the world of the grandiose sophistry of the falsely-so-called "postmodern" project: Our destiny has become "the absurd" and "truly exhausting task" of perpetual self-invention without model, purpose, or rule. Having turned ourselves into gods, Gilson maintained, we do not know what to do with our divinity.[58]

Clearly, for Gilson, just as for Maritain, the terrors of the late modern world are, in root cause, "modern," as well as moral and metaphysical; but, for Gilson, the chief clash of civilizations we face today is not between the politics of West and East, or the West and other political orders, between the Western tradition and other metaphysical and religious traditions. It is a metaphysical and moral clash between the ancient and modern West.

No wonder exists why this current conflict has become an essential effect of modern "science" falsely-so-called. Having essentially divorced itself from all moral and intellectual virtue, including wisdom and happiness, having reduced all these to its all-consuming method, like modern economics and politics, modern "science" has essentially divorced itself from all real human good and the chief end of human life: the creator-God. As a contrary of real science, modern "science" has embraced as its natual end real science's opposite, natural end: moral and intellectual vice (including foolishness and the chief natural end of foolishness: human misery).

Since the time of Descartes, "science" falsely-so-called has divorced itself from any essential connection to wisdom, virtue, and human happiness, and a creator-God (from all human good); and has identified itself with an intellectually-blind urge (misnamed "will") to power. Such being the case, having embraced a kind of intellectual Machiavellianism as its nature, why should anyone be surprised to discover such a blind urge eventually to reveal itself as the neo-sophistic inclination to dominate: naked violence, universal despotism?

Gilson maintained that, from time immemorial, we in the West have based our cultural creed and scientific inspiration upon the conviction that gods, or a God, existed. All of our Western intellectual and cultural institutions have presupposed the existence of a God or gods. No longer. All of a sudden, God no longer exists. Worse, He never existed! For Gilson, the implication is clear: "We shall have to change completely our every thought, word and deed. The entire human order totters on its base."

If our entire cultural history depended upon the unswerving conviction that God exists, "the totality of the future must needs depend on the contrary certitude, that God does not exist." The metaphysical terror now becomes evident in its depths. Nietzsche's message is a metaphysical bomb more powerful than the atomic weapon dropped on Hiroshima: "Everything that was true from the beginning of the human race will suddenly become false."

Moreover, mankind alone must create for itself a new self-definition, which will become human destiny, the human project: *To destroy*. To build the world anew, to create the new scientific world order, we must first destroy the old. The only rational justification that modern mathematical physics can give to be the sole repository of truth is a Machiavellian-like ability to torture nature to reveal secrets: to destroy. Gilson claimed Nietzsche knew that, as long as we believe that what is dead is alive, we can never use our creative liberty. Nietzsche knew and readily admitted his mission was to destroy.

If Nietzsche was speaking the truth about his project, which Gilson thought he was, Gilson maintained the he was announcing the dawn of a new age in which the aim of Nitezsche's misnamed "postmodern" culture, its metaphysical project, is to make war upon, to overthrow, traditional truths and values. To build our brave, new, scientific world order, we have to overthrow the metaphysical and moral foundations of Western culture. "Before stating what will be true, we will have to say that everything by which man has thus far lived, everything by which he still lives, is deception and trickery." As Gilson claimed Nietszche understood, "He who would be a creator, both in good and evil, must first of all know how to destroy and to wreck values."

In fact, Gilson stated, our traditional Western values are intentionally being wrecked all around us, everywhere, under our feet. He said he had stopped counting "the unheard of theories thrown at us under names as various as their methods of thought, each the harbinger of a new truth which promises to create shortly, joyously busy preparing the brave new world of tomorrow by first of all annihilating the world of today."[59]

What, then, are we who oppose Nietzsche's project to do in the face of such a cataclysm? Nietzsche's plan, his mission, is to destroy "today to create tomorrow." Gilson considered forgivable that we should not have anticipated Nietzsche's advent. "But," he said, "that we should not understand what he is doing while he is doing it right under our eyes, just as we were told he would do it—that bears witness to a stranger blindness. Can it really be that the herd of human being that is led to the slaughter has eyes and yet does not see?" Gilson's explanation for such a depth of blindness was that the announcement of a catastrophe of such an order usually leaves us "but a single escape: to disbelieve it and, in order not to believe, to refuse to understand."[60]

Whether Gilson thought Maritain suffered from such blindness, I do not know. I think he did. At the very least, Gilson clearly appeared to be saying that, if a natural law truly exists, looking today to international law for evidence of its existence and the notion of the dignity of the person that supports it historically in order to overcome contemporary Babelism cannot work. The chief reason that our falsely-so-called "postmodern" world is essentially hostile to such notions is rooted in the late modern world's essential moral, metaphysical, and political rejection of the first extrinsic principle of natural law: the existence of a creator-God.

Instead of presuming a common agreement about the existence of a natural law upon which to build a common consensus about human nature, Maritain would have been better off facing the reality of the world around him, in recognizing that the modern project is essentially rooted in a rejection of natures, or forms, in things and that Babelism in modern thought cannot be overcome unless and until, like an alcoholic incapable or self-recovery, modernity first hits bottom and accepts a common understanding that forms exist in facultatively-independent realities. If modernism and false postmodernism are built upon a rejection of the existence of forms in things and of gods, or a creator-God, upon which the classical understanding of natural law depends, how can we make appeals to that law to give us a true postmodernism based upon the common understanding of the human person that will allow for communication between substances?

In his now famous and historic 12 September 2006 address at the University of Regensburg entitled, "Faith, Reason, and the University: Memories and Reflections," Pope Benedict XVI offered to the world community a positive critique to help modernity expand its intellectual horizons to avoid real dangers that arise from what Maritain had called Babelism and Benedict called a "self-imposed limitation of reason to the empirically falsifiable."[61] Devoid of such a broadening of the notion of reason, Benedict maintained that the Western world is incapable of entering into "that genuine dialogue of cultures and religions so urgently needed today."[62]

He claimed that, while the West widely holds "that positivistic reason and the forms of philosophy based on it are universally valid," it largely cannot recognize the universal validity of forms of religious reason.[63] This puts the West in diametric opposition to "the world's profoundly religious cultures" who "see the exclusion of the divine from the universality of reason as an attack on their most profound convictions."[64] He said, "A reason which is deaf to the divine and which relegates religion into the realm of subcultures is incapable of entering into the dialogue of cultures."[65]

Put slightly differently, the Pope was saying that people cannot enter into genuine dialogue with other people, *cannot genuinely communicate between substances*, unless we enter into rational dialogue with them. Such dialogue must have at least two characteristics; it must: (1) be in touch with reality and (2) assume the rationality of the interlocutors. Unhappily, the modern Western notion of reason arbitrarily tends to limit rational discussion, *communication between substances*, to talk about mathematical being and sense experimentation, tends to view all other talk as essentially non-rational. Hence, strictly speaking, people who hold this narrow, fundamentalistic, notion of reason cannot enter into rational debate with other people about moral and religious issues because their narrow understanding of reason cuts them off from such debate about these issues.

More or less, the Pope was saying that, in relation to religious and moral issues, the modern West's narrow understanding of Cartesian and Enlightenment human reason places it in the same situation as many Muslim fundamentalistic extremists. Modern Western reason tends to be arbitrarily narrow because it tends to be essentially fundamentalistic, but in a secular way. It cannot rationally dialogue with people about moral and religious issues because it has relegated religious and moral being and talk to the sphere of the essentially non-rational, capricious, arbitrary.

The Pope well recognized, and recognizes, that this places the West in an extremely precarious position relative to religious cultures, especially to extremist elements of Islamic culture. How are Enlightened Western intellectuals supposed to dialogue with Muslims who think that God is an arbitrary Will, not subject to behaving according to mind-independent standards of rationality, like non-contradiction, when the Western intellectuals have a view of moral, political, religious reason as essentially irrational (but at the secular extreme) as their extremist Muslim counterparts?

The West's view of moral, political, and religious reason tends to be a secularized reformulation of a popular Reformation notion of the essential depravity of reason (religious reason, in the contemporary West's case), just as narrowly fundamentalistic as that of Muslim extremists.[66] Hence, strictly speaking, modern Western intellectuals cannot enter the debate because, by their own admission, because of their arrogant and unjustified presumption of their own rational superiority, they are totally incapable of conducting rational dialogue in the areas of religion, politics, and morality. Clearly, if such dialogue is to take place, it will have to occur between individuals in the West and East who do not share such hubristic and narrow understandings of rationality.

While modern "scientific" reason has to accept and base its methodology upon matter's rational structure "and the correspondence between our spirit and the prevailing rational structures of nature as given," Benedict claimed the real question remains why it has to do so? Moreover, he asserted that the natural sciences have to remand this question to philosophy and theology to answer because the natural sciences are incapable of addressing the question.[67] Benedict maintained that philosophy and theology are sources of knowledge derived from human experience, much of which in the West comes from religious traditions and Christian faith.[68]

He made special reference to Socrates' observation in the *Phaedo* that extended philosophical argumentation involving "talk about being" might incline a person to mock all such talk, and, in so doing, "be deprived of the truth of existence" and "suffer a great loss."[69] In a similar fashion, Benedict claimed that "the West has long been endangered by this aversion to the questions which underlie its rationality, and can only suffer harm thereby."[70]

He argued that to ignore theological and philosophical sources of knowledge is "an unacceptable restriction on our listening and responding" to reason, and is something we do at our peril.[71] Hence, he concluded by asserting that "a theology grounded in biblical faith enters into the debates of our time" with a program that involves "the courage to embrace the whole breadth of reason," not to deny its greatness.[72] "It is to this great *logos*, to this breadth of reason," he said, "that we invite our partners in the dialogue of cultures. To rediscover it constantly is the great task of the university."[73]

During the twentieth century, Pope Benedict XVI's predecessor, Blessed Pope John Paul the Great (b. 1920; d. 2005) was able to help colleagues introduce this *logos* to the Philosophy Department at The Catholic University of Lublin (KUL), now The Pope John Paul II Catholic University of Lublin. As a result, with the help of Mieczysław Albert Krąpiec (b. 1921; d. 2008), and other members of this Philosophy Department at KUL, the Pope was able to spread metaphysical principles of Lublin Thomism from this Department throughout Eastern Europe and severely weaken the disordered notion of science that held these people for decades under the yoke of the Babelism of "scientific socialism." No reason exists why a similar revival of Christian metaphysics throughout the West cannot do the same for the entire West in our day.

Hence, it is to this same great *logos* that this book and its yet-to-exist later volumes are devoted. In his Regensburg address, His Holiness Pope Benedict XVI attributed the attenuation of modern reason largely to a concerted effort that started in the West several centuries ago to remove the influence of classical reason, especially Greek philosophical reason, from the modern notion of science and higher education.[74] Devoid of proper self-understanding, we in the West cannot enter into rational dialogue with other cultures.

If we do not know who we are, how we came to be the way we are and think the way we do, if we do not precisely grasp our situation and its history, we cannot possibly expect rationally to listen to and understand other cultures. More than anything else today, we in the West need a *renaissance of philosophical and scientific reason*, a recovery of the understanding that a reason that is out of touch with reality, which refuses to have its judgments measured by mind-independent reality, is no reason at all, much less a scientific or philosophical reason.

If the chief cause of our contemporary, attenuated notion of reason is a loss of classical reason, its philosophical realism, and the essential connection of science and virtue to wisdom and human happiness, then nothing short of a new *Renaissance of Philosophical Reason* can restore *logos* to its proper place within world cultures. It is to this great *logos*, to this breadth of reason, that, in the spirit of

Pope Benedict, this book and its subsequent volumes seek to help contemporary readers to enter.

Why care about the contemporary separation of philosophy and science? The answer, in condensed form, is that, if we want to transcend depersonalization in contemporary science, the separation between science and wisdom, end the decline of Western higher education, reverse the West's cultural decay, and enter a new *logos* capable of transcultural and intracultural communication between substances in our dangerous contemporary age, we have to transcend the Babelism of modern thought that is essentially related to the denial of the existence of individually existing human beings naturally capable of communicating with each other independently of social science and the utopian, socialist state.

We human beings always use something we know better as the means, measure, principle for intellectually comprehending something we know less well. This means that, at some point, rationally to justify what we are intellectually doing, we have to judge everything we know on the basis of some chief intellectual principle, some assumption-less first truth, something we know best. Philosophically, scientifically, considered, this something we know best cannot be a "belief," because beliefs always depend upon someone's knowledge.

Hence, for human beings to be able to make the claim to possess a thoroughly-rooted natural knowledge (not one solely rooted a revealed theology or fantasy), some division of human knowledge must rest upon evidently known first principles, on truths we know best, or as the medieval theologians would say *per se nota* principles. At some point, to be able to exist as "philosophy," "science" at all, the human sciences must rest upon assumption-less, reality-based, knowledge. Human knowledge, philosophy, science, must have a division that, through simple intellectual consideration of their natures, can identify *per se nota*, self-evident, principles upon which all human knowing, all human science, philosophy, rest.

This division of science, philosophical metaphysics (an intellectual virtue of the human soul), must be a simple intellectual consideration, one engaged in for no practical or productive aim. It must be what the ancient philosophers called a "theoretical," "speculative," or "contemplative" knowledge. The principles it grasps must be knowable as true simply by an intellectual understanding of the natures they involve, the truths they propose to the human intellect to accept (for example, that effects presuppose causes; two things equal to a third thing are equal to each other; possessing science presupposes existing and possessing knowledge; that contradictory opposites cannot simultaneously be true).

Absent acceptance of such assumption-less, theoretical knowledge gained through personal experience of the physical world in which we live, we have no rational foundation for claiming that our reasoning processes are rooted in philosophy, science. We have no rational grounds on which to explain, justify to ourselves, or to anyone else, precisely why our reasoning is rooted in knowledge.

Absent such principles, what we call "science," "philosophy," degenerates into sophistry, into what many people, including what many mis-named "scientists" and "philosophers," today, call "belief systems." All our "science," "philosophy," becomes hypothetical, assumption-based, rooted in arbitrary beliefs that we cannot rationally explain to ourselves or to anyone else why we accept. In short, it becomes, no philosophy, science, at all.

Every division of science starts with the evident acceptance of the existence of its subject matter. Hence, for students of ethics to debate whether human freedom and good and evil exist is as ridiculous as for a medical student to debate whether physical health and disease exist.

Furthermore, as Aristotle and St. Thomas recognized centuries ago, all branches of science operate in an architectonic fashion. Lower divisions, or branches, of a science take from higher branches first principles of reasoning, definitions, rules, laws, that the lower divisions simply assume to be true; but the higher have proven or know to be evidently true. Finally, even though the notion is largely ridiculed today, every science has a chief aim, and so do the natures that these sciences study.

As Gilson noticed and Aristotle knew millennia before him, the only way that an indeterminate multitude can cease to be such and become unified into a one is by becoming an ordered multitude, parts of a whole.[75] In this world, absent unity, no individual being can act, because absent unity, no individual is this one being. All physical beings in this universe are composite, made up of parts. Parts, however, are divisions of a whole. No whole, no parts. And absent a numerically-one act (an end or aim) that can relate all the divisions of a multitude into a whole, no wholes can exist.

Parts only exist in relation to a common, numerically-one, act, or end. And these divisions of a multitude only become parts by having suitable (properly relatable) qualities. Absent this one act, and the divisions of a multitude with relatable qualities, no multitude can become united to cooperate as members of a whole. For example, no fire to fight, no suitable qualities with which to fight fires, no whole unit called firefighters can exist.

All sciences study multitudes that each science unifies into a whole. To do so, each science must have a chief aim, and study natures that have a chief aim. All sciences, moreover, are architectonically ordered. The lower sciences naturally subordinate their aims to that of a higher science.

For example, as Aristotle says, *mutatis mutandis*, the art of using directs the art of producing.[76] No chief aim that, by nature, governs the art of using something (for example, sailing a boat), and no act or art of producing it can exist. Hence, absent a knowledge possessed by a chief theoretical science, a first philosophy (metaphysics), no scientist can adequately comprehend what he or she does, or why.

In fact, in a way, all the other sciences exist to help bring into being the science of metaphysics (a highest knowledge, a first reason why) so that the practitioners of the lower sciences can have a more complete understanding of precisely what they are doing and why. For this reason, the ancient Greek poets tended to conflate poetry with all the sciences. And the discovery of a new science within the field of a prevailing intellectual culture tends to view this new science as metaphysics.

Absent the existence of a real, philosophical metaphysics, for centuries, modern and contemporary intellectuals have been unable rationally to explain and justify the existence and nature of "science," "philosophy," in terms of self-evident theoretical knowledge. As a result, these people have attempted to explain and justify these in terms of belief systems whose ultimate first principles have become reduced to utopian, socialist political projects and regimes, the bankers, politicians and judges that run them, supposedly "Enlightened intellectuals," and media elites whose propaganda helps delude the masses into believing that what their intellectual elites, politicians, judges, and educators try to pass off as science and philosophy is not what it really is: political ideology, propaganda.

Such is the condition of metaphysical justifications for the nature and existence of modern "science," "philosophy." Neither can scientifically, philosophically, rationally justify its existence, explain precisely what it does, where it gets its principles from, why they work, or why it is worth possessing for a human being.

Modern and contemporary "philosophy," "science," have never been able rationally, metaphysically, to justify the claim of modern positivists that modern mathematical physics constitutes the whole of human science. Modern and contemporary physicists cannot do this because modern and contemporary physics is formally mathematical. No mathematical formula exists capable of scientifically demonstrating that modern and contemporary physics constitutes the whole of science. Nor is this a self-evident, *per se nota*, truth.

Moreover, the first purportedly "philosophical," metaphysical attempts to offer such a justification were miserable failures, based upon fallacious, sophistical arguments. Hence, this claim has never been rationally justified. Nor is it rationally justifiable. Such attempts have been, and continue to be, the chief source of the Babelism of modern thought.

As Adler rightly understood, to be able to transcend the Babelism of modern thought, we cannot look to modern or contemporary "philosophy" or "science" for an adequate solution. Such a solution must be a philosophical metaphysics. And modern and contemporary "philosophers," "scientists," do not have the foggiest idea, much less a clear and distinct one, of just what the nature of such a study might be. Modern and contemporary "science," "philosophy," are largely responsible for the Babelism of modern thought.

We cannot turn to most students of classical metaphysics to solve this problem because most of them have no idea what metaphysics, or philosophy, is. And we cannot simply return to the classical notion of natural law, or even to the classical understanding of the human person as a "rational animal" to help us. Modernity in its fully-developed and rotting state (postmodernism falsely-so-called) has largely twisted these ideas beyond recognition, divorced them from connection with the reality in which we live our daily lives.

To reunite wisdom and science, we need a real postmodernism essentially rooted in a new understanding of the human person. And we need to recover a proper understanding of the nature of philosophy and science, a real modern philosophy; not one falsely-so-called. To that task of fulfilling these needs, I will now turn my attention.

NOTES

1.   This usage was common for St. Thomas Aquinas, for example; see Armand A. Maurer, "Introduction," in Armand A. Maurer (ed.), *The Division and Methods of the Sciences: Commentary on the* de Trinitate *of Boethius, Questions V and VI* (Toronto: Pontifical Institute of Mediaeval Studies, 3rd rev. ed., 1963), p. VIII.

2.   Maurer, "Introduction," pp. VIII–IX.

3.   For a detailed defense of this claim, see Peter A. Redpath, *Cartesian Nightmare:* *An Introduction to Transcendental Sophistry* (Amsterdam and Atlanta: Editions Rodopi, B.V., 1997).

4.   Regarding the conflation of humanism with rhetoric and poetry during the Italian renaissance, see Paul Oskar Kristeller, *Renaissance Thought: The Classic, Scholastic, and Humanist Strains* (New York: Harper & Row, Publishers, 1961).

5.   Étienne Gilson, *Unity of Philosophical Experience* (New York: Charles Scribner's Sons, 1965), p. 140.

6.   Id., p. 91; see, also, Jean-Jacques Rousseau, *Émile or On Education*, trans. Allan Bloom (New York: Basic Books, Inc., Publishers, 1979), pp. 273–275.

7.   Peter A. Redpath, *Masquerade of the Dream Walkers: Prophetic Theology from the Cartesians to Hegel* (Amsterdam and Atlanta: Editions Rodopi, B.V., 1998), pp. 91–92; see, also, Rousseau, *Emile*, pp. 285–287.

8.   Redpath, *Masquerade of the Dream Walkers*, pp. 72–73; see, also, Rousseau, *Émile or On Education*, trans. Allan Bloom (New York, Basic Books Inc., Publishers, 1979), pp. 285–287.

9.   Redpath, *Masquerade of the Dream Walkers*, pp. 15–16; see, also, Frank E. Manuel, *Isaac Newton, Historian* (Cambridge, Mass.: Harvard University Press, 1979), pp. 89–121, 139–168.

10.   John Maynard Keynes, "Newton the Man," in Bernard Cohen and Richard S. Westfall (eds.), *Newton*, (New York and London, England: W. W. Norton and Company, Inc., 1995), p. 315.

11.   Redpath, *Masquerade of the Dream Walkers*, p. 13; see, also, Redpath, *Wisdom's Odyssey from Philosophy to Transcendental Sophistry* (Amsterdam and Atlanta: Editions Rodopi, B.V., 1998), pp. 133–145.

12.   Redpath, *Masquerade of the Dream Walkers*, p. 20.

13.   Id., pp. 13–35.

14.   Redpath, *Cartesian Nightmare*, p. 20.; see Gilson, *Unity of Philosophical Experience*, pp. 125–126; for the groundbreaking work that shows how some medieval and renaissance humanists transformed the physical universe into a book and philosophy into a skill of reading that book, see Gerald Galgan, *The Logic of Modernity* (New York and London, New York University Press, 1982).

15.   Redpath, *Cartesian Nightmare*, p. 20.

16.   Étienne Gilson, *Reason and Revelation in the Middle Ages* (New York: Charles Scribner's Sons, 1938), p. 65. I thank James V. Schall, S. J. for recalling this passage to my attention; see his article, "Possessed of Both a Reason and a Revelation," in Peter A. Redpath (ed.), *A Thomistic Tapestry: Essays in Memory of Étienne Gilson* (Amsterdam and Atlanta: Editions Rodopi, B. V., 2002).

17.   Étienne Gilson, *History of Christian Philosophy in the Middle Ages* (New York: Random House, 7th printing, 1955), pp. 218–219.

18.   Redpath, *Masquerade of the Dream Walkers: Prophetic Theology Theology from the Cartesians to Hegel*, pp. 67–99.

19.   Id., pp. 101–248. For a more detailed analysis of the how, wittingly or unwittingly, the thinking of Averroes and Petrarch influenced Rousseau, see Peter A. Redpath, "Pet-

rarch's Dream and the Failed Modern Project: A Chapter Gilson Did not Write," part 1 of 2, in *Contemporary Philosophy*, 25, nn. 5–6 (2003), pp. 3-9; part 2 of 2, in *Contemporary Philosophy*, 25, nn. 5-6 (2003), pp. 52–57. I thank Karl-Heinz Nusser from the Universität München for suggesting that I add to my analysis of the influence of Averroes on Rousseau some mention of how my thesis applies in the case of Rousseau's political teaching in his *Social Contract*.

20.   For a more detailed consideration of Rousseau's influence on Kant and Hegel, see Redpath, *Masquerade of the Dream Walkers: Prophetic Theology from the Cartesians to Hegel*, pp. 67–229.

21.   For how Rousseau's understanding of tolerance is currently being used by contemporary socialists to influence the direction of the contemporary world, see Peter A. Redpath, "Reduction of Justice to Tolerance in the New Totalitarian World Order," in *Telos*, n. 157 (2011), pp. 185–192.

22.   John N. Deely, *Semiotic Animal: A Postmodern Definition of 'Human Being' Transcending Patriarchy and Feminism* (South Bend, Indiana: St. Augustine's Press, 2010), p. 10.

23.   Mortimer J. Adler, "This Prewar Generation," in Geraldine van Doren (ed.), *Mortimer J. Adler, Reforming Education: The Opening of the American Mind* (New York: Macmillan Publishing Company and London, England: Collier Macmillan Publishers, 1988), pp. 4–5; "God and the Professors," Part One, in Max Weismann (ed.), *The Great Ideas Online*, 629 (August 11, 2011), pp. 6–12 and "God and the Professors," Part Two, in *The Great Ideas Online*, 629 (August 11, 2011), pp. 1–12. I thank my friend Max Weismann, director and co-founder with Mortimer J. Adler of the Center for the Study of Great Ideas, for providing me with a copy of this article.

24.   Adler, "This Prewar Generation," pp. 4–5.

25.   Id., p. 5.

26.   Id., p. 7.

27.   Id.

28.   Id., pp. 7–9.

29.   Id., p. 9.

30.   Id.

31.   Id.

32.   Id.

33.   Id.

34.   See Plato, *Meno*, 97A–98B; see Aristotle, *Posterior Analytics*, Bk 1, ch. 11, 77a5–9.

35.   Adler, "This Prewar Generation," p. 10.

36.   Id.

37.   Id., p. 11.

38.   Id., pp., 10–11; see Plato, *Republic*, Bk. 2, 361E–367E.

39.   Adler, "This Prewar Generation," p.11.

40.   Id.

41.   Id., pp. 11–12.

42.   Id., p. 12.

43. Id.

44. Id.

45. Adler, "God and the Professors," Part One, p. 7.

46. Id., p. 9.

47. Jacques Maritain, "Allocution du Président à la première séance plénière de la deuxième session de la Conférence générale de l'Unesco, 6 novembre 1947, Son Excellence Jacques Maritain, Chef de la Délégation française," in *Célébration du centenaire de la naissance de Jacques Maritain, 1882–1973*, no editor listed (New York: UNESCO, 1982), pp. 9–33.

48. Id., pp. 16–18.

49. Id., p. 11.

50. Id.

51. Id., p. 13.

52. Id., pp. 14–17.

53. Étienne Gilson, *The Terrors of the Year 2000* (Toronto: St. Michael's College, 1949), pp. 5, 14–16.; see Friedrich Nietzsche, *"Ecce Homo,"* in Friedrich Nietzsche, *The Philosophy of Nietzsche*, no editor or translator listed (New York: Random House, Modern Library, 1954), pp. 923–933.

54. Gilson, *The Terrors of the Year 2000*, p. 28

55. Id., p. 24.

56. Id., pp. 28–29.

57. Id., p. 28. I thank John N. Deely for reminding me that postmodernism as popularly understood today is essentially (1) modernism in its natural stage of maturity: decay; and (2) should properly be called "postmodernism falsely-so-called."

58. Id., pp. 21–25, 28–29.

59. Id., pp. 16–18.

60. Id., p. 17.

61. Pope Benedict XVI, "Faith, Reason, and the University: Memories and Reflections," Apostolic Journey of His Holiness Benedict XVI to München, Altötting, and Regensburg (09–14 September 2006), Meeting with the Representatives of Science, Lecture of the Holy Father, *Aula magna* of the University of Regensburg. (URL=http://www.vatican.va/holy_father/benedict_xvi/speeches/2006/september/documents/hf_ben-xvi_spe_20060912_university-regensburg_en.html), Tuesday, 12 September 2006, p. 1.

62. Id.

63. Id.

64. Id.

65. Id.

66. Id., p. 3.

67. Id.

68. Id.

69. Id.

70. Id.

71. Id.

72.   Id.

73.   Id.

74.   Id.

75.   Étienne Gilson, *Painting and Reality* (Pantheon Books, Published for the Bollingen, Foundation, Inc., Bollingen Series 35), p. 20, n. 17.

76.   Aristotle, *Physics*, Bk. 2, ch. 2, 194b.

Two

A BRIEF EXPLANATION OF WHY I THINK I
CAN FULFILL THE CHIEF AIMS
OF THIS BOOK

As the title of Volume One of this reconciliation project indicates, I devote this present monograph to recovering our understanding of philosophy and science. Volume One's title will likely perplex those readers who were unaware that we had lost, or ever had, this understanding. If I want to resolve the separation between philosophy and science, as this book's title indicates, other readers might ask why I simply do not turn to modern and contemporary "philosophers" to do so? My succinct reply to that question is to cite a quote from my friend and colleague Curtis L. Hancock: "to do so would be like asking incendiaries to help extinguish a forest fire." My "Introduction" to this monograph answers (or, for those who have read it, has answered) why I cannot do so.

For close to twenty years I have been arguing that, for over two millennia, what has passed for philosophy and science in the West, for the most part, has not been philosophy or science. I have written a trilogy of books to defend the case that, for the most part, philosophy started and ended with the ancient Greeks, and that anyone who wishes to apply the name "philosopher" to himself or herself, if only to reject the label, needs at least to understand the maturely-developed, ancient Greek understanding of "philosophy."[1]

Still other readers might not be perplexed by the title of this Volume One, or project, but that I would have the audacity to think myself capable of fulfilling the chief aim of the larger project or of this Volume. They might find such proposals to range from immodest to hubristic, or beyond. Were I to attempt to undertake this project or Volume, on my own, I would concur with such assessments.

Over the past couple of decades, with the help of some great intellects, I have made some discoveries that I think can achieve the chief aim of this project as a whole and of the current Volume. I attribute these discoveries chiefly to the help of other people and good luck, not to personal skill. Mostly, this Volume and this project as a whole report and synthesize discoveries made by other people. I have simply been in the right place and time to have had the good fortune, as St. Bernard of Chartres (d. ca. 1130) once said, "to stand on the shoulders of giants."[2] If, in this work, I say things that appear to see farther than others before me, the chief reason is because these people are elevating me by their intellectual stature. For the most part, I am simply restating what others have already said, that I have had the good fortune to know about.

I include among these giants ancient philosophers like Plato and Aristotle, the medieval theologian St. Thomas Aquinas, the celebrated twentieth-century intellectual Mortimer J. Adler, "Christian philosophers" like Étienne Gilson and Jacques Maritain, lesser-known contemporary students of St. Thomas and great intellects like Armand A. Maurer and Charles Bonaventure Crowley (d. 1996).

When, a couple of decades ago, I first started to become convinced that we in the West had largely lost our understanding of philosophy and that this loss of understanding was a chief reason for much of our contemporary social and cultural problems, I felt hesitant to accept this view to be true. So, I can understand the trouble some readers might have accepting it. If what I say is right, much of what they now think about philosophy, science, and other matters could well be wrong. I experienced a similar difficulty when, in the late 1980s, my reading of Maritain's *The Peasant of the Garonne*, and some other works, caused me to start to take seriously Maritain's bold assertion that modern subjective idealists "impugn the basic foundation of philosophic research. They are not philosophers"; that what such thinkers practice today is a kind of "secularized theology."[3]

Gilson, no historical or philosophical ignoramus, reinforced this initial shock when I found him saying, "The magnificent 'systems' of those idealists who bear the title of 'great thinkers,' and wholly deserve it, belong to the realm of art more than in that of philosophy. . . . No more than science, philosophy cannot be a system, because all systematic thinking ultimately rests upon an assumption, whereas, as knowledge, philosophy must rest on being."[4]

I spent at least ten years doing intense, historical research to determine whether what Maritain and Gilson were saying was true. At the end of that time, I concluded it was. As a result, I had to rethink most of what I had previously learned about philosophy and its history.

During this research I had the good fortune to become familiar with some of the work of one of Gilson's most famous students: Armand A. Maurer. I communicated personally with Fr. Maurer for years and considered him a teacher and friend. Among other things, my reading of Maurer taught me that, according to St. Thomas (1) philosophy is chiefly an act of a habit of the human soul, not a body of knowledge or a logical system; (2) the subject, or genus, that the philosopher studies is not the subject, or genus, of the logician (the philosopher studies a real, not a logical, subject, or genus); (3) philosophical, or scientific universals, are not logical universals; (4) analogy is the mode of reasoning proper to the philosopher or scientist; and (5) analogy chiefly refers to an act of judgment, not to terms or concepts.

From Crowley, a cherubic and impish Dominican priest with whom I shared a departmental office for about a decade, I learned, among other things, that, according to Aristotle and St. Thomas, we cannot precisely understand the nature and divisions of philosophy without comprehending (1) Aristotle's and St. Thomas's teaching about "virtual quantity" (a concept with which virtually few of Aristotle's and St. Thomas's students have ever heard, or been familiar); and (2) that just as he had done with terms like "being," "true," and "good," Aquinas thought that we predicate the term "unity" analogously; that all the divisions of philosophy, science, essentially depend upon such an understanding; and, knowingly or not to mathematical physicists, all the laws of modern physical science involve analogously transposing to different genera the metaphysical principle of unity and its essential divisions to measure qualities, or virtual quantities.

Within the following chapters throughout this book, I will repeatedly return to the above insights from Maritain, Gilson, Maurer, Adler, and Crowley. I will also add other truths I have learned from them to help me complete this project. Having satisfied myself that I have done my best to explain to readers of this book precisely why I am doing what I am doing in this work, and precisely why I think I can do it, the time has come for the recovery to start.

NOTES

1 Peter A. Redpath, *Cartesian Nightmare: An Introduction to Transcendental Sophistry* (Amsterdam and Atlanta: Editions Rodopi, B.V., 1997); *Wisdom's Odyssey from Philosophy to Transcendental Sophistry* (Amsterdam and Atlanta: Editions Rodopi, B.V., 1997); *Masquerade of the Dream Walkers: Prophetic Theology from the Cartesians to Hegel* (Amsterdam and Atlanta: Editions Rodopi, B.V., 1998).

2 Ralph M. McInerny, *A History of Western Philosophy: From St. Augustine to Ockham.* Volume 2. *Medieval Philosophy* (Notre Dame and London, England: University of Notre Dame Press, 1970), p. 160.

3 Jacques Maritain, *The Peasant of the Garonne: An Old Layman Questions Himself about the Present Time* (New York: Holt, Rinehard, and Winston, Inc., 1968), p. 102; *The Dream of Descartes: Together with Some Other Essays*, trans. Mabelle L. Andison (New York: Philosophical Library, 1944); *Education at the Crossroads* (New York and London: Yale University Press, 1970), p. 74.

4 Étienne Gilson, *Being and Some Philosophers* (Toronto: Pontifical Institute of Mediaeval Studies, 1952), pp. 212–213.

Three

THE PRE-SOCRATIC UNDERSTANDING OF PHILOSOPHY AND SCIENCE

Before reading Jacques Maritain and Étienne Gilson, like most of my colleagues, under the influence of René Descartes, I had mistaken philosophy to be a kind of systematic logic. I mistakenly thought that the ancient Greek discovery of philosophy arose as a result of the Greek discovery of the principles of logic. By 1998, I no longer thought so.

Hence, in my *Masquerade of the Dream Walkers*: *Prophetic Theology from the Cartesians to Hegel*, I correctly wrote:

> Often, philosophy teachers assert that the problem of the one and the many was a main issue of early ancient Greek philosophy, of ancient Greek physics, or natural philosophy, the first philosophical discipline that arose after philosophical reasoning broke off from Greek mytho-poietic reasoning. This is not accurate. The whole of ancient Greek philosophy was the problem of the one and the many. For the ancient Greeks, philosophy was a study of measured being. The major Greek philosophers considered philosophy to involve knowing a multiplicity of substances and substantial properties through a one. Aristotle tells us to measure something means to know it through a one. Hence, to know a substance as a one is to measure it.[1]

A chief reason that many philosophy teachers narrow the influence of the problem of the one and the many in ancient Greek philosophy tends to be that, like me, this is what they were taught. Going back to the high middle ages, Western thinkers have largely reduced the study they call "philosophy" to the intellectual discipline of logic. The Italian renaissance was an exception because, as the great historian of Italian renaissance thought, Paul Oskar Kristeller, has meticulously shown, the mode of thought that dominated the renaissance was a combination of rhetoric and poetry. As a kind of slang, students of the time coined the term "humanist" to identify its practitioner.[2] During this intellectual renaissance philosophy was largely reduced to "humanism" (rhetoric and poetry) because the renaissance humanists were largely rebelling against the medieval reduction of philosophy to logic, or to what pejoratively they had labeled "scholasticism."

Descartes's reaction to, and critique of, the humanist education he had received at the Jesuit school of La Flèche reversed this intellectual tide and returned to the long-standing Western conflation of philosophy and logic, except this time philosophy was supposedly "systematic" logic.

In contrast, for the ancient Greeks, from its start with philosophy's Father, Thales, to its high point with Socrates, Plato, Aristotle, and Plotinus, the prevailing understanding of philosophy was never reduced to logic. Aristotle considered logic to be philosophy's tool, instrument, or organon, and ancient Greek Stoics made logic a division of philosophy, along with physics and ethics; but the reduction of philosophy to logic or a kind of logic never happened.

While all philosophers use logic, must think logically, thinking logically is not identical with philosophical thinking; and, strictly speaking, the birth of philosophy among the ancient Greeks did not start with the discovery of logic, in a formal or informal sense. Being logical is not enough to make a person philosophical.

Just as the art of medicine did not start with the practice of some sort of generic activity called "medicine," but started with studying and healing this or that specific and individual illness, the generic study called "philosophy," "science," started in ancient Greece with the study (species of philosophy, science) called "physics," with an attempt by pre-Socratic thinkers from the Greek colony of Ionia in Asia Minor (such as Thales, Anaximander [b. ca. 610 BC; d. ca. 546 BC], and Anaximines [b. 585 BC; d. 528 BC]) to understand which of the four everlasting material elements (earth, air, fire, or water) existed as the most primitive generic body, the substrate, or principle, that, somehow, contained the other three species of matter and from which the other three emerged or started to "appear."

The ancient Greek philosophers were not chiefly logicians. For all of them, from Thales through Plotinus (b. 204/5; d. 270 AD), sense wonder was a first principle of philosophical reasoning. All of them, including Plato and the "mysterious" and "mystical" Plotinus, started philosophizing from sense wonder (in Plotinus' case, in his famous *Enneads*, from wonder about sense beauty). None started philosophizing from abstract essences, faith seeking understanding, methodic doubt, impossible dreams of pure reason, the voice of conscience, Absolute Spirit's urge to emerge, or the scores of other non-philosophical principles from which, throughout Western history, non-philosophers (generally sophists of one kind or another) have claimed to begin doing philosophy.

As I have shown in my book *Wisdom's Odyssey from Philosophy to Transcendental Sophistry*, Plato's dialogues are replete with examples of his conviction that philosophy starts with sense wonder. Moreover, when Plato says that the senses are not trustworthy or not truthful, he does not mean that the senses are totally unreliable as first principles of knowing, or of philosophical knowing. In Plato's dialogues, Socrates (b. 469 BC; d. 399 BC) repeatedly starts with sensory events and returns to sensory examples to generate and, in conjunction with reason, test philosophical truths. When Plato criticizes the senses as untrustworthy or untruthful, he means that, in and of themselves, they do not provide human beings with precise, or scientific, knowledge: that is, knowledge that includes an explanation, that is not simply of the fact, but of the reasoned fact. He does not mean that they do not, or cannot, serve as starting points of human knowledge and of philosophy.[3]

Like the first teachers of the ancient Greeks (the mythological poets), all the ancient Greek physicists were sense realists, just as were the early Greek sophists, who arose historically after the philosophers as the third class of ancient Greek professional teachers.[4] While some scholars might attempt to disprove my claim that all three of these classes of thinkers were sense realists, the assertion is easy to prove. I give a detailed defense of it in *Wisdom's Odyssey from Philosophy to Transcendental Sophistry*.[5] Having done so, I will not repeat that whole argument here.

Suffice it to say, among other things, that all the early ancient Greek thinkers had a difficult time comprehending the idea of something "immaterial." No words existed in early ancient Greek to talk in such a way. Even Plato, who, apparently following Socrates, first started philosophically to conceive of immaterial being, would often do so through use of positive, not negative, terms. For example, he would call the Good "beingly-beingly-being" and an immaterial Form "beingly-being" in contrast to sensible beings that "exist." In this sense, immaterial being is what is "more-than" being or "bigger-than" being.

This difficulty of conceiving of immaterial being was not a problem that lasted just throughout early Greek philosophy. It persisted beyond Plato into the late Roman age and Christian era. It is widespread among some people in different parts of the world even today. All children, at all times in human history, experience this difficulty.

Apart from Socrates, Plato, Aristotle, and their students, who popularized the notion of "form" to introduce immateriality into ancient philosophy, virtually all the ancient Greek intellectuals (for example, stoics, atomists, epicureans) tended to revert to materialism of some sort. The situation was so prevalent that, in his famous autobiographical work, *Confessions*, St. Aurelius Augustine (b. 354; d. 430) repeatedly complains about how his inability to conceive of immaterial being had hampered for so long his conversion to Christianity.[6]

Since the first intimations of philosophical reasoning, the inclination to *wonder* about opposing reports that our sense and intellectual faculties sometimes simultaneously give us about some numerically-one subject of our experience, Aristotle tells us that, in a way (that is, analogously), even the makers of myth (the poets) are philosophers.[7]

Because the first philosophers, early ancient Greek physicists, had been first educated within, and broke off from, the ancient Greek poetic tradition, they made no initial philosophical, or scientific, distinction among intellectual disciplines like physics, mathematics, logic, and metaphysics. They had not developed logic as a separate, formal division of learning; and, initially, they had reduced mathematics and metaphysics to physics. Strictly speaking, they were not yet fully-formed, maturely-developed, philosophers.

Prior to the emergence of the new profession of philosopher, scientist, from that of the class of ancient poets, all the leading ancient Greek educators tended to be called "poets," "musicians," or "sophists." These names were predicated synonymously of them. The chief reason for this synonymous predication of these terms for professional educators is that, prior to the time of Pythagoras (who reportedly coined the term "philosopher"), the ancient Greeks identified all higher, or exceptional, forms of knowing, with "wisdom"; and they claimed that all wisdom in the form of human art or science was a gift from a god (for example, a "Muse"), an inspired knowledge given by a god to a son, or friend, of a god. For this reason an ancient epic poet like Hesiod or Homer would start a major work by invoking inspiration from a god.

In short, at this time, the ancient Greeks identified the genus "artistic" or "scientific" knowledge with divine inspiration. And they considered this genus to be the first principle of artistic, or scientific, knowledge in any human artist or scientist. In so doing, the ancient Greeks were simply analogously extending to the order of human knowing the role that they attributed to the gods within the sense world in general.

For the early ancient Greeks everything that moved was alive and had a god in it that caused it to be alive and move. For these ancient Greeks the gods existed *in*, not beyond, the physical universe. Together with everlasting matter, the gods were the generic principles (the principles that "generated," gave birth to) of all the species of change, or movement, within the physical world. Such a change could be inanimate, like a lightning bolt caused by Zeus, medical healing caused by Asclepios, the human emotion of love caused by Eros or Aphrodite, or wisdom caused by Athena.

Hence the earliest understanding that the ancient Greeks had of "science" or "wisdom" (which they did not yet precisely distinguish from each other) was of some sort of inspiration given by a god to a son or a human friend. Moreover, being the practical people that they culturally were, the ancient Greeks conceived of all knowing as practical. Hence, prior to the time of Socrates, Plato, and Aristotle, the Greeks had conflated science, poetry, music, sophistry (wisdom) with practical, not theoretical, speculative, or contemplative knowledge. Not until after Aristotle did non-practical ways of knowing start to make a little headway as the "ideal" of scientific knowledge and the highest form of wisdom.

Strictly speaking, the habit of philosophizing, the discipline of philosophy, started to develop among the ancient Greeks when some members of the educational class of poets started to wonder whether, if the gods existed in the material universe, if their influence could be known there by inspiration as an effect from a cause, why could this influence not also be known by unaided natural reason?

In short, the first of the ancient philosophers were not atheists, did not consider themselves necessarily to be breaking away from the ancient Greek theological tradition. They were simply maintaining that another way of gaining exceptional knowing of secondary causes might be open to human beings through which, without dependency upon, or appeal to, inspiration, human beings might be able to come to know about the *behavior* of the gods (secondary causes) in individually existing material beings.

While some members of the philosophizing class might, later, have become atheists, atheism was not an essential property demanded of an ancient philosopher, most of whom, from the prevailing scholarly evidence we have (including Socrates, Plato, Aristotle, and Plotinus) considered themselves to be theists. Being a theist, however, was an essential property of an ancient poet.

Moreover, while the first philosophers might not have considered themselves to be atheists, might have thought themselves to be theists, for chiefly three reasons the remaining members of the poetic class were inclined to view these philosophers as atheists. (1) The ancient Greeks were prevailingly polytheists. As such, unlike monotheists (like Jews, Christians, and Muslims), an ancient Greek could be a *complete* or *partial* atheist, could deny the existence of one or more than one god. (2) An ancient Greek could also be a partial atheist by diminishing the influence of the gods in the world. In short, the ancient Greeks tended analogously to predicate the term "partial atheist."

For this reason, at his trial recounted in Plato's *Apology*, Socrates' chief prosecutor, Meletos, represented the class of poets (something for which Plato, apparently, never forgave the poets). And Socrates raised the question against Meletos about whether Meletos was accusing Socrates of being a complete or partial atheist.[8]

Because the first of the ancient philosophers had started to introduce a way of knowing other than inspiration as an avenue to "science" or "wisdom," because they were maintaining that something other than inspiration given by a god to a son, or a human friend, could be the source of both science and wisdom, the ancient poets tended to view these philosophers as educational opponents, competitors, as people who were diminishing their influence among the ancient Greeks. Since the poets (1) understood the nature and origin of science, wisdom, in only one way (as inspiration coming from a god) and (2) knew that their gods were good, and that philosophers had exceptional knowledge (the mark of science and wisdom), they inclined necessarily to view these competitors, like Socrates, as atheists influenced by bad gods.

The general poetic suspicion of the early Greek philosophers as competitors in the commonly-accepted educational field of wisdom reinforces my claim that all ancient philosophers started their reasoning in sense wonder. Just like the poets before them, the ancient philosophers started their activity by turning toward, not away from, the sense universe to find first principles of philosophical reason in sense wonder. And they did so by consciously trying to avoid being influenced by any higher "inspiration" or external lights.

The ancient sophists also followed the lead of the ancient poets and philosophers. This third group of ancient Greek professional educators came into existence after the philosophers, after Parmenides (fl. 500 BC) had introduced a problem into ancient Greek physics that enabled the poets, and other philosophical opponents, to question the ancient Greek physicists' method of philosophical reasoning. Apparently groping toward an explicit, metaphysical understanding of science, the ancient sophists arose when some thinkers within the poetic or philosophic class started to get an increased intimation of the nature of relation, especially of real relation.

Like the ancient poets and philosophers, the sophists started their reasoning in sense wonder, in the semiotic recognition of opposition between conflicting communications (for example, what we sense as many but think of as one). Like the poets the sophists attributed the origin of this conflict to a gift, but not to a gift of inspiration. They attributed this gift to their superior birth through which some people had the ability, through language, to interfere with, overpower, and essentially alter the sense perception of other people.

Apparently influenced in part by the Greek physicist Empedocles (b. 490 BC; d. ca. 430 BC), who had maintained that we can know things at a distance because physical beings emit "films," the sophists claimed to have the ability to use speech to alter and overpower unions of emanations that arise *between* a potential knower and a potentially known being, thereby changing a sense perception before it reaches a knower. Protagoras, for example, appeared to deny that the quality "color" existed in physical things, or that the power of sight existed in human beings. Instead, he thought that the act of sight resulted from a mixing, or coincidence, outside the human person of motions simultaneously emanating from a potential seer and potentially visible being. Once mixed, supposedly, the resulting unit causes a boomerang-like effect that generates seeing to be received into the potential seer and color to be received into the potentially visible thing.[9] Apparently, the ancient sophist claimed that the power of speech could interfere with, change, the way the boomerang-effect reached, or was received by, the potential knower.

The sophists apparently attributed their special ability neither to the gods, like the poets, nor to naturally-acquired ability, like the first philosophers. The sophists accounted for their "skill" in terms of their cultural heritage, their historical roots. They simply were better born than other people. Their aristocratic birth, and/or historical, origin, accounted for their mental superiority. Hence, for the sophists (who generally tended to be lawyers, often litigators in court or before an assembly, and political advisors and mouthpieces), wisdom is a kind of linguistic, cultural gift that originates from simply being better born. Its origin is cultural, historical roots; not in nature, nurture, or the gods.

For the early Greek physicists everything that exists (even the gods) emerged, or was generated, from within some material ("chaos") that had previously existed and somehow contained whatever it generated. *This primal matter appears to have been a kind of coincidence of opposites* containing the gods (who emerge from it in a specific order) and material elements (which also emerge from it in a specific order). For this reason, the first of the ancient Greek philosophers, Thales, says that the first matter from which all things emerge is water (*hydor*) and "all things are full of gods."[10]

The chief problem these early physicists had was, just as it had been for the poets from whom they started formally to separate, to try to figure out which was the first everlasting, common matter (the genus) from which all the other species of matter, including that of the gods, had initially emerged, how did this emergence occur, and how does it continue.

The main reason that this was their chief problem is easy to explain: This was the chief problem that concerned the ancient Greek poets. The ancient philosophers were a group of ancient Greek intellectuals who broke away from the ancient Greek poets. And this problem chiefly concerned the poets because they thought that if they could answer this question they could unlock the key to understanding all the mysteries of the cosmos within which they lived.

Today, most teachers of ancient philosophy will sometimes refer to the ancient Greek physicists subscribing to a notion of evolution. Strictly speaking, the notion of evolution appears to be essentially incompatible with ancient Greek thought because evolution presupposes novelty, newness in existence, progress. Western theology, especially the notion of creation *ex nihilo* and the teachings of St. Augustine, appears to be the remote historical foundation for the modern notion of evolution.[11] The ancient Greeks tended to subscribe to a cyclical view of the universe. In such a universe, nothing new can happen. Consequently, nothing can evolve, no newness can come to be. Whatever happens simply repeats what has already existed. Such a universe has no notion of novelty, newness in the modern evolutionary, progressivist sense.

This does not mean that no one in antiquity recognized the appearance of new species or the disappearance of old ones. Some ancient physicists were aware of fossil records (as anomalies, not fossils), and even the first philosophers thought that one kind of matter was somehow the most primitive, appeared first, and somehow contained, and acted as the substrate for, the other kinds of matter.

The problem of the relationship between genera and species existed long before it started to become expressed in terms of the medieval problem of universals or modern Darwinian evolution. It comprised the chief problem of ancient philosophy. It started as a problem within ancient physics. From there it became analogously transposed into other disciplines, such as metaphysics and logic. In modern times it came back to haunt the intellectual world in terms of "biology" ("natural history").

Medieval thought simply moved this problem of the relationship between the one and the many (which first arose among the ancient Greek physicists in terms the problem of the relationship between "a real genus and a real species") to a new existential plane, which sought to trace the origin of genera and species in the mind to mind-independent principles, and attempted to understand how the transition occurs from the one mode of existence to the other.

Such a move was not entirely new. Long before Porphyry the Phoenician (b. ca. 232; d. 304), Anicius Manlius Severinus Boethius, or Peter Abailard (b. 1079; d. 1142), who introduced the problem of universals to the later middle ages, in ancient physics, Parmenides had started to move the problem of the one and the many (genus and species) to a different plane, from physics to metaphysics. In so doing, Parmenides gave ancient poets ammunition against the new method of reasoning that philosophers had started to develop. In the process, the conflict he caused would eventually help generate the philosophical discipline of metaphysics (which historically succeeds the philosophy, or science, of mathematics that Pythagoras and the Pythagoreans had started to develop) and the new discipline of logic and political profession of the sophist, or political consultant.

Parmenides is sometimes portrayed today as a metaphysician. Strictly speaking, Parmenides could not possibly have been a metaphysician for the simple reason that Parmenides thought that all being is physical. As the great historian of ancient philosophy Joseph Owens says, "Parmenides . . . appeared to Aristotle and the Greek doxographers as a physicist in the ancient sense, a philosopher of nature."[12] Like all the ancient Greek physicists before him, Parmenides starts his philosophical reasoning from sense wonder.

Parmenides existed on the frontier of the new science of metaphysics. Hence, he was unable easily or precisely to distinguish metaphysical problems from problems in physics in which his ideas had incubated. Not being fully aware that he was glimpsing complicated problems behind and beyond those that physics is able properly to investigate or resolve, Parmenides apparently thought, as Gilson observes about the medieval intellectual Peter Abailard regarding logic, that he was simply tracing back physics to its fundamental implications.[13]

Parmenides rocked the world of ancient physics by undermining one of the basic (but then still tacit) metaphysical principles upon which, unknowingly to the thinkers at the time, ancient physics rested. He called into question the ancient Greek physical assumption that an everlasting matter (genus) could generate anything. Parmenides maintained that if being is identical with unity, if the original matter from which everything is supposedly generated is essentially everlasting and one, then this matter is essentially without parts and is, therefore, essentially unchangeable. As such, nothing can emerge from it. Being (the one, unchangeable, always the same), he said, is being (one, unchangeable, and always the same); and non-being (the changeable, multiple, always different), he said, is non-being (many, changeable, always different).

The world of ancient physics stayed rocked by the thought of Parmenides at least until the time of Plato, when, as Aristotle tells us, Plato "gave separate existence to these universally predicated substances," that is, to the forms, unifying principles, in things, about which Socrates had started to speak.[14] Plato attempted metaphysically to solve the problem that Parmenides had introduced into ancient Greek physics by maintaining that, if we can separate matter as a principle of existence (genus) from another principle that causes matter to exist in different ways (Form, species), matter can be everlasting and change can still occur in the physical world.

So, Plato maintained that, while matter is everlasting in duration, considered in itself it is qualitatively indefinite, is, at best, quantified body. Another principle, which Plato called a "Form" or "Idea," makes matter specifically definite. But, unlike Socrates, Plato claimed that this immaterial principle (species) exists apart from the material world, does not exist in bodies. Physical things change by reflecting, or participating in, Forms, species, Ideas that exist apart from individually existing material beings.

By causing species to exist apart from individual beings, Plato took species out of the physical world and made them incapable of evolving or of being principles of generation existing *in* material beings. By so doing, as Aristotle notes, *Plato transformed the problem of the one and the many into the problem of universals*, the problem of how what we talk about as being general relates to what we know to exist as individual. As Aristotle says:

> But if the principles (that is, genera and species) *are* universal, either the substances composed of them are also universal, or non-substance will be prior to substance; for the universal is not a substance, but the element or principle is universal, and the element or principle is prior to the thing of which it is the principle or element.
>
> All these difficulties follow naturally, when they (that is, Plato and his followers) make the Ideas out of elements and at the same time claim that apart from the substances which have the same form there are Ideas, a single separate entity. . . .. The statement that all knowledge is universal, so that the principles of things must also be universal and not separate substances, presents indeed, of all the points we have mentioned, the greatest difficulty.[15]

In making this move, as Aristotle had recognized, like Parmenides before him, Plato had rocked the philosophical world and had moved the problem of philosophy, of the one and the many, to a new existential plane, to a new mode of existence "of the greatest difficulty": to that of metaphysics and of universals. In so doing, Plato uncovered one of the chief properties of the philosophical or scientific mind from his time to ours, the distinguishing mark of philosophical or scientific knowledge to be a claim about possessing universal truth. Just how Plato sought to resolve this problem is the issue to which I will turn my attention in the next chapter.

NOTES

1. Peter A. Redpath, *Masquerade of the Dream Walkers: Prophetic Theology from the Cartesians to Hegel* (Amsterdam and Atlanta: Editions Rodopi, B.V., 1998), p. 232; see also, Aristotle, *Metaphysics*, trans. W.D. Ross, in *The Basic Works of Aristotle*, ed. Richard McKeon (New York: Random House, 1968), Bk. 10, ch. 1, 1052b20–30; and Charles B. Crowley, *Aristotelian-Thomistic Philosophy of Measure and the International System of Units (SI)*, ed. with a prescript by Peter A. Redpath (Lanham, Md.: University Press of America, 1996), pp. 1–47.

2. Paul Oskar Kristeller, *Renaissance Thought: The Classic, Scholastic, and Humanist Strains*. New York: Harper & Row, Publishers, 1961.

3. For a detailed defense of this claim, see Peter A. Redpath, *Wisdom's Odyssey from Philosophy to Transcendental Sophistry* (Amsterdam and Atlanta: Editions Rodopi, B.V., 1998), pp. 1–62.

4. Id.

5. Id.

6. See, for example, St. Aurelius Augustine, *Confessions*, Bk. 3, ch. 7; Bk. 4, ch. 2; Bk. 5, ch. 10; Bk. 6, ch. 3; Bk. 8, ch. 1.

7. Aristotle, *Metaphysics*, Bk. 1, ch. 1, 982b15–20.

8. Plato, *Apology*, 24A–27E.

9. Peter A. Redpath, *Cartesian Nightmare: An Introduction to Transcendental Sophistry* Amsterdam and Atlanta: Editions Rodopi, B.V., 1998), p. 106. I take my interpretation of Protagoras from what Plato says about his teaching in Plato's dialogue *Theaetetus*, 167C–168C, 182A–C, and 202A–C.

10. My interpretation of ancient Greek understanding of the gods, including that of Thales, follows that of Étienne Gilson, in his masterful *God and Philosophy* (New Haven: Yale University Press), 1961.

11. Augustine, *Confessions*, Bks. 11–13.

12. Joseph Owens, *A History of Ancient Western Philosophy* (Englewood Cliffs, New Jersey: Prentice Hall, Inc., 1959), pp. 70–71; see Aristotle, *Metaphysics*, Bk.1, ch. 5, 986b1–30.

13. Étienne Gilson, *Unity of Philosophical Experience* (New York: Charles Scribner's Sons, 1965), pp. 5–6.

14.   Aristotle, *Metaphysics*, Bk 13, ch. 10, 1086b5–10; material in parenthesis is my clarification of the text.

15.   Id., 1087a1–15; material in parenthesis is my clarification of the text.

FOUR

PLATO'S ADVICE ABOUT HOW TO AVOID BECOMING A PHILOSOPHICAL BASTARD: MOVING THE PROBLEM OF THE ONE AND THE MANY TO THE PROBLEM OF UNIVERSALS

Precisely to show how Plato used the philosophical discipline of metaphysics to give birth to the problem of universals, I will start by first considering some things that, in one of his most famous dialogues, *The Republic*, chiefly through the character of Socrates, Plato told us about becoming a philosopher. As someone who, like all the philosophers before him, started philosophy as a human activity essentially related to experiencing the problem of the one and the many within the context of sense wonder, throughout his dialogues, Plato repeatedly made reference to the opposition between the one and the many and to how the peculiar way philosophers speak is connected to this opposition. The examples are so many that I need not cite all of them in particular to prove my point. Readers may simply check dialogues such as the *Meno, Symposium, Crito, Phaedo, Ion, Laches, Lysis, Charmides, Protagoras, Parmenides, Sophist, Laws*, and *Republic*. If they pay careful attention to these dialogues, they should easily be able to verify that my claim is true. Nonetheless, to prove this same point beyond reasonable doubt, I will take up this same issue in this chapter in relation to what Plato said in *Republic*, Book Seven, because, in this section of this work, Plato engaged in a sustained reflection on the pedagogy involved in becoming a philosopher.

Republic, Book Seven, starts with Plato's famous "Myth of the Cave." Plato presented this story at this point in his dialogue as an example to show how, as he just finished saying in Book Six, "Philosophy . . . the love of wisdom, is impossible for the multitude" (the many), and how strange, alien, the nature of philosophical education is likely to appear to the many.[1]

Since most people conversant with philosophy are familiar with this story, I will not go into it in detail, other than to mention that, within the context of his account, Plato made sure to indicate that "in naming the things they saw" the people in the cave would be naming appearances, but would think they were naming the things that were causing the appearances.[2] Only the person who was able to escape from the cave and, eventually, come to know the Good (which causes everything else but is the last thing seen) is the philosopher and would rightly understand how to name things.[3]

In preparing to explain the nature of philosophical education, Plato had Socrates tell Glaucon that they had to use this image of turning the soul's vision from appearances to the Good.[4] Then Socrates proceeded to explain the nature of this sort of psychic turning in more precise, less metaphorical, detail.

He started to do this by saying, "education is not in reality what some people proclaim it to be in their professions. What they aver is that they can put true knowledge into a soul that does not possess it, as if they were inserting vision into blind eyes." Next, he stated that his argument indicates the proper analogy for the change education effects is not that of filling an empty vessel.

> The true analogy for this indwelling power in the soul and the instrument whereby each of us apprehends is that of an eye that could not be converted to the light from the darkness except by turning the whole body. Even so this organ of knowledge must be turned around from the world of becoming together with the entire soul, like the scene shifting periactus in the theater, until the soul is able to endure the contemplation of essence and the brightest region of being. And this, we say is the good, do we not?[5]

Socrates then speculated that "an art of the speediest and most effective shifting or conversion of the soul, not an art of producing vision in it," might exist. But it could only do so for an eye that already possesses vision, "but does not rightly direct it and does not look where it should."

He maintained that such an art would resemble servile, or bodily, arts, inasmuch as it does not pre-exist in the soul; and we have to cause it by habit and practice. But such a liberal art, or as Socrates more precisely called it, this intellectual virtue or

> excellence of thought, it seems, is certainly of a more divine quality, a thing that never loses its potency, but, according to the direction of its conversion, becomes useful and beneficent, or, again, useless and harmful. Have you never observed in those who are popularly spoken of as bad, but smart, men, how keen is the vision of the little soul, how quick it is to discern the things that interest it, a proof that it is not a poor vision, which it has but one forcibly enlisted in the service of evil, so that the sharper the sight the more mischief it accomplishes?[6]

Plato might have had in mind Alcibiades as the sort of precocious man possessed of some intellectual cleverness but lacking in the requisite moral virtue to become a philosopher.[7] Today, we might think of one, or more, professional politician. Whatever the case, Socrates continued by saying that, had the moral part of this small-souled person's psyche "been hammered from childhood" and had it freed more the intemperate dispositions that turned its vision downward, if "it had suffered a conversion toward the things that are real and true (that is, toward first principles and causes), that same faculty of the same men would have been most keen in its vision of the higher things, just as it is for the things toward which it is now tuned."[8]

Socrates asserted that, strictly speaking, people uneducated and inexperienced in truth, and people who want to spend their lives in uninterrupted learning for the sake of learning, can never adequately rule a city, because the first live aimless lives, and direct all their actions aimlessly, and the second will not voluntarily seek to engage in politics because they believe "that while still living they have been transported to the Islands of the Blessed."

Since the wider context of Plato's consideration of education was his study of how to establish the ideal city so as to find there true justice, he had Socrates maintain that the only way he will be able to do so is to force philosophers "to live an inferior life when the better is in their power." The just city that he is founding is concerned with the happiness of the whole city, not that of one group, even of philosophers. Hence, he told Glaucon, with whom he was then speaking, that, in forcing philosophers to rule, "We shall not be wronging . . . the philosophers who arise among us, but . . . we can justify our action when we constrain them to take charge of the other citizens and be their guardians."

In this way (unknowingly describing escape from the modern city sprung from Cartesian doubt and modern subjective idealism), Socrates said, "our city will be governed by waking minds, and not, as most cities now, which are inhabited and ruled darkly as in a dream by men who fight one another for shadows and wrangle for office as if that were a great good."

Socrates claimed that philosophers "will assuredly approach office as an unavoidable necessity, and in the *opposite* temper from that of the present rulers in our cities."[9] Plato's ideal city only becomes a determinate, or real, possibility on the condition that some way of living better, some happiness higher, than political life exists.

> For only in such a state will those rule who are really rich, not in gold. But if, being beggars and starvelings from lack of goods of their own, they turn to affairs of the state thinking that it is thence that they should grasp their own good,

then it is impossible. For when office and rule become the prizes of contention, such a civil and internecine strife destroys the office seekers themselves and the city as well.[10]

Socrates said that only the life of the true philosopher looks with scorn upon political office, for this precise reason: only true philosophers are worthy of holding political office because "those who take office should not be lovers of rule. Otherwise there will be a contest with rival lovers."[11] Clearly, this is because, in Plato's mind, the philosopher is *unique*, different from, and *opposed* to the *many*, those who seek political office for personal gain.

Since rule in the ideal city necessarily demands involvement of philosophers, Socrates' next question to consider was how do we produce philosophers and how may they "be led upward to the light even as some are fabled to have ascended from Hades to the gods?" Socrates' answer was that, as he had said in his Myth of the Cave, true philosophy is that ascension to reality that is "a conversion and turning about of the soul from a day whose light is darkness to the veritable day."

All well and good. Most people who call themselves "philosophers" probably get his message. But, metaphors aside, more precisely, what did Socrates and Plato mean by this conversion and turning of the soul? Socrates immediately explained his meaning by considering the question of what powers effect this turning and conversion.

Since the general education thus far under consideration in the *Republic* had been for rulers, or guardians, Socrates maintained that this study must be useful to soldiers, but must go beyond the training in "music" (the liberal arts, or poetry, as he and Glaucon have already described music). The reason for this, as Glaucon explained, is that music had "educated the guardians through habits, imparting by the melody a certain harmony of spirit that is not science, and by the rhythm measure and grace, and also the qualities akin to these in words of tales that are fables and those that are more nearly true. But it included no study that intended to any such good as you are now seeking."

Since music, gymnastic, and the servile arts, as then popularly understood and taught, were inadequate propaedeutics for effecting the philosophical habit of mind, Socrates suggested that Glaucon and he should "take something that applies to all alike." He then referred to the "common thing that all the arts and forms of thought and all sciences employ, and which is among the first things that everybody must learn." Since this thing is common to all the arts and all forms of thought, and is something all science uses, while Socrates did not refer to it as such, at first glance, it would appear to be some sort of logical or metaphysical being because logical reasoning and metaphysical principles apply to everything we know.

The way Socrates explained this common thing, however, was as "that of distinguishing one, two, and three. I mean, in sum, number and calculation. Is it not true of them that every art and science must necessarily partake of them?" While Glaucon readily agreed, at first glance, the correct answer to the question Socrates just posed appears to be, "No," unless Socrates was referring these predicates to their subjects in some sort of metaphysical, not mathematical, way (for example, by predicating the term analogously to mean "measuring").

At the same time, in a way, what Socrates said is true, even mathematically considered, for, in a way, all linguistic development (a necessary condition for developing science), presupposes our ability to limit the length of sounds we produce to form words, and ordering words one after the other (word order), to form sentences. Both require some rudimentary arithmetical and geometrical skill. We derive our first understanding of all our concepts of measuring from our sensible experience of real quantity.

Whatever the case, Socrates' point was that mathematical study is conducive to awakening philosophical wonder in us. Hence, he said, "It seems likely that it is one of those studies which we are seeking that naturally conduce to the awakening of thought, but that no one makes the right use of it, though it really does tend to draw the mind to essence and reality."

Why? Socrates immediately explained by indicating to Glaucon that some reports our perceptions give us "do not provoke thought to reconsideration because the judgment of them by sensation seems adequate, while others always invite the intellect to reflection because the sensation yields nothing that can be trusted." Apparently, then, Plato thought that the philosophical habit of mind presupposes our experience of "reports" or "communications" from perceptions that provoke our minds to engage in reconsideration of what we have perceived and that, absent such provocation, we cannot become philosophers. Becoming philosophers, in some respect, involves semiosis and awareness of opposition.[12] (Later in philosophy's history, St. Thomas will go so far as to say all our knowledge starts with sensible signs: "Knowledge of a thing starts with certain external signs.")[13]

Glaucon thought he understood what Socrates meant and immediately said, "You obviously mean distant appearances . . . and shadow painting."

In reply, Socrates told Glaucon that he had totally missed Socrates' meaning. So, Socrates immediately clarified his point: "The experiences that do not provoke thought are those that do not at the same time issue in a *contradictory* perception. Those that do have that effect I set down as provocatives when the perception no more manifests one thing than its contrary, like whether its impact comes from nearby or afar."[14]

Socrates then illustrated his point to make his meaning more clear. He held up three fingers (the little, second, and middle). Whether he spoke of them as near or far, he said:

> Each one of them appears to be equally a finger, and in this respect it makes no difference whether it is observed as intermediaries or at either extreme, whether it is black or white, thick or thin, or of any other quality of this kind. For

in none of these cases is the soul of most men impelled to question the reason and to ask what in the world is a finger, since the faculty of sight never signifies to it at the same time that the finger is the opposite of a finger.[15]

Clearly, Plato's argument immediately above involves the problem of how we signify, or think, and talk about what we perceive, and the problem of opposition. The problem is clearly semiotic.[16] Communication from sense perception that provokes us to become philosophers changes the way we think and talk about, or signify, what we perceive. Many ways we sense things do not impel us to question, to ask the reason why. And those that do arise from sense perceptions that simultaneously involve us in a sense and intellectual experience of opposition conveyed by apparently conflicting signs. Since, in Socrates' example to Glaucon, our sense faculty never signifies to itself that a finger is not a finger, is the opposite of a finger, whence comes our simultaneous sense and intellectual experience of opposition?

Since the experience of a finger being a finger is not the cause, Socrates immediately asked Glaucon, "what about the bigness and smallness of these objects?" Or consider "the relation of touch to thickness and thinness, softness and hardness." Is it not the case that the operation of each of our senses to objects is as follows?: "In the first place, the sensation that is set over the hard is of necessity related also to the soft, and it reports to the soul that the same thing is hard and soft." In short, is it not the case that our different sense faculties report to us different objects and opposing relations, or opposites, related to those objects?

Such being the case, Socrates, again, directed Glaucon's attention to the problem of communication, signification. Simultaneously, something we perceive causes the soul to receive opposite communications, significations, reports. Hence, Socrates continued: "Then, said I, is not this again a case where the soul must be at a loss as to what significance for it the sensation of hardness has, if the sense *reports* the same thing as also soft? And, similarly, as to what the sensation of light and heavy means by light and heavy, if it reports the heavy as light and the light as heavy?"

Glaucon conceded, "Yes, indeed, . . . these *communications* to the soul are strange and invite reconsideration."[17]

Such being the case, Socrates replied that "naturally," in such cases, "the soul first summons to its aid the calculating reason and tries to consider whether each of these things reported to it is one or two. . . .. And if it appears to be two, each of the two is a distinct unit."

That is, given our experience of conflicting reports from our perception, our intellectual faculty immediately starts to consider whether our opposing communication is coming from one perceived object and perception or from two. For example, is perceiving a finger and perceiving a small, versus large, finger, one perception or two? Clearly, such determination involves counting. And if we do not, or cannot, count to two, we cannot have any perception of sensory opposition and opposing communications.

Each perception considered in itself is numerically one, and of separate, singular, objects. But considered together (thought of as two) we think of them as if they were not really separate, as not really numerically one. We are now thinking of one and one, while really separate, as not separate. Hence, of this simultaneously-and-newly-thought-of-one-and-one (considered *together* [as a unit]: this single, or separate, two considered as numerically-one unit measure, this single two), Socrates immediately said: "If, then, each is one and both two, the very meaning of "two" is that the soul will conceive them as distinct. For if they were not separate, it would not have been thinking of two, but one."

When our sense of sight so unites really separate beings, such as the "the great and the small," and thereby sends a miscommunication to the human intellect that things that exist separated and need not co-exist in reality, things that are really two (or many), nevertheless now, in this perception, do so co-exist and are not separated, but are one, Socrates maintained that "it confounds" these qualities in its report to the soul. In so doing, it compels "the intelligence" to separate them, "to contemplate the great and the small not as confounded but as distinct entities, in the opposite way from sensation."[18]

According to Socrates, this is just the sort of sense experience of opposition that gives rise to philosophic wonder. Hence, the following discussion between Socrates and Glaucon immediately ensued:

> And is it not in some such experience as this that the question first occurs to us. What is the world, then is the great and the small?
> By all means.
> And this is the origin of the designation *intelligible* for the one, and *visible* for the other.
> Just so, he said.
> This, then, is just what I was trying to explain a little while ago when I said that some things are provocative of thought and some are not, defining, as provocative things that impinge on the senses *together with their opposites*, while those that do not I said do not tend to awaken reflection.[19]

Clearly, Socrates maintained that philosophic wonder, wonder in any respect at all, is impossible absent "provocative" awareness, or sense perception that communicates to our intelligence perception of semiotic opposition, of some multitude signifying opposition to unity. Absent such semiotic sense experience, we cannot distinguish intellectual experience from sensory, much less philosophical from non-philosophical.

Immediately, Socrates asked Glaucon, "To which class, do you think number and the one belong?" That is, are number and unity visible, or intelligible, entities?

Given Glaucon's inability to conceive the answer, Socrates told him to reason the problem out from what they have already said. If we could adequately see unity through our sense of sight or some other sense faculty, unity would have no need to draw our minds to apprehend its being in cases like that of simultaneously conflicting perception of the finger just described. If we coincidentally, simultaneously, experience some opposition confounded with our sensory perception of unity "so that it no more appears to be one than the opposite," then, Socrates maintained, "there would forthwith be need of something to judge between them, and it would compel the soul to be at a loss and to inquire, by arousing thought in itself, and to ask, whatever then is the one as such, and thus the study of unity will be one of the studies that guide and convert the soul to the study of true being."

Glaucon claimed that visual perception, especially, involves such opposing communication. "For we see the same thing at once as one and as an indefinite plurality," that is, a many. For example, we see the same kind of thing (specifically, say, "finger"), as tall and short. Since experience of this sort of communicative opposition is true of unity, Socrates reasoned that it must also be true of "all number."

Moreover, since counting and "the science of arithmetic are wholly concerned with number . . . [a]nd the qualities of number appear to lead to the apprehension of truth," Socrates concluded that he and Glaucon would have to include counting and the science of arithmetic among the studies they seek. "For a soldier must learn them in order to marshal his troops, and a philosopher because he must rise out of the region of generation and lay hold on essence or he can never become a true reckoner."

That is, to become a philosopher, we must do more than sense differences or possess an art that never attempts to understand first principles and causes considered as such, like the simple art of counting, or singing, which put to right use principles whose causes a person with mathematical science and the science of music are able abstractly to consider and understand, but the singer or student of mathematics need never grasp considered as such.

Hence, Socrates maintained that counting and the scientific pursuit of mathematics are philosophically useful to us for arousing wonder in us. Philosophers are not interested in knowing about counting to buy and sell merchandise. We are interested in it because it is an area of human perception that often leads to provocative thought, which inclines us to wonder about causes and first principles. Some mathematical knowledge is a necessary, but not sufficient, condition for experiencing the wonder that generates philosophy. As Socrates said, the philosophical soul finds interest in numbering when such consideration:

> strongly compels the soul upward, and compels it to discourse about pure numbers never acquiescing if anyone proffers to it in the discussion of numbers attached to visible and tangible bodies. For you are doubtless aware that experts in this study, if anyone attempts to cut up the "one" in argument, laugh at him and refuse to allow it, but if you mince it up, *they* multiply, always on guard lest the one should appear not to be one but a multiplicity of parts.

Clearly, the numbering about which Socrates was talking as philosophically provocative is abstract, universal. The numbers that concerned him philosophically were those that involve "unity equal to every other without the slightest difference and admitting no division into parts." People who talk in such a way, he said, "are speaking of units which can only be conceived by thought, and which it is not possible to deal with in any other way."

Such abstract study of universals, Socrates maintained, appears to be "indispensable" for philosophical purposes because "it plainly compels the soul to employ pure thought with a view to truth itself" (that is, it forces us to think abstractly and generally, universally, about first causes and principles of provocative experiences, or our awareness of experienced opposition).

Socrates then described how, beyond simple counting and the science of arithmetic, such *liberal arts* as plane and solid geometry are related to astronomy and music, and how all these investigations encourage wonder in us and lead us toward first philosophy, or metaphysics.

Socrates had noticed that people who demonstrate a facility at calculation tend to be quick learners and that slow learners trained in calculation start to become better learners. Assuming he had established the worth of numbering and the study of mathematics for becoming philosophical, he proceeded to examine the specific worth of geometry, politically and in other respects.

Given the nature of his interest in education for producing good rulers, whom he also assumes to be soldiers, Plato had Socrates immediately indicate some military benefits of geometry, like constructing encampments and devising military formations in battle and on march. Socrates asserted that these will not require much geometrical skill, but will make a military officer a much different officer than he would have been otherwise.

Socrates' concern, however, was with intensive and extensive, not rudimentary, geometrical skill. He wanted to consider "whether the greater and more advanced part of it tends to facilitate the apprehension of the idea of the good." Will advanced study of geometry (that is, the *liberal art*, or *science*, of geometry) likely lead us to become more philosophical, more metaphysical? Will it change the way we look at, and tend to pursue, happiness altogether?, which is the sort of thing Socrates thought happens when we experience subjects of study that encourage philosophical reflection. Will it tend to change the way we look at everything by turning our eyes around, by turning our souls and bodies around, by forcing us to think in a totally different way than we had formerly done? Will it, in short, make us generally consider things more abstractly and reflectively related to our life as a whole?

Hence, Socrates immediately added, "That tendency" to make us better able to apprehend the idea of the good "is to be found where dwells the most blessed part of reality, which it is imperative that it," the human soul, "behold."

He mentioned that anyone with the slightest familiarity with geometricians will see how strange, how filled with opposition to the proper object of geometry, is their speech, the way they talk about what they do: "Their language is most ludicrous, though they cannot help it, for they speak as if they were doing something and as if all their words were directed toward action. For all their talk is of squaring and applying and adding and the like, whereas in fact the real object of the entire study is pure knowledge," that is, theoretical, or contemplative, study.

Strictly speaking, the object of the science of geometry is abstract, theoretical, general consideration of the principles and causes that constitute the makeup of figured bodies. This science is not chiefly concerned about how to construct individual, figured bodies. It is concerned about the principles and causes that make such construction possible. Hence, the proper, or *per se*, object that the geometrician chiefly has in view is the abstractly-and-theoretically-considered triangle, not the side of this pyramid, or how to construct this A-frame house.

For this reason Socrates said that the science of geometry studies "that which always is" (the abstractly-considered, non-moving, unchanging triangle), not "something which at sometime comes into being and passes away" (like a person's increasingly-becoming-less-slender figure).

So, because the science of geometry inclines us to think abstractly and theoretically about sensible objects, Socrates concluded, "it would tend to draw the soul to truth, and would be productive of a philosophical attitude of mind, directing upward the faculties that now wrongly are turned earthward." In short, wittingly or not, it inclines us to become more philosophical and metaphysical about the way we consider the things around us.

Next, Socrates suggested that Glaucon and he consider whether the liberal art of astronomy might be of benefit for their political and philosophical education. Glaucon immediately recognized its worth for agriculture, navigation, and, more so, "to the military art."

Glaucon's reaction bemused Socrates, who commented that, apparently, Glaucon had responded the way he did, emphasizing astronomy's practical, not theoretical, benefit, out of fear of what "the many" might suppose were he to recommend "useless studies." Socrates commented that, after we have been blinded by our "ordinary," (that is, daily practical) pursuits, we have a difficult task realizing that every soul has an intellectual faculty that theoretical study purifies and refreshes, "a faculty whose preservation outweighs ten thousand eyes, for by it only is reality beheld. Those who share this faith will think your words superlatively true. But those who have and have had no inkling of it will naturally think them all moonshine."[20]

After Glaucon admitted that he spoke, asked, and answered, questions for his, not anyone else's, sake, Socrates told him they needed to back track a bit because they had made a mistake in their order of investigation. The natural order of scientific investigation, and philosophical learning, requires that we first study solid geometry, or as Socrates called it, "the dimension of cubes and of everything that has depth" (a deep body, as opposed to a surface body) after we study plane geometry (which studies the surface body).

The reason for this, Socrates said, is that, properly considered, astronomy studies "solids in revolutions," not "plane surfaces."[21] Consequently, even though Socrates maintained that the thinkers of his time only "languidly pursued" such studies "owing to their difficulties," the proper order of investigation requires that we understand the principles and causes of solid bodies and the way they behave before we attempt to study the principles and causes of movement of solid bodies, as does the science of astronomy.

At this point in their conversation Glaucon attempted to move Socrates along to investigate other sciences to include in the city by agreeing with Socrates that they should incorporate "geometric astronomy" among those disciplines that he would now praise on Socrates' principles. By this Glaucon meant he would not praise theoretical astronomy on the basis of the *practical way the many* praise it, or, as Glaucon more precisely put it, not on the basis of its "vulgar utilitarian commendation," because, "it is obvious to everybody . . . that this study certainly compels the soul to look upward and leads it away from things here to those higher things."

Socrates, however, immediately replied that this appears to be evident to everyone but Socrates. "As it is now handled by those who are trying to lead us up to philosophy, I think that it turns the soul's gaze very much downwards."

Socrates said he responded in this negative fashion because he thought Glaucon had "put a most liberal interpretation on the 'study of higher things.'" Apparently, Glaucon would incorrectly call someone a "contemplative using higher reason" (not higher vision) anyone whose head were thrown back to learn something about decorations on a ceiling. Strictly speaking, Socrates said, the only sort of study that "turns the soul's gaze upward" is "that which deals with being and the invisible." Strictly speaking, he claimed that any person who studies a subject whose matter (that is, its generic subject) concerns sensible reality (that is, sensible qualities), "whether gaping up or blinking down . . . never learns—for nothing of the kind admits of true knowledge—nor would I say that his soul looks up, but down, even though he study floating on his back on sea or land."

While, Socrates said, we have to regard heavenly bodies, "these sparks that paint the sky, . . . decorations on a visible surface, . . . as the fairest and most exact of material things," we have to recognize that such realities "fall far short of the truth," by which he meant, in this instance, "the movements . . . of real speed and real slowness in true number and in all true figures both in relation to one another and as vehicles for the things they carry and contain," Socrates maintained that we apprehend such realities "only by reason and thought, . . . not by sight."

That is, while all species of heavenly mobile body (heavenly mobile body being the astronomer's generic subject) are worthwhile subjects of consideration inasmuch as a species of such a generic subject are of a more immaterial kind than an earthly body, and their motion is closer to the divine [because it is perpetual]), precisely considered, the philosopher's job is abstractly (and, therefore, exactly) to consider (reason about) the principles and causes (or, as Socrates said, "the truth") of the properties, the necessary and essential accidents, of such species of body as they move across the visible surface of the sky, including the effects these specific bodies produce through their properties (like acting on each other in relation to time [speed], or twinkling, going through retrograde motion), as these specific bodies act through principles and causes they effect through the power of their generic subject (that is, inasmuch as they are species of heavenly body involved in circular movement). The philosopher, in short, considers proximate, *per se* effects in light of their proximate, *per se* causes.

Socrates maintained, further, that, while astronomy has to use such complicated, visible, surface decorations as models to help us study the principles and causes of the motion of heavenly bodies, we should not expect that mapping the heavens in this sort of architectural fashion will give us the absolute truth, the exact conclusion, about the mathematical ratio of their movements. The astronomer is in the same sort of situation as would be any geometrician who happened upon the blueprints or diagrams of a craftsman or painter like Socrates' ancestor Daedelus. While he might admit such a person's workmanship to be beautiful, he would not expect that the mathematical ratios would exactly match those that exist in the physical world.

Socrates thought that, when astronomers reflect upon the motions of the stars, they will likely agree with him that heaven's architect fashioned the heavens and everything in them in the most beautiful and best possible way for the nature of the whole. And when they consider the order of heavenly motions, the regularity of the relation between night and day, month to month, to year, of the motion of star to star, they will have to consider absurd the belief that heavenly realities, bodily and visible things, exist "forever without change or the least deviation" and that the astronomer's "unremitting quest is the realities of these things."

That is, they would have to admit that astronomers will never find the principles and causes (the permanent realities) of the motions of heavenly bodies through bodily vision in what these bodies reveal to human sight. They will only get at these principles and causes through abstract, intellectual consideration and reasoning from visible effects in abstractly-considered specific bodies to invisible causes in abstractly-considered generic bodies.

Socrates explained that, if we want to transform astronomy and the soul's natural power of intelligence from being useless to being *truly useful* (that is, abstract and theoretical study), we will have to attack problems in astronomy the way we do in geometry, "and leave the starry heavens alone." That is, we cannot expect to find principles and causes with our external vision. We have to reason to these, abstractly, by turning our minds away from the visible effect to seek the invisible cause.

We have to do the same sort of thing with our ears in one of astronomy's mathematically-related sciences: music. Just as our eyes are fashioned for astronomy, the orderly motion of whose sensible object fixes their movement and attention and limits our gaze, Socrates maintained our ears are fashioned for music, because harmonic movements of audible sounds fix and limit what we musically hear. He added he agreed with Pythagoras that many other mathematically-subalternated sciences like astronomy and music can exist, suited for other sense faculties.

As in the case of astronomy, Socrates claimed that, in his time, musicians made the same mistake as astronomers. Instead of looking for inaudible causes (in this case, numbers) of the harmony of audible sounds that account for their mathematical proportion, a harmony, some students of musical theory tried to hear these inaudible causes (numbers, the causes of the harmonies) with their ears as if they were sensible, minima notes that exist between notes, while others maintained the strings are the cause.

> They talk of something they call minims and, laying their ears alongside, as if trying to catch a voice from next door, some affirm that they can hear a note between and that this is the least interval and the unit of measurement, while others insist that the strings now render identical sounds, both preferring their ears to their minds.

"Their method," Socrates said, "exactly corresponds to that of the astronomer, for the numbers they seek are those found in these heard concords, but they do not ascend to generalized problems and the consideration (of) which numbers are inherently concordant and which not and why in each case."[22]

Socrates realized that the task of reforming the methods of human investigations and arts to transform them into sciences is daunting. He knew that experts in practical pursuits are not experts in philosophical reasoning, or what he called "dialectic." At the very least, he had hoped that the study Glaucon and he had been conducting had gone far enough to show "the community and kinship" of these studies and to allow them "to infer their affinities." If, at least, he had been able to show how they are alike, their work had helped come closer to achieving his goal and has not been in vain.

Socrates maintained that people who cannot give explanations, who cannot give or follow an argument in discussion, will never be able to know anything about the things he said "must be known," that is, philosophy's real subject and generic method. They resemble people still held prisoner within Plato's mythical cave.

For this reason, at this point in the dialogue, Socrates re-turned to the cave analogy to elucidate the way we have to proceed to do philosophy, dialectic. He asserted that the human mind has an ability to achieve progress in learning by following the "law of dia-lectic," which he thought is a law regulating the operation of the human mind that we see imitated in the faculty of sight. He reported he had already described this likeness in Glaucon's and his attempt to use the faculty of sight to find first principles and causes, or, as he said, "to look at living things themselves and the stars themselves and finally the very sun."

Dialectic's law, however, "belongs to the intelligible" realm, in human reason's power of abstract and contemplative considera-tion that results from the wonder caused in us by sensibly-perceived-and-reported provocative communications. We see this law at work, in short, "when anyone by dialectic attempts through discourse of reason and apart from all perceptions of sense to find his way to the very essence of each thing and does not desist till he apprehends by thought itself the nature of the good itself, he arrives at the limit of the intelligible, as the other in our parable came to the goal of the visible."[23]

This "limit" of the intelligible about which Socrates spoke immediately above is what Plato called "the Good." This was clearly Socrates' meaning because he identified this limit with the Sun, or the Sun's light, that was the goal in his Myth of the Cave, to which he directly referred here. He called "the Good" a limit of the intelli-gible because an intelligible limit, as a limit, is that beyond which we cannot intellectually go. As such, it is an indivisible, or, as Plato often called it, "the One." For this reason, also, while Plato did not say so here, the highest, or maximum, as a limit, is an indivisible, one, and a measure, because we always measure everything, even things we know, in terms of a one. Hence, we measure our knowledge in terms of intelligible indivisibles, or intellectual, but not necessarily mathematical, ones, units, first principles, or *per se nota* starting points.

When Plato said that "dialectic attempts through discourse of reason and apart from all perceptions of sense to find his way to the very essence of each thing" he was not thinking like dissatisfied young Descartes, fresh out of school at La Flèche, hoping entirely to escape from sensory input, clean out all the intellectual junk he has stored for years in his spiritual attic to follow the whispering voice of conscience (in addition to whatever handy dreams or divine signs might reinforce this voice) calling him to get in contact with his pure reason in the hidden recesses of his mind.

Plato's understanding of dialectical progress involved initially receiving conflicting communications from sensible being trustworthy enough to start us on, and reinforce along the way, our abstract, philosophical quest for invisible first principles and causes of a *per se* effect that relates to a proximate and *per se* subject. Plato did not entirely distrust the human senses. He thought that their formal object, the world of becoming, as he would often call it, has some reality, but is incomplete and imprecise in nature. He thought it "exists," but is somewhat false, because he identified truth and reality with precision, exactness, permanence, unity, and completeness. And he maintained sensible reality lacks the level of reality (unity) that he would call "true being," the "really real," or "beingly-being" (which level of reality entities in the World of Forms possess), and the Good has, to which he refers as "beingly-beingly-being" or the "really, really, real" (or, sometimes, as beyond being, or not-being).[24]

To explain dialectic's nature and method more precisely, Socrates started a short, but detailed, exegesis of part of the Myth of the Cave at the point where a prisoner had broken free from his subterranean world and had ascended to the world above. When he first exited the cave, this escaped inmate had a "persisting inability to look directly at animals and plants and the light of the Sun." He was only able to see divine-like reflections in the water and shadows of real beings cast by the Sun, similar to the shadows he had seen in the cave cast by a light that, compared to the Sun's light, is as unreal as shadows. Socrates maintained that the practice of the arts and sciences as Glaucon and he had been describing them shows their power to stir the human soul upward to contemplate the best realities, just as, in the fable he had told, the best sense organ, sight, "was turned to the contemplation of what is brightest in the corporeal and visible region."

Such being the case, Glaucon urged Socrates to show him (1) the nature of dialectic's power, (2) its divisions, and (3) its methods, so that they can come to the end of their journey and rest.

In reply, Socrates told Glaucon he would show Glaucon these things, not their image, if he could; but, unhappily, he was unable to show Glaucon the real truth as it appears to Socrates, whether it appears rightly to Socrates or not. Still, Socrates had to affirm that the real truth must be something like what they had affirmed. And they may properly state that only dialectic's power could show it, and only to a person experienced in studies they have described (that is, like theoretical geometry, astronomy, and music).

Still, Socrates maintained that no one will be able to refute their claim that no other method of investigation exists that tries progressively and universally to determine what each thing really is (that is, the principles and causes of the behavior of things). Mostly all the other arts have human opinions and wants as their object, are totally concerned with generation and composition, care and cultivating "things that grow and are put together." Those few arts, like geometry and its subalternate studies, astronomy and music, dream about being, but never reach it, because their method of investigation always starts with assumption, belief, not with absolutely, or assumptionless, first principles of knowing, *per se nota* truths.

Evidently, Socrates did not use the Latin. Instead, translated into English, he said: "The clear waking vision of it (reality or real being) is impossible for them as long as they leave the assumptions which they employ undisturbed and cannot give any account of them. For where the starting point is something that the reasoner does not know, and the conclusion and all that intervenes is a tissue of things not really known, what possibility is there that assent in such cases can ever be converted into true knowledge or science?"

Socrates claimed that dialectic is the only method of inquiry that eliminates assumptions, hypotheses, to advance "up to the first principle itself to find confirmation there." Only philosophy, as he had described it, utilizes a starting point of scientific investigation that is entirely assumption-less, is not based upon any hypothesis. *Philosophy uses no assumptions because it finds confirmation, not in a system or systematic logic, but in awareness of the first principle of knowing considered in itself.* It does not take its first principles from the conclusions of another, higher science. Philosophy is the science that, with dialectic's help, knows the first principles that all the other sciences assume. Clearly, what Socrates had in mind as philosophy, science, is not philosophy, science, generically considered, science as a genus. It is the specific philosophy, science of metaphysics, first philosophy.

For this reason, Socrates continued by saying that when the soul's eye, the human intellect, is buried deep in a kind of primeval mud,

> dialectic gently draws it forth and leads it up, employing as helpers and co-operators in this conversion the studies and sciences which we enumerated, which we called sciences often from habit, though they really need some other designation, connoting more clearness than opinion and more obscurity than science. "Understanding," I believe, was the term, we employed. But I presume we shall not dispute about the name when things of such moment lie before us for consideration.

Clearly, this passage indicates Plato thought that, while he called studies like geometry and its subalternate disciplines of astronomy and music "sciences," or "philosophy," he was predicating the terms "science" and "philosophy" analogously, and chiefly of the assumption-less, non-hypothetical, theoretical science of metaphysics. Toward the end of the *Republic* Book Six, Socrates had described to Glaucon a divided line of learning, ascending from the lowest form of human learning to the highest. He now revisited what he had said about the divided line toward the end of Book Six to express his thinking more precisely.

He recalled how he had given a simile of a straight line, cut in two, with each half, similarly subdivided. The result was a four-fold division of two major sections, one representing higher learning, the other lower. The two subdivisions of higher learning he had designated "knowledge"; the lower two he had called "opinion." The higher division he had subdivided into (1) science and (2) understanding. The lower division he had subdivided into (3) belief and (4) imagination. Socrates stated that knowing relates to being, and opinion relates to becoming. Expressing this in a proportion, he said that as being is to becoming so science is to belief and understanding to imagination.

Socrates then stated they would give the name "dialectician" to the person who can give an account of the being, or essence, of each thing to himself and others. But they would deny this designation to the person unable to do this because this person does not "possess full reason and intelligence about the matter."

He added that, in the same way, denial of this designation applies to the person who cannot "define in his discourse and distinguish and abstract from all other things the aspect or idea of the good." *Socrates thought that truly (that is, precisely) to know something is to know it philosophically or scientifically. And this means to know it abstractly. This involves being able to explain something in terms of its first principles and causes, to be able to state the reasons why something is the way it is in terms of principles we have abstracted from our experience of the being of things.*

He described someone incapable of doing this to be like someone going through life half-awake, dreaming his way through. He said we would say of such a man that he "does not really know the good itself or any particular good, but if he apprehends any adumbration of it, his contact with it is by opinion, not by knowledge, and dreaming and dozing through his present life, before he awakens here he will arrive at the House of Hades and fall asleep forever."

Especially in an ideal city, where philosophers will be rulers, Socrates maintained we cannot neglect having children learn that discipline whereby they will be able "to ask and answer questions in the most scientific manner." For this reason, Socrates said he had put this study of dialectic higher than all others, like "a coping-stone," so no higher learning could be put above it and to make their discussion of studies complete.[25]

Having thus completed their investigation into the nature, division, and methods of the sciences, Socrates stated that what remained for them was to determine to whom to assign studies and how. In the *Republic*, Book Six, Socrates had already stated that traits of a philosophical nature included: quickness at learning, memory, courage, and magnificence.[26] Toward the end of Book Seven, he reiterated many of these traits, and recalled something else he had said in Books Six and Seven, "Our present mistake . . . and the disesteem that has in consequence fallen upon philosophy are, as I said before, caused by the unfitness of her associates and wooers. They should not have been bastards, but true scions."

So as not to be a philosophical bastard, Socrates maintained we have to be industrious, not half-hearted. A true philosopher loves learning and hard work. We must also hate mistakes in ourselves and others, as much as we hate lies in both. No true philosopher "cheerfully accepts involuntary falsehood," is undisturbed when convicted of ignorance, or "wallows in the mud of ignorance as insensitively as a pig." True philosophers are also temperate, courageous, and great-souled.

Socrates maintained that, since philosophers will be rulers or their advisors, we have to be careful that philosophical natures possess, and can recognize in others, temperance, courage, and greatness of soul. Otherwise, we will undermine, not preserve, our city, and "we shall pour a still greater ridicule upon philosophy."

Moreover, we cannot take Solon's advice that, as we get older, we will be able to learn many things. We must train the young for philosophy through liberal education. Or, as Socrates stated:

> Now all this study of reckoning and geometry and all the preliminary studies that are indispensable preparation for dialectic must be presented to them while still young, not in the form of compulsory education. . .. Because . . . a free soul ought not to pursue any study slavishly, for while bodily labors performed under constraint do not harm the body, nothing that is learned under compulsion stays with the mind. . .. Do not . . . keep children in their studies by compulsion but by play.

After a period of primary education in the liberal arts, at about age twenty, Socrates said, those who will be given preference to higher learning in philosophy would have to demonstrate their ability to unify "the studies which they disconnectedly pursued as children in their former education into a comprehensive survey of their affinities with one another and with the nature of things." That is, they would have to be able to show how all their *many* former studies are *one* with each other and the world.

"That," Socrates maintained, "is the only instruction that abides with those who receive it." This is the only kind of learning that lasts. "And," he added, "it is also . . . the chief test of the dialectic nature and its opposite. For he who can view things in their connection is a dialectician; he who cannot is not." That is, the person who can intellectually comprehend how many things are one, the person who can reason abstractly and metaphysically, is the philosopher. The person who cannot do this is not.

Socrates warned, however, about the dangers of premature study of dialectic. He did so, among other reasons, because Plato tended to conflate philosophy, which he called here "dialectic," with first philosophy, or metaphysics. Socrates thought that premature study of metaphysics is dangerous, because metaphysical study requires that a person be able "to disregard the eyes and other senses and go on to being itself in company with truth." Because most young people are not prepared to embark upon such a rigorous journey in abstract reasoning about most general first principles and causes (first principles and causes that all arts and science take for granted, or assume), he noted how great is the harm cause by the way the Greeks were treating dialectic in his time: "Its practitioners are infected with lawlessness."[27]

Sad that Descartes's Jesuit instructors at La Flèche did not take this warning to heart. Premature study of metaphysical subtleties by precocious youth under the influence of sophists often winds up producing sophists (like Descartes), and eventually, in their wake, corrupt lawyers, judges, politicians, bankers, and intellectuals, much as sophists like Protagoras and Gorgias had done in Socrates' and Plato's time and, as Adler, Maritain, and Gilson recognized, subjective idealists and other "philosophical bastards" have done in modernity's early and late phases.

Socrates maintained that the situation of such prematurely metaphysically-exposed youth is similar to that of an intelligent, spoiled rich kid, doted over all his life by family flatterers, and raised by others like an orphan, almost as if by adopted parents. When he reaches physical adulthood he perceives that he has no parents, and does not know how to find his natural ones. A young person in that sort of situation would likely start to have a higher opinion of his flatterers and those who raised him, would be more inclined to listen to them and live by their rule and less inclined to disobey them in great matters, than he would his natural parents.

From childhood rearing, Socrates said, we have received specific convictions about higher things, great, important, matters, such as about the nature of truth and the honorable. We have been raised from childhood under obedience to these convictions. At the same time, practices opposite to what we have learned exist "that have pleasures attached to them and that flatter and solicit our souls." Such practices do not corrupt decent people because they continue to honor and obey what they have been taught.

But what are such people to do when they run into questions about the highest and most important things, questions we commonly call "metaphysical" and "moral," when they find their traditionally-held beliefs about what they hold to be true about everything refuted by subtle arguments they cannot adequately answer? What is the honorable person to do, Socrates asked, "when he has had the same experience about the just and the good and everything that he chiefly held in esteem"? How will he conduct himself thereafter regarding respect and obedience to his former beliefs?

Glaucon's answer was that, inevitably, this person will disrespect and disobey the former beliefs.

And, then, Socrates wanted to know, what will happen to him? He will now be in a situation where he ceases to honor his former metaphysical and moral principles, will think they are no longer binding on him, and he will be unable to discover true ones. Such a person will be like putty in the hands of any flatterer or dictator who comes along, and will adopt the life the flatterer or dictator desires. In so doing, like American youth of the pre-World War II generation, and many Western youth of today, such a person will become rationally ungovernable, a rebel against traditional law and morality.

Plato gave us a similar warning in his classic work the *Gorgias*, in which we find Socrates critiquing the famous sophist Gorgias for making the same absurd and grandiose claim, which Descartes would later make: that he possessed one art, or *the* specific method, to know everything, and "without learning any other arts . . . to prove in no way inferior to the specialists." The discussion continued:

> SOCRATES: Therefore when the rhetorician is more convincing than the doctor, the ignorant is more convincing among the ignorant than the expert. Is that our conclusion, or is it something else?
>
> GORGIAS: That is the conclusion in this instance.
>
> SOCRATES: Is not the position of the rhetorician and of rhetoric the same with respect to the other arts also? It has no need to know the truth about things but merely to discover a technique of persuasion so as to appear among the ignorant to have more knowledge than the expert.
>
> GORGIAS: But is this not a great comfort, Socrates, to be able without learning any other arts but this one to prove in no way inferior to the specialists?[28]

Socrates did not think so. For this reason, in the same work, in his discussion with the corrupt politician Callicles, Socrates told Callicles (who, like Gorgias' student, Polus had admired the despot Archelaus as the happiest of men) that men like Archelaus are the most miserable of men and fools. Callicles' problem was that *confounding sophistry with wisdom eventually tends to turn a person into a dictator or a panderer to dictators.*[29]

Rightly considered, Socrates thought the practice of dialectic, or the generic practice of philosophically-abstract reasoning common to all the specific sciences, is ordered toward enabling us to become metaphysicians, to help us to understand the first principles and causes about everything, especially about the highest, or most important things for us to know as human beings. When it is not rightly ordered, the knowledge that had been philosophy, science, tends to degenerate into sophistry, ideology, and argument for the sake of victory (propaganda), not truth; tends, in short, to produce philosophical, scientific, bastards.

No wonder, then, so many contemporary descendants of Descartes, Kant, and Hegel glory in thinking that their philosophical work is chiefly to get students "to question their belief systems."

Such thinking is not philosophical. It is a secularized understanding of St. Augustine's reduction of philosophy to theology in which philosophy becomes reduced to "faith seeking understanding."

As a result of the perennial dangers of mistaking sophistry for philosophy, we have to be careful not to introduce students too early to philosophical argumentation involving metaphysical issues. When this happens, when young people "first get a taste of disputation," Plato thought they "misuse it as a form of sport, always employing it contentiously, and, imitating confuters, they themselves confute others. They delight like puppies pulling about and tearing with words all who approach them."[30]

Plato maintained that the person who "makes a jest and sport of mere contradiction" is a sophist, not a true philosopher or dialectician. When young people run into such sophists, mistaking them for philosophers, and start to imitate them, he thinks "they quickly fall into a violent distrust of all that they formerly held true, and the outcome is that they themselves and the whole business of philosophy are discredited with other men."[31] As Mortimer Adler recognized, they become like contemporary students have become under the influence of modern subjective idealists and their subjective critique: moral and metaphysical relativists.

Socrates and Plato did not object to questioning traditional beliefs. Socrates was put to death for refusing to stop questioning the poor educational practices of his time fostered by poets and sophists. Both philosophers objected to confounding philosophy with sophistry and sophistry with metaphysics. Hence, Plato had the character Socrates maintain that his requirement would be that "those permitted to take part in such discussions must have orderly and stable natures, instead of the present practice of submitting it to any chance and unsuitable applicant."[32]

Because Plato also tended to conflate philosophy, science, as a generic habit with the specific scientific habit of first philosophy, or metaphysics, he ended Book Seven of the *Republic* by recommending, in striking similarity with his student Aristotle, that the study of metaphysics, or dialectics, start about age fifty. At this time, he said of those who would have passed all prior tests and would have been approved to become philosophers:

> We shall require them to turn upward the vision of their souls and fix their gaze on that which sheds light on all, and when they have thus beheld the good itself they shall use it as a pattern for the right ordering of the state and the citizens and themselves throughout the remainder of their lives, each in his turn, devoting the greater part of their time to the study of philosophy, but when the turn comes for each, toiling in the service of the state and holding office for the city's sake, regarding the task not as a fine thing but a necessity. And so, when each generation has educated others like themselves to take their place as guardians in the state, they shall depart to the Islands of the Blessed and there dwell. And the state shall establish public memorials and sacrifices for them as to divinities if the Pythian oracle approves or, if not, as to divine and godlike men.[33]

NOTES

1. Plato, *Republic*, trans. Paul Shorey, in Edith Hamilton and Huntington Cairns (eds.), *The Collected DialoguesIncluding the Letters* (New York: Pantheon Books, Bollingen Series 71, 1966), Bk. 6, 494A. My addition in parenthesis.
2. Plato, *Republic*, Bk. 7, 515B.
3. Id., 515B–518B.
4. Id., 517B.
5. Id., 518C.
6. Id., 518D–519A.
7. See Socrates' discussion with Alcibiades in Plato, *Symposium*, 213B–223D.
8. Plato, *Republic*, Bk. 7, 519A–B.
9. Id., Bk. 7, 519B–520E. Italics are my addition.
10. Id., 521A.
11. Id.
12. Id., 521B–523C.

13.   St. Thomas Aquinas, *Commentary on the Metaphysics of Aristotle*, 2 vols., trans. John P. Rowan (Chicago: Henry Regnery, Co., Inc., 1961), vol. 1, Bk. 5, l. 19, n. 1048.

14.   Plato, *Republic*, Bk. 7, 521B–523C. Italics in the block quote are my emphasis.

15.   Id., 523D

16.   See my treatment of the semiotic nature of wonder and the relation of semiotic experience to philosophy's origin in my article related to John N. Deely's groundbreaking work in semiotics, "Platonic Reflections upon *Four Ages of Understanding*," in *Semiotica* 179 (2010), pp. 83–101.

17.   Plato, *Republic*, 523D–524B. Italics are mine.

18.   Id., 523D–527C.

19.   Id., 527C. The first two italicized words are from Plato's dialogue. The third (italicized phrase) is mine.

20.   Id., 527C–528E.

21.   Id., 528B.

22.   Id., 528E–531C. I add the "of" in parenthesis to clarify the translation.

23.   Id., 531C–532B.

24.   Id., 532B–534E.

25.   See, for example, Plato, *Parmenides*, 142A–144E; *Sophist*, 256E–259E; *Republic*, Bk. 6, 509B; *Timaeus*, 87D; see, also, Étienne Gilson's lucid exposition of the problem of reality and being in Plato in *Being and Some Philosophers* (Pontifical Institute of Mediaeval Studies, 1952), pp. 1–18.

26.   Id., Bk. 6, 503C.

27.   Id., Bk. 7, 535C–538A.

28.   Plato, *Gorgias*, trans. W. D. Woodhead, in Edith Hamilton and Huntington Cairns (eds.), *The Collected DialoguesIncluding the Letters* (New York: Pantheon Books, Bollingen Series 71, 1966), 459B–D.

29.   Id., 482C–527E.

30.   Plato, *Republic*, Bk. 7, 539B–C.

31.   Id., 539C.

32.   Id., 539D.

33.   Id., 534E–540C.

Five

THE POST-PLATONIC UNDERSTANDING OF PHILOSOPHY AND SCIENCE: PHILOSOPHY'S FAILURE TO TRANSITION FROM PAGAN TO CHRISTIAN CULTURE

In the preceding chapter, among other things I wanted to show: (1) that, to help students avoid bastardizing, misunderstanding, philosophy's, science's, nature as a perpetual quest to resolve the problem of the relationship between the one and the many, Plato had moved philosophy, science (that is, its subject-matter and method), toward a new existential plane in which the ancient Greeks would start to consider philosophy, science, chiefly as theoretical and metaphysical activities (not as practical and physical activities); that (2) with the help of Parmenides, Plato (not Porphyry the Phoenician or Anicius Manlius Severinus Boethius) had introduced the problem of universals into philosophy as a new way of considering philosophy's subject matter; (3) that the initial introduction of this problem into philosophy and science had happened within the discipline of metaphysics, not within the discipline of logic; and (4), as Plato well understood, when it is not rightly ordered, knowledge that had been philosophy, science, tends to degenerate into sophistry, ideology, and argument for the sake of victory (propaganda), not truth; tends, in short, to produce philosophical, scientific, bastards: fools, political panderers; not, strictly speaking, philosophers, scientists.

 Among other reasons, I had need to do the above things because, just as many contemporary philosophers falsely-so-called tend to present the problem of the one and the many in antiquity as if it had been a problem unique to Greek physics (as the starting point on the road to the Greek discovery of logic, in which philosophy supposedly reached full bloom), so they also tend to speak of the problem of universals as if this had been a problem first discovered and articulated by logicians during the Christian middle ages. As a result, some contemporary "philosophers" still tend to speak of medieval "philosophy" as though it had dealt almost entirely with the problem of universals, as if the Christian middle ages gave birth to this problem. Worse, as a result, they tend to misunderstand philosophy's nature and cannot precisely report philosophy's, science's, history.

A chief aim of the preceding chapter was to show beyond reasonable doubt that, in actuality, this problem of universals arose in Greek antiquity, within the newly-developing discipline of metaphysics as philosophical reasoning was transitioning beyond physics and mathematics to the discovery of the philosophy or science that would later be called "metaphysics." Just as the practice of philosophy had preceded the origin of its name among the ancient Greeks, so, too, did the practice of metaphysics. Another main aim of the chapter was to show that this transition occurred as part of the maturation of the ancient Greek understanding that all philosophical, scientific, problems are simply different instances of the philosophical, scientific, problem of the one and the many.

1. How the problem of universals contributed to the medieval Christian misunderstanding of philosophy's, science's, nature

Initial aims of the present chapter are to show: (1) precisely how the third-century A. D. Greek Aristotelian commentator Porphyry and the Roman humanist Boethius misunderstood the problem of universals; and, (2) how, by so doing, they tended to introduce into medieval thought a misunderstanding of philosophy's, science's, nature that would encourage thinkers from that time to our time to confound philosophical (scientific) and logical genera and species, reduce philosophy, science, to the discipline of logic, and misunderstand philosophy's, science's, history.

Porphyry had first presented this problem to medieval intellectual history in his famous *Introduction* (*Isagogue*) to a logical work of Aristotle (the *Categories*) by saying: "At present, regarding genera and species, I shall refuse to say whether they subsist or whether they are placed in the naked understanding alone or whether subsisting they are corporeal or incorporeal, and whether they are separated from sensibles or placed in sensibles and in accord with them. Questions of this sort are most exalted business and require very great diligence of inquiry."[1]

After announcing that he would later consider the nature and mode of existence of genera and species, as Étienne Gilson has well said, as a good teacher, at the start of a work in logic written for beginners, Porphyry postponed until later problems that "belong to advanced metaphysics." Such problems involve examining the mode of existence of genera and species, what many thinkers have commonly called "universals," or some have often mistakenly called "general ideas"; for example, whether they are subsistent realities considered in themselves, mind-independent realities, or simply mental conceptions; material or immaterial; and, supposing they are immaterial, examining whether they exist apart from material things or do so only as existentially united to them.[2]

Gilson well understood that the problem of universals is chiefly metaphysical, not logical, because it is "one of those fundamental problems which the human mind stumbles upon every time it tries to grasp, beyond all particular sciences, the conditions that make knowledge itself possible." When some practitioner of a particular science, or art, confronts such a problem, that person tends not to recognize that this problem falls outside the order of questions proper to that practitioner's specialization. In some cases, Gilson observed, that person will attempt to resolve this problem according to the methods of his or her discipline, as if it were a problem proper to that person's discipline, as if he or she were simply tracing back his or her discipline to its fundamental implications.[3]

Gilson presented Peter Abailard as a prime example of a medieval thinker who made the error of mistaking the problem of universals for a logical problem and then attempting to solve this problem by logical methods. Gilson remarked Abailard did so because, in Abailard's time, some scholars had already tended to conflate science, philosophy, with logic. Questions like, what is a definition? difference? species? genus? are the proper objects of speculation for a logician. Questions like, what is the nature of our ideas and their relation to things?, and, do general substances exist inside or outside the mind?, are not. Properly speaking, as Plato well recognized, such questions are concerns of metaphysics, not of logic, or physics.

Yet these were exactly the kind of properly metaphysical questions that would naturally arise in the mind of any normal human being who also happened to be a great logician because, as Gilson indicated, they arise on the border that divides logic from normal human metaphysical interest. "An almost invisible line indeed," Gilson says. "Yet as soon as you cross it, you find yourself in an entirely different country, and if you do not notice it, you get lost."[4]

Evidently then, long before the birth of St. Thomas in the thirteenth century, medieval thinkers were lost about the nature of philosophy, science, did not know what it is. And part of the reason they were lost goes back centuries before to the sixth century AD when, to help preserve classical learning, the Roman humanist Boethius sought to use the work of Porphyry to help pass on the logical works of Aristotle to future generations.

2. Why, before the start of Christianity, ancient pagan culture had largely lost its understanding of philosophy's, science's, nature

Philosophy's, science's, birth within ancient Greek culture had been hostile. In a sense, it initiated a "Battle of the Arts" about which Plato talks in Book Ten of his famous *Republic* that has continued unbroken until this day. This fight existed within pagan antiquity until philosophy's death within Roman culture around the time of Marcus Tullius Cicero (b. 106 BC; d. 43 BC) in the first century BC when Cicero generally defined philosophy, in his *On Duties*, as "devotion to wisdom" and, in his *Tusculan Disputations*, as "expeller of vices and explorer of virtue."[5] This battle remains hostile today, largely against philosophy's spectre in the postmodern period false-ly-so-called, because what the leading ancient Greek philosophers like Socrates, Plato, Aristotle, and Plotinus had understood by philosophy was not transmitted to early Christian thinkers (or, if so transmitted, was rejected by those few thinkers who understood it). While thinkers within the liberal arts today still carry on the Battle of the Arts, we largely do so not understanding precisely what the fight is about.

Even though its initial roots had presupposed the theism of the ancient poets, and philosophy could not have arisen without this theism, from its start in ancient Greece, philosophy had been attacked by some poets as atheistic. As philosophers became increasingly successful in liberating the ancient Greek intellect from the superstition, magic, and myth common to their prior mytho-poietic mode of knowing, toward true intellectual enlightenment, to some extent, the philosophers increased skepticism about the gods within Greek culture.

As Parmenides, the sophists he helped generate, and poets started to undermine ancient Greek confidence in the philosophical method of ancient Greek physics, this skepticism started to turn toward philosophy, science, and its generic method. By removing the gods from the physical world, by causing them, like Forms, to exist essentially apart from the physical world, and formally initiating the study of metaphysics, among other things, Plato sought to remove the negative influence of morally-degenerate, poetically-misconceived gods from Greek politics; and reverse increasing Greek skepticism about the gods, philosophy (science), and the ancient Greek intellectual ability to solve the problem of the one and the many. To reverse these trends, in part, he devoted his famous school, the Academy, founding it as a kind of religious-political-intellectual brotherhood devoted to the goddess of wisdom, Athena.

Plato's dematerialization of the gods and the soul were so alien to the widespread materialism of ancient Greek culture that not even his brilliant student Aristotle was able to reverse the trend. Aristotle attempted to rejuvenate life into philosophy, science, by reintroducing forms into the physical world. To a degree, he was successful; but by totally depersonalizing the gods, by making the most perfect of physical forms move the planets and look up to an impersonal Unmoved Mover who accounted for all movement and life in the universe, Aristotle helped undermine the influence of ancient Greek religion and increased Greek skepticism and the hostility of many Greeks toward philosophy.

A short time after, Roman political expansion and Greek political decline further increased Greek skepticism about, and hostility toward, philosophy. Within the context of their increasing doubt, the ancient Greeks started to turn away from the more metaphysical speculations that Plato and Aristotle had introduced into later Greek philosophical thought. As they did so, even in Plato's Academy, the methods of the poets, sophists, and philosophers, scientists, increasingly started to resemble each other.

Plato's Academy had no set curriculum, and Aristotle's Lyceum had lost many of Aristotle's works, which had been bequeathed to Aristotle's friend Theophrastus, and then lost to antiquity for several hundred years. From the start these schools were largely intellectual discussion groups. Almost immediately after Plato's death his Academy became overrun by skeptics. And Aristotle left no school of sufficient power to counteract the onslaught of skepticism.

In addition, the poets and others pointed to Greek political decline as a sign that, as a result of philosophies that had turned their backs on the traditional gods, the gods had turned their backs on the Greeks. While the more theoretical philosophies of Plato and Aristotle had helped undermine the classical poetic view of the gods, and the influence of the traditional poets, the critique of theoretical philosophy by the lesser Socratic schools, like the Megareans, cynics, stoics, and epicureans during the Hellenistic and Roman Imperial ages, had seriously damaged ancient Greek and Roman trust in philosophical metaphysics and theoretical philosophy as legitimate intellectual disciplines.[6]

As this was happening, according to an ancient Christian tradition, "under a special inspiration of the Holy Spirit," seventy or seventy-two, philosophically-conversant, Jewish scholars produced a Greek version of the *Jewish* Scriptures. The first Christians would later adopt this as the *Catholic* Old Testament. As a result, according to Pope Benedict XVI, prior to the advent of Christ, the ancient Greek philosophical notion of rationality, the best of ancient Greek *logos* (as Benedict calls it) as part of reality and God's nature, entered into Biblical faith. Benedict calls "this inner rapprochement between Biblical faith and Greek philosophical inquiry . . . an event of decisive importance from the standpoint of the history of religions, but also from that of world history": A World-historical event, as Georg Hegel might say.

As a result, Benedict says, "Many cities saw the formation of a circle of the 'God-fearing,' of pious 'pagans,' who neither could nor wanted to become full-fledged Jews, but participated in the synagogue liturgy and thus in Israel's faith. It was in this circle that the earliest Christian missionary preaching found its first foothold beyond the Jews, and began to spread."[7]

While some early Christian apologists and Church Fathers would later interpret this event as a "revelation of reason," *not faith*, by the Holy Spirit to prepare pagan culture to be rationally receptive to the subsequent Christian revelation, many ancient Greeks likely saw this as simply the formation of one more philosophical school. Because of the increasing strength of its cynicism, skepticism, practical nature, and communal spirit, neither Christianity nor the last great theoretical, metaphysical, philosophical movement of the ancient pagan era, neo-Platonism, could overcome the force of philosophy's degeneration into a kind of quasi-religious cult.

As I have said in my book *Wisdom's Odyssey from Philosophy to Transcendental Sophistry*, the neo-Platonic movement was "the last great attempt by the ancient pagan intellect to combat revelation and explain the workings of the entire physical universe through unaided reason alone."[8] As such, neo-Platonism was "a kind of philosophical Protestantism reacting against the death of purely natural reason, and its reincarnation within an alien universe," with its own entirely new, theological notion of being and knowing."[9]

As this happened, Greek and Roman materialism continued to increase, as did the stoic influence that sought to return the influence of the gods, especially Zeus, to the physical world. Simultaneously, some Greek and Roman poets attempted to bring the gods back down to Earth by allegorizing the teachings of the philosophers. These attempts became so pronounced that the Roman stoic Seneca mockingly commented, "All the schools of philosophy find their doctrines are in Homer."[10] Increasingly, before the end of the pagan era, the distinction among philosophers, poets, and sophists had started to become blurred, with philosophers becoming largely identified as individuals who belonged to a quasi-religious community involved in a practical life largely removed from the world and its concerns.

In short, by this time and the time Boethius came on the scene, the ancient Greek and Roman "philosophers" had largely lost their understanding that philosophy started in sense wonder and that the chief problem that always concerns the philosopher is the problem of the one and the many. They had virtually forgotten what philosophy's subject matter and method had been.

During the first-century AD, the prevailing ancient Greek understanding of a philosopher was of someone who lived in a community, was a member of a school, and lived in a distinguishable way according to the principles of a master. "Philosophy" was understood chiefly to signify love of a way of thinking developed by a great teacher and pursued by members of a school. This was the prevailing understanding of a philosopher, scientist, wise man, that existed by the time Christian evangelists and apologists like St. Paul traveled to Greece to seek to convert the Gentiles:

> Gilson notes that in the second century people could often as easily recognize a philosopher on the street as today we can identify a member of the clergy. A philosopher did not live, talk, or dress like other people. Often as not, a philosopher believed that philosophy's most important work was to seek after God. For such people, to convert to Christianity was to move from a religiously-quickened philosophy to a religion receptive to philosophical quickening.[11]

Crucial to note about what Gilson says is that "a religiously-quickened philosophy," a poetically-inspired physics, was precisely the sort of reasoning away from which the pre-Socratic philosophers had sought to move human reason. Greek philosophy arose out of a dissatisfaction of religiously-quickened Greeks with their mythological theology. Since such people started their reasoning in sense wonder and were seeking to reason under no intellectual light higher than natural reason, Aristotle reasonably said that, analogously speaking, even the myth-makers deserve the title "philosopher."

Even when they did so like inspired poets, in an extraordinary way, the ancient Greeks claimed they knew their gods through a completely natural, not a supernatural, mode of knowing, or "belief." Hence, transition from being a poet to a philosopher did not involve accepting the existence of a generically new and superior way of knowing, or act of supernatural, or even natural, faith. If anything, for an ancient Greek poet, this involved opting for an inferior way of knowing over a superior one.

Hence, philosophy's "Father," Thales, deserves the title even though he said "all things are full of gods" because, a few centuries later, the "gods" (*the principle of opposition within matter*) to which Thales was referring, Socrates and Plato will recognize were theomorphisms of first principles (secondary causes), of the notion of forms (starting points of different species of motion and principles of opposition in physical things), toward which Thales was groping. In talking about the gods, the poets were personalizing, mythologizing, first principles of natural motion. Socrates, Plato, and Aristotle were doing the reverse, demythologizing first principles.

In a way, even though physics was philosophy's first activity, philosophy started as a metaphysical quest on the part of a religiously-quickened people who were dissatisfied with the nature and behavior of the gods portrayed in Greek mythology. These individuals were seeking to move away from a mythological, imaginative, understanding of first principles and toward an intellectually-conceived, de-mythologized understanding of these same principles. Such people merit the label "philosophers." Such does not appear to be the case when the movement happens in the opposite direction, even if the God of such a people is all good and is initially conceived of them as such in a non-mythological way.

3. How the early Christians first started to misunderstand philosophy's nature, and how this was later corrected

Given the prevailing understanding of philosophy to which they were exposed, early Christian apologists saw this philosophical pursuit of the ancient Greeks as a quest for the real wisdom that only comes from and through supernatural revelation. Some of them reasoned. "If philosophers are lovers of wisdom, they must be lovers of the gods. Lovers of the gods, however, might reasonably be expected to show dissatisfaction with the behavior of the gods portrayed in Greek mythology, and they might be expected to search for and welcome a way of understanding the gods which displayed their gods as good."[12] Hence, the first ancient Christian writers, the "Apologists," claimed for themselves the title "philosopher," and, by the late fourth, early fifth century, St. Augustine had reportedly coined the term "Christian philosophy" to refer to the supernatural revelation of natural reason that the ancient Greeks had been seeking.[13]

Nonetheless, like the first philosophers before them entering the world dominated by the ancient poets, in entering Greek culture, the first Christian evangelists came into an intellectual world generally hostile to their claims to possess a supernatural revelation from a creator-God.

The ancient Greeks tended to consider the perpetual existence of the world as a self-evident truth. And they considered the existence of an infinite, all-powerful, all-good, God to be ridiculous. They tended to identify infinity with chaos, imperfection; and, in light of the evident existence of evil in the physical universe, the epicureans, especially, found the existence of an omnipotent, omnibenevolent God intellectually incoherent. "How could such a 'God' permit such a state?" they mused. A god might be all-good, or all-powerful, one or the other; but not, simultaneously, both.

As a result of their views of gods and the world, many ancient Greeks considered the early Christian apologists to be of the same intellectual nature as their ancestors had considered Alexandrian Jews to have been centuries before them: cultureless barbarians. And they told the Christians as much, just as their ancestors had said the same thing to the Alexandrian Jews who had preceded them.

As the Greeks did so, Christian apologists started to defend themselves against such critiques the way Alexandrian Jews had done centuries before them, by fabricating a history in which Moses became the first philosopher. The Alexandrian Jewish thinker Artapanus (ca. third or second century BC) had gone so far as to maintain that Moses, whom the Greeks, he said, call "Musaios," was Orpheus' teacher and that Moses had "invented ships and machines for irrigation, implements of war, and philosophy."[14] Reportedly, even the great Jewish thinker Philo of Alexancria (Philo Judaeus, b. 20 BC; d. 50 AD) followed Artapanus' line of argumentation about

Moses being a philosopher and Judaism being the origin of philosophy.[15]

Early Christian apologists like Eusebius (b. 236; d. 399) and Lactantius (b. ca. 240; d. ca. 320), Clement (b. ca. 150; d. ca. 215) and Origen (b. 184/85; d. 253/254), nurtured this apocryphal, initial Jewish apologetic conflation of philosophy, science, with an esoteric teaching transmitted to the ancient Greeks from Biblical revelation. By so doing they were starting an apocryphal tradition about philosophy's, science's, history. They would pass both these erroneous traditions on to St. Ambrose (b. ca. 337–340; d. 397), who would pass them to the greatest of the early Christian intellectuals after St. Paul: St. Augustine.

By the fourteenth and fifteenth centuries, for political purposes designed chiefly to elevate the status of their disciplines within academia and the Battle of the Arts, Italian renaissance humanists would revive these fabricated traditions about philosophy's, science's, history and origin. Their doing so accounts for much of the renaissance humanist interest in the Jewish cabala and hermeneutical writings.

As used by the first Christian apologists, philosophy, science, did not begin in sense wonder. It was not a study of the problem of the one and the many. It was not a mode of uninspired reasoning utilizing principles initially and solely derived from the sense world without the help of God, or gods. Philosophy was the Catholic religion. As former Cardinal Prefect, The Sacred Congregation of the Catholic Faith of the Roman Catholic Church, Joseph Ratzinger (now Pope Benedict XVI) has rightly observed, "The identification of Christianity with philosophy was based upon a particular understanding of philosophy which had gradually come to be criticized by Christian thinkers and was definitely abandoned in the thirteenth century."[16]

True, during the thirteenth century, St. Thomas Aquinas had criticized and abandoned this understanding of philosophy because, as he said, "The seven liberal arts do not sufficiently divide philosophy."[17] But, St. Thomas was not long dead and buried before, in the fourteenth and fifteenth centuries, humanists of the Italian renaissance would revive and widely spread throughout Europe the erroneous identification of philosophy, science, with an esoteric teaching that only the Christian theological poet supposedly had the skill to decode.

If, as Pope Benedict has rightly said, hundreds of years had passed before Christians had started to come to understand that philosophy is not identical with Christianity, up to that time the medieval Christian understanding of philosophy, science, and its history was, and had to have been, wrong. If, in turn, that misunderstanding was revived, not overturned, during the Italian renaissance, the Italian renaissance understanding of philosophy, science, and its history was, and had to have been, wrong. If Descartes had based his understanding of philosophy, science, and its history upon the popular view of philosophy, science, coming out of the Italian renaissance, he could not have understood what philosophy, science, and its history had been prior to his time. His understanding of philosophy was, and had to have been, wrong.

In short, with the exception of some early works in neo-Platonism that never transmitted to early Christians a precise understanding of the maturely-developed ancient Greek notion of philosophy, philosophy, science, never entered the Christian middle ages. It had largely disappeared from the West before this time. Moreover, strictly speaking, the Christian philosophy that passed into the later middle ages was revealed theology, not philosophy. On this point, Pope Benedict XVI appears to concur with me on the basis of his claim that, by the thirteenth century, Christian thinkers had started to realize that, strictly speaking, what the earlier apologists had called "philosophy," or "Christian philosophy" could not be philosophy. It was revealed theology.

But Benedict also appears to agree with me on the basis of two other things he has said:

(1):

> Philosophy is the search by pure wisdom for an answer to the final questions of reality. Philosophical knowledge is exclusively that knowledge which can be gathered from reason and can be gathered without the teaching of revelation. It achieves its certainty exclusively from argumentation, and its statements have only the value of arguments presented in their defense.
>
> Theology is the examination of God's revelation in an attempt to understand. It is faith which seeks insight. It does not determine its own content, but receives it from revelation.[18]

And (2):

> Faith cleanses the heart. It is the result of God's initiative toward man. It is not simply a choice that men make for themselves. Faith comes about because men are touched deep within by God's spirit, who opens and purifies their hearts.[19]

Based upon these two statements by Pope Benedict, strictly speaking, the notion of a Christian philosophy appears to be, inherently, an oxymoron. I say this not to denigrate Christian reason, but to make intelligible the unique theological mode of reasoning to which the meeting of ancient pagan philosophical reason and Christian belief eventually gave birth.

In quotation "1" above, by "pure wisdom" Pope Benedict appears to mean purely natural knowledge, knowledge completely unaided by any higher intellectual lights, knowledge, as he says, that "can be gathered from reason" and "without the teaching of revelation," what St. Thomas Aquinas would call "*revelabilia.*" Such knowledge would exclude knowledge that is not philosophically impartial, that is not received and judged in a formally philosophical way.

Philosophy is chiefly an act of a philosophical habit. To be philosophical more is required of an act than that it be about philosophical content, about things knowable to unaided human reason. Such an act much also be performed the way the habit of philosophy, science, demands it be done.

To act courageously a person must do more than choose the same act that a courageous person chooses. Such an act must be done the way a courageous person does it. A courageous Christian does not behave in identically the same way as a courageous pagan. He does so with supernatural help, through a now-supernaturally-infused habit. Choosing with the assistance of the grace of the Holy Spirit, a Christian can display acts of courage that he could never perform as a pagan. Christian courage contains a supernatural element as part of its essence that radically transforms it to a higher level of perfection than the habit, virtue, of natural courage. Analogously speaking, the same is true about the mode of knowing that had been philosophy or science when it exists in a Christian soul. Its species changes.

In a complete sense philosophy's formal object does not consist in a being of "eidetic visualization." It consists in a being known as this known being essentially relates to, is received into and judged by and through a naturally-acquired and exercised habit of mind. The Christian philosopher's formal object, however, must always consist in a being known somewhat supernaturally abstracted from the being of physical things and somewhat supernaturally received into and judged by the Christian knower.

By definition, philosophical, scientific, acts must, in some way, be related to sensible content uninspiredly received and judged. But, as Pope Benedict says in quotation 2 above, Christian faith essentially enters into the human "heart" (that is, the will) creating within it a supernatural *docilitas*, docility, teachability completely unavailable to the non-believer. I reiterate, "We cannot abstract from living faith the way we can consider the color of an apple apart from the existence of an apple."[20] To try to do so is to falsify faith, become a non-believer. For Catholics, the human will is an intellectual appetite within an intellectual faculty. By entering the human heart, faith's content enters the human intellect. Even a pagan whose intellect was being inspired by the Holy Spirit would not, strictly speaking, qualify as a philosopher to the ancient Greeks. Even more so would not a Christian.

As I have argued in detail in an article entitled "Philosophizing within Faith," the habit, activity, the leading ancient Greek thinkers called "philosophy" can never exist in a believing Christian's soul the way it does in that of an ancient, pagan Greek.[21] Such a habit is not some sort of body of knowledge in a different location.

As Pope Benedict says, the grace of revealed faith gives to the human will a supernatural docility, a "supernatural teachability" not available to the non-believer. Because the human will is the intellectual appetite, is part of the human intellect, by entering into the human "heart," human will, this supernatural docility enters into the human intellect, makes the intellect more teachable. By so doing, it makes the Christian intellect incapable of receiving a form without some influence of revelation. For grace is a revelation.

While, as Pope Benedict says, philosophical knowledge (1) "is exclusively that knowledge which can be gathered from reason and can be gathered without the teaching of revelation" and (2) "achieves its certainty exclusively from argumentation, and its statements have only the value of arguments presented in their defense," I maintain that the philosophical habit alone (1) can never fully constitute the way the believing Christian gathers what the ancient Greeks called "philosophical knowledge" and (2) can never fully constitute the way a believing Christian knows with certainty.

As the medieval theologian John Duns Scotus (b. ca. 1265; d. 1308) rightly observed, the ancient Greek philosophers held nature to be complete, without the need for grace to bring it to perfection.[22] In such a world being becomes reduced to uncreated, everlasting, being. But in a created universe being no longer contains the necessity of its own existence within its essence. In such a world, the order, division, and methods of the sciences become radically altered. "In a finished universe philosophy reigns supreme. In a created universe, it does not. In such a universe, philosophy must always exist in a fashion which is open to theological regulation in its exercise and specification."[23]

Strictly speaking, a human scientist acting as an uninspired researcher does not conceive and judge in light of information, content, plagiarized from, or donated to him, by other people, even by God. Strictly speaking, a scientist, philosopher, acts solely in light of (1) his own research, consistent with the specific and generic aims of science; (2) principles that essentially relate to his subject matter that he has been able to abstract through uninspired natural ability alone, not supernatural help, from the being of sensible things; or (3) information gathered with the help of other scientists who abstract their intellectual content in a completely, but-not-more-than, natural way from the being of sensible things.

Because being a Christian essentially involves being a believer, having supernatural faith, Christians can never abstractly derive the generic and specific content of philosophical reason as an act of pure reason, pure natural wisdom alone. Christian reason must always be an act of more than pure reason, more than pure natural wisdom, must always involve the influence of faith. Nor can Christian certainty ever be derived exclusively from argumentation. It must always involve faith in God. Faith in God must enter into the essential definition of "Christian philosophy."

Another way to recognize that, strictly speaking, a Christian can never be a "philosopher," "scientist," as the ancient Greeks understood this term is to do something many students of St. Thomas do not do in attempting to answer the question whether a Christian philosophy is possible: actually follow St. Thomas's understanding of philosophy and science and recognize that, strictly speaking, according to St. Thomas, the formal object of a science, its proper subject, is an intellectually-considered being that is an abstractly-considered and judged being. According to St. Thomas, strictly speaking, science is the act of an intellectual habit of abstraction. Thinking scientifically, or philosophically, involves thinking abstractly. Infusion of grace, however, is not an act of abstraction.

Moreover, Thomas adds that scientific habits like those of the speculative sciences are ordered, essentially related, to abstractly-considered natures. Scientific habits are essentially divided according to distinctions in objects that are essential to, necessarily related to, the habit they activate.[24] Just as we cannot distinguish sense faculties according to just any distinction regarding objects of sense, like sensing a dog or a rose, but according to differences that essentially activate these faculties (like color essentially relates to sight inasmuch as it activates it, and, thereby, enables us to distinguish sight from hearing), so we distinguish scientific habits in the same way, by means of an essential, or formal, object that activates these habits.

St. Thomas says that intellectual abstraction can be of two kinds: (1) chiefly through simple, or absolute, consideration of a nature, or simple apprehension and (2) abstraction chiefly through judgment.[25] *The first form of abstraction is essentially conceptual.* It relates to the intellect as a passive power helping to bring the intellect to act. In this form of abstraction, the intellect does not consider the existence or non-existence of what the intellect thinks about (for example, to think about the shape of a ball without considering the nature of being a ball). *The second form of abstraction relates to the intellect as an active power terminating in the act of judging.*

In this first sort of abstraction, St. Thomas says we may, with no error involved, omit from the object of our intellectual consideration (not think about) what exists united to it, or is *existentially one*, even necessarily so, with it in reality so long as, in so doing, we are not omitting from it part of its essence, something without which it cannot be what it is and its nature becomes unintelligible. The reason we can engage in this form of abstraction in the example given is that such a consideration (thinking about a ball) bears no essential relation to the intelligibility of a shape. While all balls might have circular shapes, we can understand what a circular shape is (its nature, essence, what its concept expresses) without ever thinking about a ball.

In this form of conceptual apprehension, we can, and must, make judgments to determine the genus and specific difference that adequate conceptual expression of a nature demands. As a result, we cannot omit from the object of our consideration, from the concept about which we think (in this case, shape), and the judgments we make about the intelligible content of a nature, anything that exists united to said nature in reality and upon which this nature necessarily depends for its intelligibility as being what it is, nothing essential to its nature and definition as shape.[26]

Similarly, philosophy, science, essentially involves apprehending and *judging* truly about the way natures exist in reality (are related to each other independently of the way they are related to, are *conceived* by, the human intellect). Such being the case, we cannot omit from the second form of abstraction, existential judgment about our scientific objects, real relations that exist united to the natures of these objects in reality, or deny of them real relations that exist separated from them in reality. In the case at hand, for example, we cannot omit from our existential judgment how this shape is really related to this ball, that it is the shape *of* a ball.

In the case of a Christian philosopher, in reality, strictly speaking, living faith is an essential part of, is essentially related to, the nature and definition of a Christian. Living faith is an essential part of the intelligibility of the nature of being a Christian that we grasp through simple apprehension of the nature of a Christian. And abstracting intelligible content with no supernatural assistance is an essential part of the nature and definition of a philosopher.

In reality, strictly speaking, these two natures (Christian and philosopher) cannot simultaneously co-exist in one and the same being. These two natures cannot be united, really related, to comprise one nature. They cannot be united as a scientific habit because they attempt to conceive as united in one intellectual habit natures that cannot co-exist, cannot be really united, in one intellectual habit. Hence, if we judge them to be united, really related, in existence, we say something false. The Christian soul is essentially incapable of receiving into itself an essentially pagan habit of mind, which is what philosophy, as the ancient Greeks understood and practiced it, essentially is.

In becoming Christian, the habit of abstracting and reasoning that, for a non-believer, had been philosophical, scientific, is displaced and replaced by an essentially Christian habit, intellectual form, that, through supererogatory grace, orders the human intellect in a supernatural way to the chief aim of a higher genus, supernatural happiness. In so doing, the reasoning that had been philosophical becomes, something more-than philosophical, more-than scientific, essentially theological: Christian wisdom.

The habit of abstracting and reasoning the ancient Greeks called "philosophy," "science," can never exist in a believing Christian's soul the way it does within the soul of an ancient, pagan Greek. A believing Christian can never abstract first principles of natural reasoning from the being of sensible things in identically the same way as does a non-believer. To some extent, by faith, the Christian already knows by higher principles and a grace-filled method, what the intellect of a philosopher seeks to uncover by sense wonder and totally natural abstraction alone. Hence, while, from an external, historical observer's standpoint, the activities of a Christian philosopher and that of a non-believer might appear identical, from a practitioner's standpoint, they cannot be identical.

The act of faith and the grace of the Holy Spirit are contained within the intellect of the believing Christian. As Gilson, following St. Thomas, has so forcefully shown, the person, not the senses or intellect, knows.[27] We sense with our intellects and intellectualize with our senses. Consequently, when Christians engage in sensory abstraction, strictly speaking, they do so with the assistance of grace.

As St. Thomas has said, principles we derive through faith, not abstraction, are theological, not philosophical.[28] Faith received through grace is a revelation and a theological principle.[29] Sensing with faith is always a condition, first principle, of a believing Christian's soul. Hence, strictly speaking, in a believing Christian's soul, no act of philosophy, science, can be a non-theological act.

For this reason, the highest form of argumentation for a Christian philosopher must always be the argument from authority. The chief first principle for a Christian philosopher, his highest and chief principle of certainty is, "God says it is true." This can never be the case for an ordinary philosopher, scientist, a non-believer whose highest form of authority must always consist in principles essentially abstracted in a totally unsupernatural way from the being of sensible things.

During the thirteenth century, St. Thomas Aquinas appears to have been the first Catholic theologian to recognize that the methods used by a Christian and an ancient pagan to study things in a philosophical way were essentially different. While, content-wise, Christians might study the same subject-matter as an ancient Greek philosopher, method-wise they cannot do so in the same way. Strictly speaking, however, philosophy's subject-matter, its formal object, includes its content and method. Hence, strictly speaking, the subject-matter of Christian philosophy and non-Christian philosophy can never be identical.

At best, when talking about philosophy, science, the way the ancient Greeks practiced it and the way a Christian practices it, we predicate the term "philosophy," "science," analogously. The reason for this, again, is that philosophy's, science's, method, which is a first principle of philosophy, science, essentially involves a habit of abstraction. Because the habit of abstraction that Christian and non-Christian philosophers use to derive their content-principles of philosophical reason are not essentially identical, these two activities cannot be essentially identical. At best, they can be somewhat the same, somewhat different: analogous.

Somewhere during the 1250s, when he composed his *Commentary on the* de Trinitate *of Boethius*, or before, St. Thomas had come to realize that the common view of his theological predecessors about the ancient Greek way of doing philosophy, science, was wrong. To provide himself with a more suitable and closely philosophical tool to do theology, in his *Commentary*, St. Thomas distinguished two methods of investigation open to the theologian.

(1) The traditional method was chiefly exegetical. Its history went back to Church Fathers like Hilary and Ambrose. It held longstanding authority among the undergraduate faculty of Liberal Arts at the University of Paris, who had been schooled to reduce philosophy to the traditional *trivium* (grammar, rhetoric, logic), or one of its divisions, illumined by revelation. This method, utilized by Peter the Lombard in his famous *Sentences*, proceeds solely on the basis of argument from authority. It makes reference solely to the authority of Scripture and Church Fathers.

Later, in the "Prologue" written for his famous *Summa theologiae*, St. Thomas explained that, to avoid superfluous material and needless repetition that breed boredom and confusion, sound pedagogy dictated that a book like his *Summa*, written, as Thomas said, for "beginning students" should have a compatible structure, should be clear and concise. Hence, in the *Summa* St. Thomas utilized a second method of theological investigation, one that he said was inspired by St. Augustine and used by Boethius in his *de Trinitate*.

(2) The second method, chiefly scholastic, is divided into two parts. It starts in a similar way to the traditional method, by accepting as presuppositions arguments from authority based upon Scripture, the Church Fathers, the magisterial Church. To this it adds reasoned arguments from first principles derived through abstraction by natural reason from sensation.[30]

Because a Christian theologian's chief first principle of reasoning is the argument from authority, either of the above two methods is appropriate for such a theologian to use. A Christian theologian can totally avoid the use of philosophy and still be a theologian, as numerous theologians in the East and West had done prior to St. Thomas. Like St. Augustine, who tended to mistake philosophy with the Christian-inspired liberal arts in general, or rhetoric in particular, a Christian might use either, or both, of these as ancillary tools.

But if a Christian theologian chooses to study theology as a "Christian philosopher," *mutatis mutandis*, such a theologian must imitate the method of natural reasoning used by the ancient philosophers. He must use arguments and principles of reasoning rooted in, and abstracted by natural reason *with the help of supernatural faith* from, the being of sensible things. As an Aristotelian might put it, such a person has to use "the language of proof or demonstration." The methods of the Christian and ancient philosophers must use the same language, of demonstration. Still, these two methods are not essentially identical.[31]

Prior to St. Thomas, strictly speaking, the scholastic method of philosophizing within revealed theology called "Christian philosophy" did not exist. In large part, this was due to the fact that, prior to St. Thomas, Christian theologians did not have anything close to a proper understanding of the practice of philosophy in which the ancient Greeks had actually engaged. While the scholastic method of doing theology practiced by Boethius and St. Augustine had involved using reasoned arguments from first principles derived through abstraction by natural reason from sensation, such a procedure alone does not make argumentation philosophical.

Liberal artists and people engaged in the use of experiential reasoning use identically the same procedure. Boethius largely confounded philosophy with logic or the liberal arts. And St. Augustine equivocated about philosophy's nature, at some times identifying it with the liberal arts or rhetoric, at other times confounding philosophy with theology (faith seeking understanding); and, at still other times, conflating it with using the liberal arts, or rhetoric, as a tool of faith seeking understanding.

St. Augustine was not a Platonic philosopher anymore than St. Thomas was an Aristotelian one. Both were Christian theologians who read pagan philosophers to deconstruct and mine their thought in the service of Christian theology. The difference between the two is that, unlike Augustine, St. Thomas actually had a precise understanding of what, around the time of Aristotle, in their golden age, the ancient Greeks meant by "philosophy."

Hence between St. Thomas and the decline of ancient pagan antiquity with the Emperor Justinian's (b. ca. 482; d. 565) closing of the ancient pagan philosophical schools in 529 AD, no precise understanding of what philosophy for the ancient Greeks had been actually took root among theologians in the Christian West, and the same was true for their counterparts among Jews and Muslims in the Middle East. As Ernst Robert Curtius rightly noted, by the sixth century AD, philosophy and poetry had largely been reduced to rhetoric:

> The assimilation of philosophy to rhetoric is a product of neo-Sophism. Rhetor, philosopher, sophist now mean the same thing to the Latin West too. Thus by the time pagan Antiquity came to an end there existed six different notions of philosophy preserved by Cassiodorus (sixth-century AD) which were transmitted to medieval Christianity: 1. Knowledge of what exists and how it exists; 2. Knowledge of divine and human things; 3. Preparation for death; 4. Assimilation of man to God; 5. Art of arts and science of sciences; 6. Love of wisdom.[32]

Between the sixth and ninth centuries, apart from John Scotus Erigeuna's neo-Platonic musings mixed together with Christian theology, nothing closely resembling ancient Greek philosophy appears in the West. Revival of Christian learning by the Emperor Charlemagne in the ninth century gave birth to cathedral and monastic schools to help restore Western literacy. But, as this happened, stress was placed upon those subjects chiefly related to literary restoration: the *trivium* of grammar, logic, and rhetoric. During this time, together with Scripture, the writings of Boethius and St. Augustine held chief authority. Hence, the Battle of the Arts became revived again with Christian intellectuals disagreeing with one another whether philosophy was chiefly grammar, logic, or rhetoric (largely in that historical order).

By the thirteenth century, as literacy had begun to rise again and universities had started to become established, a new Battle of the Arts began as the lost philosophical works of Aristotle, especially his physics and metaphysics, started to become available to Christian scholars. Consequently, only toward the end of the middle ages, with the work of St. Thomas Aquinas, did medieval Christians start to understand what philosophy, science, actually had been for the ancient Greeks. Prior to this time, for more than 1200 years, the understanding of philosophy, science, as the leading Greek philosophers Socrates, Plato, Aristotle, and Plotinus had actually conceived it, had largely, if not entirely, become lost to the West.

As a result, strictly speaking, no history of medieval philosophy, science, has actually ever been written. Nor could one ever have existed before the time of St. Thomas. The chief reason for this is that a correct history of a subject depends upon a proper understanding of the subject's nature. Throughout the middle ages up to Aquinas, no proper understanding of philosophy, the ancient Greek maturely-developed understanding of science, existed within the Christian West (or within the Middle East for that matter).

As a result, understanding St. Thomas's teaching about Greek philosophy, science, is crucial to giving an account of philosophy's, science's, nature and history. No recovery of our understanding of the Western understanding of philosophy, science, and no ending of the contemporary separation of science and wisdom can occur without a detailed study of St. Thomas' understanding of philosophy, science, as the ancient Greeks practiced it. Hence, it is to that study to which I will now turn my attention.

NOTES

1.   Étienne Gilson, *Unity of Philosophical Experience* (New York: Charles Scribner's Sons, 1965), p. 8.

2.   Étienne Gilson, *History of Christian Philosophy in the Middle Ages* (New York: Randhom House, 1954), p. 98.

3.   Gilson, *Unity of Philosophical Experience*, pp. 5–6.

4.   Id., pp. 10–11.

5.   Peter A. Redpath, *Cartesian Nightmare: An Introduction to Transcendental Sophistry* (Amsterdam and Atlanta: Editions Rodopi, B.V., 1997). p. 7.

6.   Peter A. Redpath, *Wisdom's Odyssey from Philosophy to Transcendental Sophistry* (Amsterdam and Atlanta: Editions Rodopi, B.V., 1997)., pp. 1–38.

7.   Joseph Ratzinger, Pope Benedict XVI, *Jesus of Nazareth*, trans. from the German by Adrian J. Walker (San Francisco: Ignatius Press, 2007), Part 1, pp. 169–180; and Pope Benedict XVI, "Faith, Reason, and the University: Memories and Reflections," Apostolic Journey of His Holiness Benedict XVI to München, Altötting, and Regensburg (09–14 September 2006), Meeting with the Representatives of Science, Lecture of the Holy Father, *Aula magna* of the University of Regensburg. (URL=http://www.vatican.va/holy_father/benedict_xvi/speeches/2006/september/documents/hf_ben-xvi_spe_20060912_university-regensburg_en.html), Tuesday, 12 September 2006.

8.   Redpath, *Wisdom's Odyssey*, p. 36.

9.   Id.

10.   Id., p. 42.

11.   Id., p. 41.

12.   Id.

13.   Id., p. 40–42; see, also, Joseph Owens, *Towards a Christian Philosophy* (Washington, DC: The Catholic University of America Press, 1990), p. 1; and Joseph Cardinal Ratzinger, *Faith, Philosophy, and Theology*, in *Pope John Paul II Lecture Series* (College of St. Thomas, St. John Vianny Seminary, 1985) pp. 9-14;

14.   Redpath, *Cartesian Nightmare*, pp. 7–9; see, also, Brian P. Copenhaver and Charles B. Schmitt, *Renaissance Philosophy* (Oxford and New York: Oxford Univeristy Press, 1992, pp. 329–332; and Ernst Robert Curtius, *European Literature and the Latin Middle Ages*, trans. Willard R. Trask (New York: Published for the Bollingen Foundation by Pantheon Books, 1952), pp. 39, 205–212.

15.   Redpath, *Wisdom's Odyssey*, pp. 42–43; see, also, Curtius, *European Literature and the Latin Middle Ages*, p. 212; see, also, Giovanni Reale, *A History of Ancient Philosophy*, Vol. 4. *The Schools of the Imperial Age*, ed. and trans. John R. Catan (Albany: NY: SUNY Press, 1990), pp. 177–190

16.   Ratzinger, "Faith, Philosophy, and Theology," p. 11.

17.   St. Thomas Aquinas, *Commentary on the* de Trinitate *of Boethius, Questions V and VI. St. Thomas Aquinas: The Division and Methods of the Sciences*, ed. and trans., Armand A. Maurer (Toronto: Pontifical Institute of Mediaeval Studies, 3rd rev. ed., 1963), q. 5, a.1, ad 3, p. 11; Curtius, *European Literature and the Latin Middle Ages*, p. 213,

18.   Ratzinger, "Faith, Philosophy, and Theology," pp. 9–14.

19.   Joseph Ratzinger, Pope Benedict XVI, *Jesus of Nazareth*, trans. into English by the Vatican Secretariat of State (San Francisco: Ignatius Press, 2011), Part 2, pp. 58–59.

20.   Redpath, *Wisdom's Odyssey*, p. 61.

21.   Peter A. Redpath, "Philosophizing within Faith," in Curtis L. Hancock and Brendan Sweetman (eds.), *Faith and the Life of the Intellect* (Washington, DC: The Catholic University of America Press, 2003).

22.   Owens, *Towards a Christian Philosophy*, pp. 77, 79.

23.   Redpath, *Wisdom's Odyssey*, pp. 60–61.

24.   Aquinas, *Commentary on the* de Trinitate *of Boethius, Questions V and VI. St. Thomas Aquinas: The Division and Methods of the Sciences*, q. 5, a.1, reply, p. 7.

25.   Id., q. 5, a.2. reply, pp. 22–23.

26.   Id.

27.   Étienne Gilson, *Thomist Realism and the Critique of Knowledge*, trans. Mark A. Wauck (San Francisco: Ignatius Press, 1986), pp. 172–173.

28.   St. Thomas Aquinas, *Summa theologiae*, 1, q.1, a. 6, ad 3.

29.   St. Thomas Aquinas, *Commentary on the* de Trinitate *of Boethius, Questions I–IV. St. Thomas Aquinas: Faith, Reason, and Theology*, trans. with an intro. and notes, Armand A. Maurer (Toronto: Pontifical Institute of Mediaeval Studies, 1987), q. 3, a. 1, ad 5, pp. 65–70.

30.   Id., see Thomas's "Introduction" and questions I–IV.

31.   Id.; see, also, Ralph M. McInerny, *A History of Western Philosophy*, Volume 2. *From St. Augustine to Ockham* (Notre Dame, Ind. and London: University of Notre Dame Press, 1970), p. 54–59; Gilson, *History of Christian Philosophy in the Middle Ages*, pp. 140–178.

32.   Curtius, *European Literature and the Latin Middle Ages*, p. 212.

Six

ST. THOMAS'S AND ARISTOTLE'S TEACHING ABOUT THE NATURE OF PHILOSOPHY, SCIENCE, AS A STUDY OF THE PROBLEM OF THE ONE AND THE MANY

As is well known, St. Thomas Aquinas's teaching about, and understanding of, philosophy, science, is heavily influenced by Aristotle. This is so true that, even though their two ways of thinking are essentially different, to separate them, to treat St. Thomas's understanding of philosophy, science, separate from the teaching of Aristotle would be impossible. For this reason, and to avoid unnecessary repetition, I did not engage in a separate study of Aristotle's understanding of philosophy, science, until now, preferring to study his teaching and St. Thomas's understanding of it together.

Before I do so, however, I need to make some remarks about unusual use of four terms by St. Thomas and Aristotle that can easily get readers confused: "matter," "subject," "object," and "principle."

Historically in the West, in philosophy truly- and falsely-so-called, the term "matter" has referred chiefly to a potency or quantity. When St. Thomas uses the term "matter," he generally means potency, not quantity. The reason for this is simple. Strictly speaking, matter and quantity can never be identical because a thing can change its quantity (its size, for example) without changing its matter. While perhaps useful in some ways, the modern and contemporary identification of matter with quantity, or physical extension, dimensive being, cannot be right.

To complicate the linguistic confusion, St. Thomas often synonymously uses "matter" and "subject" (which I often translate as "subject-matter"). In native English we still often conflate these terms today. For St. Thomas the subject, or matter, of a science is that about which a science chiefly thinks or talks, what a science chiefly studies or considers, the formal perspective under which we think about the intelligible content of a science, the nature that a science studies, or both.

St. Thomas understands a substance to be chiefly a facultatively-independent, or real, being. This is a being that has within itself its own act of existence (*esse*) as an intrinsic principle distinct from its nature and from the nature and existence of other beings. The subject of science, however, is a dematerialized and abstractly-considered substance (a substance about which a scientist chiefly and abstractly conceives, judges, and talks): a real being thought, judged, and talked about in relation to some real difference that activates a knowing faculty or habit. Considered as a subject of a science, a substance includes as part of its nature what we think about and how we think about it. Hence, even though quantity and matter are not identical, quantity can be the matter, or subject, of a science; and, in a way, so can quality.

In this sense (as the subject of a science), further to complicate the language difficulty, for St. Thomas, a subject can be an "object," a being (*ens* or substance) about which we think or talk considered as thought or talked about.

Today, virtually all people who call themselves "philosophers," including students of Aristotle and St. Thomas, think that philosophical principles are linguistic or logical premises. They do this because they tend to reduce philosophy to a branch of the traditional *trivium*: grammar or logic. Aristotle and St. Thomas, however, predicate the term "principle" analogously. And they understand the term chiefly to refer to a starting point of being, becoming, or knowing.

So conceived, anything that exists can be a principle. A complete nature that possesses its own, individual act of existing (a substance) can be a principle. So can the parts of an existing substance (form, matter, the act of being). St. Thomas calls God and the Devil principles, God being the exterior principle of all moral good; the Devil being the exterior principle of all moral evil.[1] And, by analogous extension, so can logical premises be principles; but, in the chief and highest sense, a principle as subject of a science, is an abstractly-considered *ens* or substance. This sense of principle includes human faculties and habits as much as it does what essentially activates a faculty or habit.

Given these caveats, readers should have a somewhat easier time following Aristotle's and St. Thomas's amazing teaching about the nature of philosophy, science, that starts immediately below.

2. Why Aristotle maintained that philosophy, science, starts is wonder with the problem of the one and the many and essentiallly depends upon the existence of an immaterial first cause for its existence and intelligibility

Like his teacher Plato, Aristotle thought that philosophy is essentially (1) a study of the one and the many, and of opposites; (2) unity is related to plurality as a measure to a being measured; and (3) measures of things are chiefly facultatively-independent indivisibles, unities, ones, forms. Aristotle simply relocated such measures from a Platonic World of Forms to individually-existing, numerically-one subjects so as to make his understanding of philosophy more coherent.

While what I have just said in the above paragraph might sound strange to some readers, even to those familiar with Aristotle and St. Thomas, that Aristotle thought the way I am saying is easy to show simply by reading his *Metaphysics*. Consider, for example, the way he started the last Book of this work: "All the philosophers make the first principles contraries: as in natural things (that is, in physical beings), so also in the case of unchangeable substances (that is, in metaphysical beings)."[2] Aristotle included the pre-Socratics, Socrates, and Plato in the phrase "All the philosophers."

Since Aristotle maintained that contraries are extreme differences, opposites, belonging to the same genus, and that species that share a common genus share a common matter, he was maintaining that all philosophers prior to him, including Plato and Socrates, wittingly or not, thought that opposition was the first principle of everything. Moreover, since Aristotle maintained that the opposition between the one and the many was the ground of all other opposition, by considering first principles to be contraries, Aristotle believed that all philosophers prior to him were studying the problem of contrariety, were involved in attempting to understand the opposition between the one and the many.

Nonetheless, Aristotle rejected the then-commonly-received notion that contrariety can be the first principle of everything because, he maintained, the notion of contrariety involves the notion of being generated from a common matter or subject; and first principles must have no underlying subject. Hence, he stated:

> But all things which are generated from their contraries involve an underlying subject, and none can exist apart; a subject, then, must be present in the case of contraries, if anywhere. All contraries, then, are always predicable of a subject, and none can exist apart, but just as appearances suggest that there is nothing contrary to substance, argument confirms this. No contrary is the first principle of all things in the full sense; the first principle is something different.[3]

Moreover, Aristotle did not reject the notion that philosophy essentially involves studying opposites and that we initially derive the problem of the one and the many from conflicting communications about sensible measures we first uncover, as the pre-Socratics, Socrates, and Plato maintained, in experiencing opposition in the being of sensible things. Whatever the first principle is, Aristotle claimed that it involves the notion of being one, because a principle is a one and indivisible, and being one involves the notion of being a measure.

He explained that being a measure involves being homogeneous with the thing measured. This is the case, he said, in music (a quarter-tone in a scale), in spatial magnitude (a finger, a foot, or something similar), in rhythms (a beat or syllable), in heaviness (a definite weight, an indivisible limit), "and in the same way in all cases, in qualities, a quality, in quantities a quantity (and the measure is indivisible, in the former case in kind, and in the latter to sense), which implies that the one is not in itself the substance of anything."

Aristotle immediately added, "And this is reasonable" (that is, that the one not be the substance of anything). For, he said that, while substances are composites of matter and form:

> "the one" means the measure of some plurality, and 'number' means a measured plurality and a plurality of measures [that is, of things measured]. Thus it is natural that the one is not a number; for the measure is not measures [that is, things measured], but both the measure and the one are starting points. The measure must always be some identical thing predicated of all the things it measures, e.g., if things are horses, the measure is "horse," and if they are men "man." If they are a man, a horse, and a god, the measure is perhaps "living beings."[4]

Aristotle thought that all divisions of philosophy, not just metaphysics, study a substance considered *per se*. He maintained that all human knowledge originates in the being of sensible things. Sensible things are composite beings, complexes of opposites of form and matter, or act and potency, in, and from, which we derive our knowledge of first principles.[5] Aristotle even attributed to Socrates, Plato, and Plato's followers the procedure of deriving universals from sensible singulars.[6]

Strictly speaking, for Aristotle, a universal (*katholou*) is a kind of whole. As an object of science Aristotle grounds our knowledge of universals in individual, sensible, beings. While these things are changeable, composite, and contingent in nature, they contain an unchanging, permanent, principle, a one or unitary whole (a form) *that universally and necessarily relates* to all individual things that contain it. As such, individual, contingent, sensible beings contain necessity of the appropriate kind to act as the object of scientific knowledge, or subject of a science.[7]

Aristotle considered philosophy to be identical with science: certain knowledge demonstrated through causes.[8] He maintained that philosophy, or science, considers a multitude of beings, a genus, a many (contrary opposites), and tries to demonstrate essential properties of the genus by reasoning according to necessary principles, or measures, universals, or ones, to the genus.[9]

Aristotle thought that causes are principles, and principles are starting points, and measures, of being, becoming, or knowing.[10] For this reason, he thought of philosophy as a study of causes, principles of effects, which we first encounter in our experience of sensible being.

He considered principles to be measures because principles are starting points and points are ones, unities, or indivisibles. He said that points are ones, indivisibles, with position, principally spatial position or position in a continuum. Principles, then, are indivisibles, ones.[11] As known, they are indivisible intelligibles, limits of knowing.

As is well known, Aristotle considered being and unity convertible concepts. In reality, what we call being and one are identical. They differ only conceptually, in reason. We derive our idea of unity by adding the concept of indivisibility and principle to our idea of being, just as we derive our idea of number by dividing a unity (a continuum). *Hence, Aristotle thought that the notion of unity adds to being the ideas of being a principle and privation of division.*[12]

In his *Posterior Analytics* Aristotle said that demonstration demands that a one exist "in many and about many" and that science involves knowledge of the fact that something is and demonstration of the reason why. He claimed that demonstration must make manifest a thing's proximate, or fully commensurate, cause.[13] Demonstration, requires a middle term, *a one that is the same in many*, or a one unequivocally predicable of a many. If no one something exists the same in a multitude, in a many, no one intelligible content exists unequivocally predicable of a many. Lack of such a uniform content existing in a many makes demonstration, and philosophy, science, impossible because it makes universal predication impossible.[14]

Because Aristotle maintained that demonstration involves knowledge of the fact and of the reason why, he asserted that science requires necessary, or *per se,* predication, predication of a proximate, not a remote, cause. Such a cause is the proximate principle of substance and its essential accidents, accidents that have their cause in a proximate subject and necessarily and always inhere in the subject.[15] For Aristotle, no science considers accidents as such because no science can study an infinite number of things, can be involved in infinite predication. Science can only study accidents that have determinate causes in a subject.[16]

In making such statements, Aristotle appears clearly to have been following the lead of Socrates and Plato as Plato described the nature of *per se* predication in his dialogues. Aristotle did not develop the notion of *per se* predication. We have already seen many examples of it in Book Seven of Plato's *Republic* involving Socrates' discussion of the division and methods of the arts and sciences of arithmetic, geometry, astronomy, and music. And it is present as far back as Book One of the *Republic*, where Plato portrayed Socrates utilizing it in conversation with the sophist Thrasymachos.

At that point in the dialogue, Thrasymachos had just ridiculed Socrates for needing a nurse to wipe his nose because Socrates thought that, strictly speaking, the art of shepherding concerns the welfare of sheep, not the monetary benefit of shepherds. In reply, Socrates told Thrasymachos, that, precisely speaking (that is, predicating the term *per se* of its proximate cause or subject), the art of shepherding relates to a different generic subject than does the art of money-making. It concerns a different matter, a different proximate cause, generic subject, or genus.[17]

This is one of the first instances, if not the first, of the explicit articulation of the notion of *per se* predication in philosophy's history. Clearly, Plato had this notion consciously in mind when he wrote Book Seven of his *Republic*. The notion of *per se* predication underlies this Book because, as is clear from our study of the *Republic*, Book Seven, Plato thought that we can distinguish the different arts and sciences based upon the different psychological powers to which different matters relate in unequal ways for possible human investigation.

Aristotle took from Plato his notion of an order of the arts and sciences, he often referred the hierarchy of the arts and sciences, and he started his *Metaphysics* with reference to it. *For Aristotle, science, or philosophy, studies the many different ways many things relate to one proximate subject: the way many beings, more or less, share, participate, in the unity of a primary, or chief, subject.*

Every science, not just metaphysics, therefore, chiefly and *analogously* studies the principles and causes of substances to understand the properties of the many species of which we predicate a genus.[18] Hence, Aristotle said that as many parts of philosophy exist "as there are kinds of substance."[19] And, following Aristotle, Aquinas stated, "demonstration is concerned with things which are *per se* in something."[20]

Aristotle claimed that science, or philosophy, chiefly studies the principles and causes of a proximate substance and its *per se* accidents. It does not study just any substance and any accidents.[21] It studies proper, essential, accidents (properties) of a proximate substance. Through these substantial principles we come to know the proper accidents, or properties, of all the species that belong to the genus.

Aristotle maintained that no science could possibly study all the accidents that relate to its subject because we can *relate* an infinite number of accidents to a subject. Science, however, must study a finite multitude. The scientist's study bears only on those accidents that are essential properties of its subject, such as intrinsic shape and size relate to a geometrical figure.

Similarly, just as no science can depend for its intelligibility upon the relation of an infinite number of accidents to a subject, no science can depend for its existence and intelligibility upon an infinite number of principles. For this reason, Arisotle thought that the existence of an Unmoved Mover was a necessary condition for the intelligibility of all science, not just physics. Hence he defended this teaching both in his *Physics* and his *Metaphysics. If such be the case, and the science of physics is a necessary condition for the existence of all other divisions of philosophy, science, then the whole of philosophy, science, necessarily depends upon the existence of theism, or an analogue closely akin to it, as a first principle.*[22] (Hence, the origin of philosophy from Greek mythologological speculation about the gods appears to have been a necessary condition, not a historical accident).

For Aristotle, then, in some way, all philosophy, every science, involves coming to know how a many is essentially one. He maintained that (1) as many species of being exist as species of unity exist; (2) just as we can predicate the term being analogously, so we can predicate the term unity analogously; and (3) one science, metaphysics, has the job to study these species of unity: "the same and the similar and the other concepts of this sort." [23]

Since being and unity are convertible notions, Aristotle maintained that we can analogously predicate unity of all the different genera. Hence, he claimed that we may refer almost all contraries to unity as to their principle.[24] St. Thomas Aquinas explained Aristotle's meaning thus:

> since being and unity signify the same thing . . . there must be as many species of being as there are species of unity, and they must correspond to each other. For just as the parts of being are substance, quantity, quality, and so on, in a similar way the parts of unity are sameness, equality and likeness.

For things are the same when they are one in substance, equal when they are one in quantity, and like when they are one in quality. And the other parts of unity could be taken from the other parts of being, if they were given names. And just as it is the office of one science [first] philosophy to consider all the parts of being, in a similar way it is the office of this same science to consider all the parts of unity, i.e., sameness, likeness, and so forth.[25]

Aristotle viewed a genus as a kind of whole. Philosophically or scientifically considered, he thought of it as a generic body, the immediate, proximate, first, or proper subject, principle, of different *per se* accidents, unities, or properties within the genus.[26] Aquinas explained that this sense of genus is not the same as the sense of genus as signifying the essence of a species, which is the way the logician uses the term "genus":

This sense of genus is not the one that signifies the essence of a species, as animal is the genus of man, but the one that is the proper subject in the species of different accidents. For surface is the subject of all plane figures. And it bears some likeness to a genus, because the proper subject is given in the definition of an accident just as a genus is given in the definition of its species. Hence the proper subject of an accident is predicated like a genus.[27]

Since surface is the immediate subject of all colors and plane figures, it is the referential source of being and intelligibility of all surface bodies, the proper subject (proximate principle) of all the accidents that emanate from a proximate subject. We must refer color and figure to surface, must include surface in their essential concept and definition, to comprehend their natures. By proximately subjectifying them, surface gives quantitative unity to all plane figures. For this reason, when geometricians predicate surface of different plane (surface) figures they predicate surface analogously as a common matter or subject.

In so doing, analogously, geometricians resemble logicians. When geometricians and logicians predicate a genus, both include the genus in the species's definition. And both predicate the genus that signifies the essence of a species. In both cases, the definition of the species refers to its subject genus (and, tacitly, to the chief aim of the genus), its substance, for its intelligibility.

But logicians do not predicate their genus of their subjects as *per se*, or proper, accidents of a proximate, and *per se, generating subject*. They totally abstract from such a concrete understanding of a subject. The substance the geometrician studies is a surface body as a *per se* cause, proximate principle, of *per se* effects, the proper subject, generator, of an accident, not the essential definition of the logician. The logician's abstract logical universal in not identical with the scientist's, or philosopher's, concrete universal because the logician and the scientist, or philosopher, consider the same subject under distinct formal aspects. The logician considers it abstractly and as existentially neutral, does not consider the genus as a generator of something else. Even if the philosopher, scientist, uses abstract reasoning initially to grasp his formal object, he always views this formal object concretely and as existentially related, *as a causal principle of real species*.

As St. Thomas, following Avicenna (ibn Sina, b. 980; d. 1037) says in his *Commentary on the* de Trinitate *of Boethius*, "principles can be called common (by which St. Thomas means "universal") in two ways: by predication, as when I say form is common to all forms because it is predicated of all; second, by causality, as we say that the sun, which is numerically one is the principle of all things subject to generation."[28] *Hence, according to St. Thomas and Aristotle, philosophical universals are not logical universals, principles common as a result of common predication or reference of some one essence to a multitude. Philosophical universals are causal universals, principles that, in light of this cause's chief aim, es-*

tablish a universal relationship between a numerically-one cause and the many effects of which it is the universal cause.

As part of their essential scientific activity, scientists, philosophers, look for the *per se* subject of an activity by referring the activity to an existing *per se* property, as an effect caused here and now by a numerically-one *per se* subject acting through a *per se* property as through a *per se* accident. Flowing from the form or matter of its substance, such a *per se* property, and the contrary opposites that necessarily flow from it, act as external signs of necessary, intrinsic relationships between a substance's form and the parts of a substance that essentially relate to it.

For example, through his *per se* habit of music, Socrates the musician (the numerically-one *per se* proximate subject, or cause, of music), not Socrates the human being or philosopher (incidental, remote, subject, or cause, of music), is now producing a kind of music (the *per se* action) as a result of his possession of a numerically-one *per se* musical property, his numerically-one musical habit or quality, a *per se* accident that necessarily flows from his habit's essential relation as a qualitative property to Socrates' form as a human being.

Socrates produces the music because of his existing, numerically-one musical ability or habit, not because of his philosophical ability, or habit, or because he is a human being. All musical action presupposes production by an existing, numerically-one, musical quality and a numerically-one existing musical subject. Socrates' action is musical. Therefore, Socrates' action presupposes production by musical quality and an existing musical subject.

Hence, despite the fact that, logically considered, and according to the logician's way of abstract talking or predicating, and, in truth, Socrates is essentially a human being, philosophically and scientifically considered, and according to the philosopher's and scientist's way of talking or predicating terms, being human is incidental to being a musician. Precisely speaking, predicating philosophically, or scientifically, causally and proximately *per se*, being a musician involves a principle and cause more proximate to music production than being a human, just as being a geometrical body involves a principle and cause more proximate than being a material body. Strictly speaking, the musician generates music through "the acquired art of music," not "the natural act of being a human."

The generic body, or subject, the philosopher, scientist, studies in music is the musical, not the human, body, or subject. Similarly, the subject of study in ancient and contemporary physics is the mobile, not the corruptible or incorruptible, body, whether, logically and abstractly considered, matter is essentially corruptible or incorruptible.

The essential way of reasoning and talking, and the skills, of the philosopher, or scientist, are radically different from the logician's. Consequently, Aristotle maintained that, philosophically or scientifically considered, we cannot reduce one proximate subject (genus) to another. Generically diverse beings in a philosophical or scientific sense are those "whose proximate substratum is different, and which are not analyzed the one into the other nor both into the same thing (e. g., form and matter are different in genus)."[29]

Aquinas clarified Aristotle's meaning by referring, as I have just done, to the idea of a proximate subject as *a subjectifying common matter*, a proximate generating principle, of necessary accidental species. He said: "A solid is in a sense reducible to surfaces, and therefore solid figures and plane figures do not belong to diverse genera, . . . but celestial bodies and lower bodies are diverse in genus inasmuch as they do not have a common matter."[30]

That is, philosophically, or scientifically, considered (whether corruptible or incorruptible), solid and plane figures are species of surface bodies. Both are kinds of surface body. Surface body proximately causes both of them and the necessary accidents that are subjectified in them. So considered, surface body is their proximate, or subjectifying, common matter, their generic matter. They share surface body as a proximate, or subjectifying, common matter, genus, or common material subject or first principle. This is the reason we can study them in one science.

Logically considered, we can include celestial bodies, sublunary bodies, surface bodies, and mobile bodies in the same genus because all are species of body. But they do not belong to a common science because, as bodies, they share no proximate, subjectifying (that is, real) common, generating matter, or genus. They share a remote matter, an abstract "body."

In ancient physics, celestial and sublunary bodies share no proximate, subjectifying, existential, common, generating matter. The proximate matter of celestial bodies is everlasting. The matter of sublunary bodies is corruptible. Considered as such (as corruptible, as opposed to incorruptible, bodies), celestial and sublunary bodies are separate, not identical, subjects of philosophical, or scientific, study in ancient physics. They share no proximate subjectifying cause and, therefore, constitute diverse genera.

In physics they share a common matter for philosophical, or scientific, purposes of study *as mobile* (not as corruptible or incorruptible) bodies because this last formal difference (being mobile) distinguishes them relationally as essential accidents in reference to a common principle, cause, and proximate, numerically-one, generating subject, and accounts for their essential being as proximate causes of motion. For this reason, classical physics, natural philosophy, can study both just as geometry can study both as species of suface body.

Recall that Aristotle tells us that all science chiefly studies substance. This means philosophy, physics, mathematics, and metaphysics study substance, that substance is a first principle of all scientific study. Metaphysics, however, studies immaterial and material substance as part of its subject, even though, logically considered, immaterial and material substance cannot be reduced to a common "matter," subject, being, or body. Immaterial substance has no matter. And part of metaphysics involves studying beings that have no bodies at all.

Logically considered, apparently we should not include corruptible bodies as part of the study of metaphysics. And metaphysics should not be a science because science involves study of specific multitudes in terms of a common, or generic, matter. And immaterial substances have no matter. Nonetheless, as a philosophical discipline, philosophers can claim that metaphysics studies a "common matter" by saying that metaphysics studies common being as its matter, or proximate subject, or priniciple, somewhat like the mathematician studies what St. Thomas called "intelligible matter" as the common matter of quantitative beings.

Moreover, philosophers, and scientists, can justify their right to make such distinctions by rightly maintaining that their way of predicating terms essentially differs from the way logicians predicate terms. Logicians predicate terms univocally using existentially-neutral, universals (relations), universals that abstract from the notion of sharing a proximate subject as the cause for inclusion within the genus. Philosophers predicate terms analogously using concrete, existentially-related, universals, universals that include the notion of sharing a proximate subject, principle, and cause for inclusion within the genus.[31]

Hence, another crucial point to understand about the way Aristotle and St. Thomas consider the way of talking of a logician and that of a philosopher, scientist, to be different is that, talking "scientifically," "philosophically," Aristotle and St. Thomas do not use the term "substance" in the same way as does an Aristotelian logician. Properly speaking, anyone familiar with Aristotelian logic would expect an Aristotelian not to consider a quantified or qualified body to be a substantial body. We would expect the Aristotelian logician to call such bodies, "accidental bodies." Nonetheless, *just as in the case of the use of the term "genus," scientifically or philosophically considered, Aristotle and St. Thomas predicate the term "substance" analogously, and chiefly to mean a "subject genus" (a one) considered as the principle, generator, of a multitude of species (a many).* Hence, for scientific, or philosophical, purposes, Aristotle and St. Thomas consider a scientific, or philosophical, substance to be a substantial body, a quantified body, or a qualified body.

Inasmuch as philosophy, science, studies real being, or substance, as the proximate cause of *per se* accidents within an ordered multiplicity of beings, or a genus, Aristotle maintained that every science studies opposites and first principles because every science studies a multiplicity of differences of perfection and privation according to a principle of unity.

Every science considers opposition, negation, completeness, privation, possession, and necessity, precisely because it studies substances through a principle of unity. Opposition, negation, completeness, privation, possession, and necessity, however, essentially relate to the idea of being one, unity, not to the idea of being many, multiplicity.

The one is undivided, does not possess, is deprived of, division, and is the opposite of division or plurality. Plurality, not number, is the first-conceived opposite of unity and the ground of all division and difference. Hence, Aquinas maintained, we derive the idea of unity from the idea "of order or lack of division."[32] The concept of unity entails, depends upon, negation and privation (species of opposition) for its intelligibility.

Aristotle held that our idea of "unity" includes an implied privation, "a negation in a subject," like blindness in a human being.[33] He added that we can reduce all our concepts of necessity to that which can be in only one way.[34] Hence, our notions of unity, privation, and opposition even precede our notion of necessity!

Aristotle appears to have contradicted himself by maintaining that our idea of unity includes an implied privation because he also had held that the one is the principle by which we know number.[35] His reply to such an objection was that sensation is the starting point, or first principle, of all of our knowledge, even our knowledge of notions like unity, cause, and principle.[36]

He maintained that our first perception is of a many, of composite things, that we first confusedly grasp as a one. Hence our first positive concept of unity and plurality, even of being, is a conflation in which we do not precisely distinguish unity and plurality. We confusedly identify them together as a coincidence of opposites. Perhaps this is why the ancient Greeks initially understood being as chaos and why the ancient physicists thought of all philosophy in terms of contrariety.

Whatever the case, Aristotle held that we derive all our concepts, definitions, and first cognitions of first principles by privative negations of the way we sensibly perceive them as composite beings. *He thought of unity as the most primary privation, consisting of negation in a subject.* Since Aristotle maintained that plurality stems from unity, and causes diversity, difference, and contrariety, he viewed diversity, difference, and contrarity to be effects of unity's pluralization, and claimed that we know first principles negatively in reference to the way we perceive their contraries.[37]

Hence, Aristotle said that "all things are contraries or composed of contraries, and unity and plurality are the starting points of all contraries."[38] Since contraries are extreme differences within a genus that relate as most complete and most deprived possession of a form, as Plato recognized in Book Seven of the *Republic*, contrariety, as such, is a kind of plurality (because difference is a pluralization of unity, and an opposition between possession and privation, which Aristotle calls the fundamental opposition). This means that contrariety consists in the greatest distance of difference, or inequality, between extremes of species within a genus.[39]

Aristotle thought that all otherness derives from dividing and, thereby, pluralizing, unequalizing, unity. And he claimed that unity, or what is undivided, is the principle of all sameness, equality, and similarity. Similarity, equality, and sameness are simply analogous extensions of the metaphysically-conceived notion of unity. Aristotle referred to them as unity's "proper accidents" or "parts." As such, he considered them to be the principles of all plurality. Since, in turn, Aristotle held that plurality grounds all difference, he maintained that similarity, equality, and sameness are the principles of all difference.

For Aristotle, in short, difference is pluralization of unity, and unity's opposite. The analogous extensions and properties of unity, however, are unities. To be similar, equal, or the same, therefore, is, analogously, to be one.[40]

Hence, to be dissimilar, unequal, or different is to be many, a pluralization of unity and the respective opposites of being similar, equal, and the same. Moreover, *predication of sameness, equality, and similarity is simply analogous predication of unity just as predication of difference, inequality, and dissimilarity is simply analogous predication of multiplicity or plurality.*

Since the one and the many are opposed, since, along with being and privated being, they are the principles of all opposition and contrariety, they (1) are the primary contraries into which we reduce all other contraries and (2) make all other contraries intelligible as their first principles.[41]

This being so, if Aristotle is correct, as Charles Bonaventure Crowley rightly recognized, the principles of similarity, equality, and sameness and their opposites and contraries (dissimilarity, inequality, and difference) are the first principles of all per se *accidents and of the relative first principles of all philosophy and science for all time.* This must be the case because they constitute the most fundamental oppositions between unity and plurality. The opposition between unity and plurality is the first principle of all other oppositions and is the principle into which all others are reduced and made intelligible. Since science, or philosophy, studies the principles of opposition within a genus, it must chiefly study the opposition between, or problem of, the one and the many related to the principle kinds of *per se* subjects.[42]

2. What the knowing being contributes to forming the subject, formal object, of a science

According to Armand A. Maurer, Boethius' threefold division of the speculative sciences into physics, mathematics, and metaphysics (which Boethius passed on to the later middle ages) is based upon the hierarchy of forms that exist in reality in differing degrees of separation from matter. "Thus natural science studies forms as bodies along with the bodies themselves in which they exist. Mathematics studies, apart from matter, forms of bodies that must exist in matter (*e.g.* lines, circles, numbers). Theology studies forms that are entirely separate from matter (*e.g.* God)." [43]

As Maurer rightly notes, in such a view, "little need exists to investigate the subjective acts by which the different objects of the sciences are rightly grasped. The intellect follows more or less passively division of forms it finds ready-made in the world."[44] Such an understanding of philosophy, turns science into largely a spectator activity, an act of viewing, or, as Maritain called it, "eidetic visualization."[45]

Maurer rightly praises St. Thomas for showing the dynamic and

essential role played by the operations of the intellect in the determination of the subjects of the sciences. The sciences are no longer considered as differentiated according to distinctions the mind itself makes in the course of its investigation of reality. It is no longer a form in the Boethian sense, even though he sometimes uses the language of Boethius. Each science is said to have its own subject (*subjectum*), which differentiates that science from every other. By the subject of science St. Thomas does not mean the things considered by science or its subject-matter. The term (that is, 'subject' or 'subject-matter') also designates the formal perspective (*ratio*) under which these things are considered in the science.[46]

A chief reason St. Thomas places such an emphasis upon the dynamic aspect of the intellect in the nature of science is because *the human intellect is an active as well as passive power.* Another reason is because, following Aristotle, *St. Thomas maintains that complete scientific understanding involves grasping activities in light of Aristotle's famous four causes: material, final, efficient and formal.*

Two of these causes (efficient and formal), however, are extrinsic to the human intellect and relate to it as to a determinate passive (receiving) power just as a colored physical substance activates the faculty of sight as a determinate passive power. The other two causes (material and final) exist within the human intellect and relate to it as to a determinate active power that generates the act of knowing in response to the intellect's activation as a determinate passive power just as the faculty of sight generates the act of seeing upon activation by its formal object: *suitably-intense* color.

In referring to the intellectual faculty and faculty of sight as "determinate" powers, I mean they contain within themselves intensive quantum limits (qualitative limits) of receiving and generating action. For example, not all color is sight's formal object. Sight's formal object is color properly relatable to the seeing faculty: suitable, or fitting, color—not too much or too little color to activate or destroy the seeing power.

St. Thomas tells us that, in the case of the speculative sciences of physics, mathematics, and metaphysics, we derive the formal object of such sciences "according to differences between objects of *speculation*," which we derive partly "from the side of the power of the intellect" and partly "from the side of the habit of science that perfects the intellect."

Because all three sciences are intellectual considerations made by active powers, with solely and chiefly speculative aims, they must involve the human intellect in their operation of simply wondering about occurrences flowing from a proximate subject in the hope of simply knowing the *per se* principles of these occurrences. Hence, we derive the formal object of speculative science *partly from the side of the power of the intellect* because this formal

object essentially and chiefly activates our intellects as active powers through the first and highest aim of a person to think speculatively, not practically, about a subject of consideration. Our scientific
habits are *speculative* precisely because they conform to the ontological exigencies of the human intellect as an active, judging, power
chiefly aiming at thinking speculatively, not practically.

According to St. Thomas, *our intellects are immaterial faculties*. Because knowing is the union of two beings in a living act in
which neither the knowing being nor the thing known can change
while becoming or being united, *from the side of the intellect immateriality is an essential condition for any kind of knowing*, and especially scientific knowing.

In any kind of material reception of one being into another,
human experience shows that the receiver and what is received become somewhat changed. As the popular medieval metaphysical
maxim says, "Whatever is received into a receiver is received according to the capacity of the receiver."

Knowing is a living act, a way in which human beings exercise living while simultaneously uniting with another being. In the
act of knowing, a union occurs between a living subject, a knower,
and something known, an intelligible content. Some being is received into the knower that is other than the knower. In being
known, neither the knower nor the thing known can change in any
way because, strictly speaking, knowing involves exact identity.
And this is especially true in the case of scientific knowing.

Since our intellects are immaterial faculties, *immaterial*, or
dematerialized, being, being removed from the identity conditions of
matter and motion, essentially activates them, moves them from being passive to active powers. St. Thomas tells us that one of the necessary identity conditions of the formal object of speculative science
is that it be a proximate subject *immaterially, or abstractly*, considered. The formal object of speculative science must, in some way, be
a dematerialized object considered in a dematerialized way. Hence,
while what makes our thinking *speculative* is that we think about an

abstractly-considered proximate subject for a solely intellectual aim: to understand its nature, in part and from the side of the intellect, what makes our thinking *scientific* is that *a dematerialized being* activates our knowing habit.

Moreover, because all three speculative *sciences* are habits, or qualities, of judging inhering in our intellectual faculty that *express necessary relations*, St. Thomas tells us that all principles that give them specifically *scientific ways of existing*, that is, *necessary ways of existing* must activate them. Just as aiming at thinking chiefly for speculative aims is the formal difference that makes speculative science *speculative*, because immateriality *and necessity* comprise the distinguishing difference of *thinking* scientifically and *that about which we think* scientifically (something whose existence expresses necessary relation), *immateriality and necessity* comprise the distinguishing difference, the formal object, that makes speculative, or any other, scientific habit *science*.

Science is a habit of thinking about what must be. Hence, what makes our speculative way of thinking *scientific* is that we possess our immaterial, speculative habit of thinking, judging, *in relation to* an immaterial consideration of necessary, not contingent or incidental, *relations* of beings or activities to a proximate subject in which they essentially inhere.

We can think speculatively about what is not a subject of science (something contingent, what need not be or can be in more than *one* way, or what is incidental to a proximate subject); and we can think scientifically about what is not a subject of speculation (a subject of productive science).

What makes a subject of speculation a *scientific* subject is that, through its intrinsic accidents, properties, and the distinctive kinds of oppositions they produce as principles of action and signs of the form of their subject (*and necessary relations existing within a subject*) our habit of knowing reacts to, and judges with necessity about, some *necessary relation* in the speculatively-considered being that we know: that something in this being *is* a *one and unchangea-*

ble principle upon which something else proximately and necessarily relationally depends, *necessarily exists*, for its being and intelligibility.

Hence, St. Thomas tells us that we differentiate the speculative sciences according to the degree to which our different intellectual habits operate in separation from, or connection with, matter and motion.[47]

Furthermore, he adds that we use *different methods* of doing this in different sciences. He says that we take the methods of the sciences "from the powers of the soul" because these powers operate in different ways to dematerialize what, when dematerialized, becomes their formal objects. By "powers of the soul," St. Thomas means intellect, interior and exterior senses, and their respective habits. And we determine how our powers (intellectual habits) operate by *relating their immaterial mode of operation* to their respective, abstractly-considered subjects (formal objects). Hence, we take the methods of the sciences *from* the different formal objects, or identity conditions, that determine a proximate subject to be *one and unchanging*, in this way, not that way in relation to this or that habit.[48]

As a result, the ancient physicist's proximate subject is a qualified body because an intrinsic quality gives a surface (quantified) body another, non-dimensive, way of being in a unified and permanent way. This is the formal object, scientific subject, that activates the intellectual habit of natural philosophy, or physics. The mathematician's proximate subject is quantified material being, the surface body, because this inhering accident (quantity) extends a substantial body so as to possess a dimensional unity and permanence. This is the formal object that activates the intellectual habit of mathematics. And the metaphysician studies substantial being that need not exist in matter, that has the unity and permanence of a substance that might be capable of existing in a dimensively extended body through the accident of quantity, or might be completely immaterial. This is the formal object that activates the intellectual habit of metaphysics.

Scientifically, we proceed in this way because we derive scientific principles partly from the natural constitution of our faculties and their habits and partly from the way things exist according to facultatively-independent relations, ways of being one, as Crowley recognized. Scientifically, we think the way we can (*according to the way our powers are capable of operating in relation to different ways of dematerializing beings that are capable of becoming formal objects*), not the way we wish. The being of things and the way this *essentially relates* to the natural capabilities of our natural faculties and habits, not our dreams, determines the methods by which we can think about objects at all or scientifically. The being of things and the natural constitution of our knowing powers, not our dreams, provide the unity and necessity that *relationally* ground all knowledge and science.

According to St. Thomas, on the part of the knower, we use the external senses and human imagination as starting points, first principles, for scientific knowing. To know scientifically, directly, or indirectly (through effects, negations, relations, and signs), with the help of the external senses and imagination, we must penetrate a thing's nature by means (such as sense images and concepts) adequate to reveal the principles of its essence. The reason for this is that a thing's essence, what a real definition expresses, contains the real principles (the evidence) by means by which we judge truth within a science, a science's truth conditions or measures. For this reason, even today "scientific" textbooks like biology and chemistry tend to start with definitions of terms.

We judge about things scientifically chiefly according to what a thing's essence, its real definition, is capable of revealing to us about that thing, not according to what the senses reveal or can reveal. Strictly speaking, no such thing as "empirical science" exists.

The reason for this is that, in and of themselves, the human senses are incapable of recognizing truth and falsity, which are the measures of all knowledge, including science. Science is chiefly an act of the intellect, reason, not of the senses. Until intellectually de-materialized, a nature, essence, can reveal nothing to an intellectual faculty or habit. Hence, science chiefly resides in making intellectual judgments about the nature of something through principles (evidence) indirectly abstracted by the intellect from the nature in question as this nature is directly presented to the human intellect through an adequate image, or adequate images, existing in the human imagination.

In defining a nature or essence, we are engaged in an act of abstract consideration of that essence or nature. Scientific definition involves, is an act of, abstract consideration of a nature in which we *judge*, distinguish parts of, a thing's essence. Hence, St. Thomas says that we define things according to the way we abstract (dematerialize) an essence (evidence) from individual material conditions, or better, from the human imagination, from the way we imagine a thing to be.

The reason for this is that, strictly speaking, intellectual apprehension, abstraction, dematerialization, starts from what the human imagination is able to reveal about a thing's essence: evidence. For this reason, a dull imagination is a hindrance to scientific reasoning, and a sharp one is a great aid.

Moreover, while we scientifically judge with our intellects, we always do so with the help of other faculties, chiefly with that of the imagination. While all human science remotely starts with the external senses, with sense wonder, intellectual knowledge always proximately involves the human imagination from start to finish. No matter what the kind of knowledge involved, nor what its formal object, human intellectual activity always proximately involves use of images to reveal evidence (principles contained in essences or real definitions), which, following Aristotle, St. Thomas says "are related to our intellect as colors to sight."[49]

The human imagination, then, is the proximate principle of all intellectual knowledge, including that of metaphysics. All intellectual knowledge proximately starts in the imagination and remotely in the external senses. But not all intellectual knowledge concludes, terminates, in the imagination or external senses.

According to St. Thomas, some intellectual knowledge (for example, physics) terminates judgments, concludes its reasoning, in the external senses. Other human knowledge (for example, mathematics) terminates its judgments, concludes its reasoning, in the imagination. And still other intellectual knowledge (for example, metaphysics) terminates its judgments, concludes its reasoning, in the intellect.

St. Thomas thinks that the reason for this is that intellectual judgment terminates its reasoning in that faculty capable of finally revealing to (dematerializing for) a person, through an adequate image, the definition that expresses the essence, or nature, that contains the principles through which the intellect judges. *The principles contained in essences, natures, that definitions express are the truth conditions, measures (indivisibile intelligibles, ones, limits), by means of which, with which, the intellect judges.* They comprise intellectual *evidence*, revealed through the images in which and through which the intellect sees the principles contained in essences. Such being the case, the intellect concludes its judgments, ends its reasoning, in the faculty finally capable of adequately producing, the images that adequately express the definitions, natures (evidence), by which, and with which, the intellect judges truth or falsity in relation to its subject.

According to St. Thomas, because qualities are subjectified in surface bodies and sensible qualities are the proper objects of external sense faculties, external sense faculties are capable of producing images that adequately express the essence (and principles contained therein) of qualified bodies, the subject of the science of physics. For this reason, in dematerializing the imaginable content that activates the human intellect as its formal object, St. Thomas says the physical scientist engages in a kind of conceptual and simple apprehension common to all three speculative sciences, abstraction of an essence, a necessary intelligible content, from accidental particulars, details, or "parts" upon which its intelligibility does not depend, but theirs do. He labels this kind of abstract, concept-generating, intellectual operation "*abstractio totius*" abstraction of a whole.

Being subjectified in surface bodies means that qualities are subjectified in, exist in, quantified bodies. Such being the case, we cannot understand the nature of sensible qualities without referring our understanding of them to a dimensive, or quantified, body. For example, figure is the quality of a surface body. Hence, we cannot think about a figure without thinking about a surface body. This is a necessary relation about which we must think to think scientifically about qualitative being and opposing actions that proceed from it. The order of intelligiblilty demands this. But the reverse is not true. A surface body can exist without this or that particular quality. Hence, we can think about a surface without thinking about its color.

Since dimensive, or quantified, body, or simply quantity, is not the proper object of the external sense faculties, the external sense faculties are incapable of producing an image of a quantified body capable of revealing to the human intellect the nature or essence in which the intellect can find its evidence, first principles, by means of which to make judgments of truth or falsity about mathematical being. To acquire such an image, the human imagination must be able to abstract, dematerialize, quantitative aspects of physical things (like length and size) that do not reveal themselves to, escape the notice of, the external senses. In doing this, the mathematician achieves the definition of an essence through a concept that abstracts from, does not include, sensible matter.

Because quantity is an accident of a material substance, the object of mathematical consideration must contain in its concept and definition reference to matter as part of its intelligibility. The "matter" in question cannot be the concrete, sensible, or "qualitative," matter that physicists consider, because mathematicians abstract from (do not essentially consider) this in their concepts, definitions, and judgments). Instead, this is a kind of quantified matter (subject) that gives a substantial body surface dimensions, surface unity and permanence, and is apprehensible by the human imagination. Properly speaking, analogous to the matter of the physicist, we might call this underlying principle "imaginable" matter. However, because, to some extent, all material being is imaginable, such a term is even less helpful than the term apparently used by several thinkers during the high middle ages: "intelligible matter."

Hence, while the mathematician need not think about or imagine sensible matter in forming mathematical concepts and definitions, he may not do so from intelligible matter because, properly speaking, the concept of quantity is only intelligible as a dimensive, or extended, body, an accident inhering in a substantial body. This notion of matter must enter into the concept and definition of mathematical quantity.[50]

St. Thomas calls the mental operation of conceptualization through which the intellect of the mathematician dematerializes this image of quantified being "*abstractio formae*," apparently because it involves considering one form (quantity) without considering another form (quality).

Because the intellectual abstraction (intellectual dematerialization) of the mathematician is more removed from immediate relation to the external senses, it is more highly intellectual, requires more intellectual effort to attain than the intellectual abstraction used by the physicist. To achieve it, the mathematician must possess the abstraction skill dematerializing power (*abstractio totius*) of the natural philosopher, physicist, and an intellectual dematerializing ability of a higher intensive quantity. Hence, properly speaking, the mathematician is more scientific than is the physicist, more deserving of the name "scientist."

The third, and final, form of intellectual operation involved in speculative science is that of the metaphysician. In his *Commentary on the* de Trinitate *of Boethius*, St. Thomas calls this kind of mental activity "*separatio*" ("separation"), but Maurer claims St.

Thomas drops the use of this term later in his *Summa theologiae*, where St. Thomas "speaks of two modes of abstraction, one through judgment, the other through apprehension. The term 'separation' does not appear."[51]

Because even in his *Commentary on the* de Trinitate, Thomas "uses the verb 'to abstract' to designate the act of 'separating,'" Maurer finds nothing surprising about abandoning the use of the term "separation" later on.[52] Because of the difficulty of the problem under consideration (how scientists, philosophers, come intellectually to grasp their subjects), Maurer claims St. Thomas went through three redactions of Reply to Question Five, Article Three of this *Commentary*, each time realizing more completely the existential character of judgment and the role judgment plays in all divisions of science, especially the role of judgment in metaphysics. As Maurer says,

> In judgment . . . the intellect does not simply know *what* things are. Rather, it grasps them in their very existence. For when we affirm that the grass *is* green, we understand how grass exists, namely as green; and when we judge a man is not a stone, we understand how he does not exist, namely as a stone. That is why St. Thomas says that the first operation of the mind (that is, abstraction through simple apprehension) is directed to the essence of a thing, whereas judgment is directed to it existence.[53]

A crucial point to note about what Maurer says above is that, strictly speaking, Maurer should not have said that the "intellect" grasps what things are in their existence. He should have said, as he well understood, that the person, not the intellect, grasps existence because, according to St. Thomas, the person, not the intellect knows; and neither the senses nor intellect grasp the existence or essence of anything without the assistance of the other faculty. Gilson adds that, for St. Thomas, the existing man, the individual person, not the intellect or senses, grasps the existence (*esse*) of anything; and we sense with our intellects and intellectualize with our senses.[54]

Throughout our total knowing process, the individual person, not some faculty, knows. Hence, whenever in this book I say that this or that faculty does something, I should always be understood to mean that the person, through use of said faculty, does the act in question. Moreover, we never know anything without the use of sense images—not even metaphysical objects, about which we have to form an image negatively, through negative judgment from a physical image to be able to think about them. For this reason, St. Thomas maintains that negative judgments are the distinctive mark of metaphysical intellectual operations.

By saying this, St. Thomas does not mean that *only metaphysicians* grasp the existence of things, or that existence is an activity that human beings can only apprehend through negative judgment. As Maurer rightly notes, "only in negative judgment do we grasp the separation of one thing from another."[55] And when we say something like "Fido exists," in a positive judgment we unite, do not separate, existence from a subject. Because, in his *Commentary on the* de Trinitate *of Boethius*, St. Thomas says that "separation" (which he there calls a "negative judgment") is the unique form of judgmental abstraction used by metaphysicians, some students of St. Thomas mistakenly interpret him to be saying that only metaphysicians grasp existence and that human beings can apprehend existence only through an act of negative judgment.

The claim that we can only apprehend existence through negative judgment is evidently false because we human beings, including physicists and mathematicians, frequently make positive judgments expressing existence. Existential judgments are not the proprietary possession of metaphysicians. All scientists, philosophers, engage in making existential judgments, as distinct from the existentially-neutral judgments of logicians that simply join a subject term and predicate term together through use of a copula "is."

Were this not the case, judgments of truth and falsity would be irrelevant to every science other than metaphysics. Only the metaphysician could talk about reality, or we could only do so through use of metaphysical principles, something that is obviously false. Even if the formal mode of apprehensive abstraction that the mathematician uses causes the mathematician to talk about mathematical entities as if they have no contact with reality, if a mathematician says that a six-foot long piece of wood is actually five-feet long, that claim is a mathematical and existential one about the length of the wood.

Both mathematics and classical physics start their reasoning by making judgments about really existing beings; but St. Thomas thinks that classical physics, natural philosophy's mode of investigating truth, follows more closely the natural procedure of the human mind to reason from effects to causes. It must take into account the existence of motion and sensible qualities, while mathematical reasoning abstracts from (does not consider) these modes of existing and deduces its conclusions chiefly through use of formal causes, not through final and efficient causes, through the way the imagination helps mathematicians grasp quantitative modes of existing that transcend the notice of the external senses. Hence mathematical science does not abstract from modes of existing in a surface body or from existential judgments. It abstracts only from those, like motion, not essential to dimensive existence in a substantial body.[56]

Continuing, St. Thomas says, "the philosopher of nature and the metaphysician treat of essences as existing in reality; and therefore they say there are different genera wherever they find diverse modes of potency and act, and consequently diverse modes of being."[57]

Driving home the point about the existential nature of scientific judgments of the metaphysician and physicist as distinct from the existentially-neutral premises of the logician, Maurer explains:

From the point of view of the logician, material and immaterial things can be brought under the same logical genus (for example, substance), because he considers them only as concepts in the mind. From the point of view of the natural philosopher or metaphysician, however, they do not come under the same genus because these philosophers consider the natures of things as they actually exist in reality, and in actual existence the substance of material things is not the same as that of immaterial things. Hence from a logical point of view, the genus of substance is predicated univocally of all substances; but from the point of view of the natural philosopher and the metaphysician, it is predicated analogically.[58]

Considering what St. Thomas and Maurer say about the nature of existential judgments and abstraction, chief among the reasons negative existential judgments are a distinguishing difference of metaphysical intellectual activity is that the subject metaphysics studies is a nature or essence that, even if it happens to exist in matter, does not depend upon matter for its existence.[59] Metaphysics studies being *qua* being, being in general. By this, Thomas says he means the genus metaphysics studies consists of species of beings that include some that, even if they do, at times, exist in matter, can exist without it.[60]

According to St. Thomas, every science investigates a genus, a multitude of species, with respect to a chief aim. He states that we divide science considered as a whole on the basis of the chief end, or aim, of science considered as a whole, human happiness, because, by perfecting our intellectual operations, the whole of art and science chiefly exists to enable us to become happy. Because human happiness is twofold (theoretical and practical), philosophy has two main, or generic, divisions: theoretical and practical.[61]

Each of the special arts and science, in turn, has a special end, or aim, related to its respective nature as a habit (arts and sciences being habits, virtues) of perfecting the person through perfection of intellectual operations.[62] Hence, *relation of a habit to a different multitude, order, genus, of being through which intellectual operation is perfected accounts for the division of the sciences.*[63]

What St. Thomas says means that, to some extent, promoting human happiness enters into the nature, definition, of any authentically-conceived "science." This is so true that philosophy's, science's, historical development was not possible prior to the existence of a moral culture that could generate its existence. *Moral and political culture are the basis of the existence of all leisure. Leisure is the basis of the existence of the liberal, or "speculative," arts. And existence of the liberal arts is a necessary condition for the fully-developed exercise of philosophy, science.*[64]

Generically and specifically considered, philosophy, science, is chiefly speculative science. Secondarily, analogously, it is practical, or productive. Absent the time to devote to politically-unfettered research, study of any branch, division, of philosophy, science, becomes impossible. Hence, regarding philosophy's, science's, historical development, Aristotle reports that, after all the arts needed to provide for the necessities of human life had been discovered, the liberal arts originated in Egypt with the discovery of the liberal art of mathematics.

What made this discovery possible was that *a priestly class* economically supported by the community had come into existence. As St. Thomas says, "the mathematical arts, which are speculative in the highest degree, first discovered in Egypt by the priests, who were given the time for study, and whose expenses were defrayed by the community, as we read in *Genesis* (47:22)."[65]

Only after the origin of the liberal arts, with the start of the development of democratic modes of communicating and the existence of a leisure class somewhat supported *by the community*, could the practice of philosophy have come into existence. Democratic, republican, or, at a minimum, a relatively-just form of community that, at least by not overtly attacking it, facilitates support of the existence of a leisured class, is a necessary condition for the practice of philosophy, science.

Hence, any purported "philosopher," "scientist," that does not practice his activity in such a way as to promote the moral and political culture that enables philosophy, science, to exist and be freely exercised, engages in a behavioral contradiction, is, strictly speaking, no philosopher, no scientist. Since divorcing philosophy, science, from wisdom, virtue, the human soul, human happiness promotes a moral and political culture that undermines the necessary conditions to promote the existence and politically-unfettered exercise of philosophy, science, strictly speaking, those who do this cannot be scientists, philosophers. Properly speaking, as Plato well described them such people are scientific, philosophical, "bastards."

Furthermore, if a limit to human choice (a finite number of desirable beings from which to choose), a natural end of human desire (a highest human good), is a necessary condition for having a finite number of principles of choice in the present, denying the existence of such a highest good (what most people call "God") makes the practice of philosophy, science, impossible. Little wonder, then, that, like philosophy and science, the liberal arts started with a *priestly class*, a group of religious people.

Some modern "scientists" and "philosophers" falsely-so-called tend to glory in the claim that no natural aims or ends exist in reality. Such a claim is the statement of a fool or ignoramus. If what they say is true, modern science can contribute nothing to wisdom and moral culture, helping human beings improve our lives, become wiser, happy. So conceived, modern science is worthless. If so, why would anyone seek to possess it?

While we can use some sense faculties to know some things without relating them to another order, genus, of beings, St. Thomas maintains, "it belongs to the reason alone to know the order of one thing to another."[66] Since, as he says at the start of his famous *Summa contra gentiles*, the job of the wise man to order things and govern them well, to some extent the essential job of any science, directly or indirectly, is to contribute to making human beings wiser.[67] Citing Aristotle's *Metaphysics*, St. Thomas says elsewhere, "the order of the parts of an army among themselves depends on the order of the whole army to the leader."[68]

While the claims I cite in the above paragraph surely are true, I do not think these are assertions to which most contemporary "scientists" (mathematicians or mathematical physicists) would subscribe. Given their inclination to be "value neutral" regarding all claims that they cannot numerically measure, while I could be wrong, I think most would not want to take a stand on such issues. Beyond this, I have never found any of them not trained in classical thought who could give me anything close to a well-reasoned explanation of precisely what is the nature of modern science, where, strictly speaking, science exists, where it gets its principles from, or precisely why these principles work.

In saying this, I do not deny—I celebrate—the many marvels of modern mathematics, mathematical physics, and modern technology as real human goods that have immeasurably improved my life; and I am convinced that many of the practitioners of these studies engage in their work with the best of intentions (while simultaneously not realizing the behavioral contradiction they practice when claiming that science has no real end or good that, by nature, it pursues).

My point is not that contemporary mathematics, mathematical physics, and the technology they have helped generate produce no amazing effects in areas like medicine, transportation, entertainment, and so on. They do. Nor is it to deny that many of the practitioners of modern "science" falsely-so-called are not well intentioned. They are. My point is that we human beings think the way we can, not the way we wish. Because, according to most of their leading practitioners, this world we inhabit contains no real natures, no intrinsic principles of unity or good (even within individual scientists), as an act of a human intellectual habit existing in this world, mathematical physics does not exist, can have no chief aim, and has no identifiable practitioner or practitioners. Such being the case, what is this strange entity, precisely where does it exist, and precisely what is its proximate cause?

According to their principles, not mine, *amazingly*, the leading practitioners of these disciplines cannot, with rational consistency, celebrate as "scientific goods" the wonders I say they produce. Nor can they rationally explain precisely what they do that makes their activity scientific, precisely where science exists, and precisely what generates it. Because they deny the existence of individual natures and habits, with rational consistency, they cannot even say *they* produce anything, much less anything scientific or good.

Having no chief aim, by nature, these disciplines cannot be theoretical, practical, or productive sciences. If they contribute anything to human happiness, they must do so incidentally, not as part of their nature. At best, contemporary mathematics and mathematical physicists appear (incoherently) to adopt the view of Sir Francis Bacon (b. 1561; d. 1626) that the essence of modern and contemporary science is the ability to force the universe around us to reveal its secrets.[69]

Just what makes such an act of violence, cosmic despotism, an essence, or one of "science," appears to me to be rationally inexplicable. Since, from the modern "scientific" perspective, no real essences or aims exist in the physical universe, even within scientists, this Baconian claim that such an activity is practical or productive and comprises the nature of modern or contemporary "science" is rationally absurd.

Practical and productive knowledge presuppose practical, and productive aims existing in individual habits of individual intellects that exist in individual souls existing within the physical universe. No practical and productive aims existing in such intellectual habits, within such souls, no practical or productive science. If no real goods exist at which science naturally aims, what poses as "science" might be able to make the state of existing things different.

For the simple reason that it has no nature, by its nature, it could never essentially improve them or make them worse. At best, science so-conceived appears to be a blind act of emotion performed by no one.

Being totally aimless by nature (better, lack of nature), modern mathematics and mathematical physics have no way rationally of differentiating among theoretical, practical, and productive pursuits. They have no way of explaining how science is an act of this individual. In fact, the practitioners of these disciplines generally do not appear to claim that science is an individual act. They appear to claim that science is a team effort, a social project, in which no team member individually possesses science, but, somehow, some collective does.

To me this situation resembles that of a marvelous chef who, at times, can create culinary masterpieces and, at times, can only destroy meals. All the while this poor soul cooks, he has no idea of what he is doing or why; nor can he tell anyone else.

In contrast to the widespread contemporary view of the aimless nature of facultatively-independent beings, St. Thomas maintains that a twofold order exists in things: (1) of parts to some whole (of some multitude to each other); and (2) the order of things to an end. The second is more primary. As St. Thomas says, "the order of the parts of an army among themselves depends on the order of the whole army to a leader."[70] In the human person the intellect, reason, is related to the other faculties that the intellect can direct like a leader is related to all the parts of an army. Its end holds together the order of the parts to each other and to the end of the whole. In so doing, it transforms the parts and the aim from being an unrelated multitude into being parts of a whole.

Thomas claims, that, through its habits of art and science, in four ways human reason is involved in ordering its interior and exterior acts, bringing them into relation as parts of the whole act of human science—in relation to: (1) natural things, beings that reason studies and does not make (natural philosophy, physics); (2) psychological entities that, by its thinking, reason generates within itself (logic, "which is concerned with the order of the parts of discourse to each other and the order of principles among themselves to conclusions"); for example, when reason generates order among its concepts and words (signs, meaningful sounds, of concepts); (3) the order of operations it generates in the human will; and (4) "that which by its thinking it makes in the exterior things that it produces, as in the case of a box or a house."[71]

By ordering all the habits of the human knowing faculties through art and science, as it extends our knowledge of all the orders of being, the human intellect brings the operations of these faculties, and of itself, to perfection in relation to the chief aim of human life: human happiness.

In saying that arts and sciences help bring the human faculties to perfection, St. Thomas means that these activities help bring these activities to mature development, completeness. Hence, objecting to what he says by saying that only God is perfect or that perfection cannot exist in this world is specious.

We commonly call things around us "imperfect," "incomplete." We can do so only because we realize that they have within them a determinate possibility for completeness, maturity. Hence, while nothing in this world is absolutely perfect the way God is perfect, each thing that exists possesses some level of perfection according to the virtual quantum intensity of its nature.

Also, in saying that art and science help perfect human faculties and activities, St. Thomas is not claiming that artistic and scientific activity never involve making mistakes. Even the best professional baseball player has a hitting percentage of under "500" out of a possible "1000." And even the best swimmer sometimes drowns. While art and science facilitate our ability to excel ordinary human achievement to judge and choose rightly, they do not guarantee doing so. While they cannot fail in their nature, they can fail to become exercised or completely so.

Through natural science, physics, the human intellect improves our ability to know about all physically existing natures. In so doing, it helps perfect our external sense faculties, increase our knowledge of physical beings and the way they act, and assist human reason in the pursuit of human happiness by helping a human being to understand how properly to relate to all physical being.

Through mathematics, among other things, the human intellect helps perfect the human imagination to become a tool for higher forms of abstract reasoning so that, through such perfection, as Plato recognized, human beings become more completely aware of the existence of immaterial realities and of the fact that human happiness involves knowing the natures of such beings. Beyond this, the human intellect becomes able to know about the existence of natures whose operations escape the notice of the human senses unaided by mathematically-regulated technologies.

And, through metaphysics, human reason most completely liberates human reason from the slavery of ignorance, extending human awareness to a knowledge of immaterial beings and immaterial ways of knowing that are most highly intellectual and least like that of a slave.

In perfecting the operations of the will, the human intellect perfects all the practical and productive arts and the faculties through which these become exercised, thereby perfecting the human person in his or her many ways of knowing and the relationship among all the human faculties to each other, to reason, and to a person as a whole.

While each individual science is a generic habit that, in a way, gives unity to all the species of scientific acts within that genus, generically considered, science is an architectonically-arranged, essentially-related, order of habits that gets its generic unity from the chief aim of science: perfection of the human person, human happiness. Each species contains within itself the essential elements of its genus, which are maximized in the species that is the maximum in a genus, which is the measure of all the other species within a genus.

For example, the genus "athletics" is a whole that contains within it all the species of athletics related to it as parts of a whole, maximized in one genus (for example, gymnastics) that contains, in a most perfect way, the athletic ability aimed at in each species of athletics. Similarly, for example, the genus "firefighter" is a whole that contains within it, as parts related to a whole, all the species of firefighters with more or less perfect abilities to fight fires. Again, the genus courageous human being contains within it all the species of courageous human beings with more or less perfect abilities to attack dangers.

Whatever kind of species we talk about, each species contains within it its genus. Genus plus formal difference produce species. And the real species expresses a thing's specific nature, its real definition. Such being the case, no species belonging to any genus can exist apart from, can properly express its definition and nature, without having an essential relation to the chief aim of its genus. And no genus of human activity can exist without having some essential relationship to human happiness.

For example, strictly speaking, no species of athletics can fulfill its proper definition if it refuses to aim at perfecting the harmonious operation of bodily movements. No species of firefighting can fulfill its proper definition if it contributes nothing to putting out fires. And no species of courageous human being can fulfill the specific nature, definition, of being courageous without possessing the specific inclination to attack danger.

Strictly speaking, no genus considered as a genus can exist in a condition in which its specific members behave as if they are essentially unrelated to (1) each other; (2) the genus; (3) cooperatively to fulfilling the chief aim of its genus; (4) producing a human good that, in some way, improves some human capacity to arrive at human happiness. Consequently, any firefighter who thought he had no essential relationship to other firefighters, no professional responsibility to try to put out fires, and did no human good that helped human beings live happier lives, would be mistaken about his nature. If he thought that he constituted the whole of the firefighting art, most people would consider him delusional. Any shipbuilder who thought that his art comprised the whole of human knowledge, that his art, in and of itself, knew everything knowable about sailing, or was totally worthless, would not understand his art. He would not know the origin of some of his essential principles. Making the appropriate changes, the same would be true of any courageous person or athlete. Such people would be delusional.

Why, then, do we not consider equally delusional any "specific" science, like contemporary mathematical physics, that considers itself to constitute the whole of science and truth, or that thinks it has no essential relationship to producing a human good, wisdom, or contributing to human happiness? Virtually no "scientist" today can tell other people precisely what are scientific principles; what makes them scientific; what is the point of origin of a "scientific principle"; what is the essential nature of the scientific good; and precisely what science essentially contributes to fostering human happiness Yet, a real scientist should be able to explain all these things. Being able to relate one kind of knowing to another is a normal act of human reason. Hence, anyone claiming to be a "scientist" should possess it.

Because all science involves rightly relating, ordering, parts to a whole, every specific science has to have the ability to know the parts that comprise it and how these relate to each other and to this specific science as a whole. Beyond this, every specific science has to know how, as a part of an architectonic order of sciences, its activity relates to that of other sciences and to its genus and the generic aim of science.

While each specific science, philosophical discipline, contains parts that it must understand so as completely to comprehend the nature of its subject, each whole, specific science, philosophical discipline, is part of science, philosophy, as a generic whole comprised of an architectonically-arranged order of habits. Hence, to fulfill its nature completely as a science, each and every science, division of philosophy, must understand precisely how it relates to those sciences higher and lower than it.[72]

Human "science" does not exist in an intellectual vacuum. Strictly speaking, "science" refers to both a generic and specific habit existing within the individual habit of an individual scientist. To be scientific, an individual person has to know precisely how his specific science relates to other kinds of knowledge, other sciences. The claims of modern positivism are ludicrous, if for no other reason than, because they claim the truths of the sciences of mathematics and physics do not depend upon truths of ordinary grammar, language usage. Indeed, at times, people who take pride in calling themselves "scientists" maintain that science achieves no truth or good.

Ridiculous. Strictly speaking and generically considered, science is a generic habit that generates specific and individual habits of science. As a generic habit, in light of its chief aim, science is contained within, and gives unity to, all the species of science that flow from it as their common principle or common matter. And as a specific habit, in light of its chief aim, science is contained within, and gives unity to, all the individual acts of science that flow from it as a common principle or common matter. Since the only way to unify a multitude is to order it, the generic habit of science architectonically orders, essentially relates, comprises as parts of a whole, the specific and individual habits of science (like metaphysics, mathematics, and physics) in terms of an order of more or less perfect possession or privation of the generic principle of science and its chief aim.

Since every genus is divided by opposites of possession and privation of a generic principle, the highest member of the genus, the most perfect species, maximally participates in the nature of the genus. In so doing, it maximally contributes to fulfilling the chief aim of the genus and becomes the measure in light of which we know all the less perfect members of the genus.

For this reason, we use the best athlete or general to know and measure the less good and worst, and the most courageous of human beings to know and measure the leas courageous and most cowardly. Hence, in science, we use the most perfect species of science, metaphysics, as the means of knowing, judging all the inferior divisions of science, philosophy.

As St. Thomas says, if we study carefully what makes a person suited to rule, we can understand the nature of metaphysics and the kinds of objects it studies. "For just as men of strong intellect are by nature rulers and masters of others, while those robust in body and weak in mind are by nature subjects . . . so the science that is most intellectual should be naturally the ruler of the others: and this is the science that treats of the most intelligible beings."[73]

From the viewpoint of the causes it knows (the highest), the universality of the principles through which it knows these causes (the most remote from sensation, least particular, and most dependent upon pure intellection to grasp), and the immaterial mode of being of what it knows, metaphysical science is the most highly intellectual, most worthy, of the name "science," and most deserving to rule over other sciences as a leader over followers. For this reason, all the other sciences analogously have to borrow some of their first principles of scientific reasoning, as well as the name "science," from metaphysics; not vice versa.[74]

Little wonder then that in separating itself from "first philosophy," metaphysics (natural wisdom in its highest form), and the chief principles that generate natural wisdom (for example, God, human happiness, virtue, and the human soul), having turned the chief aim of science into that of becoming nothing, or, at best, vocational training, technological manipulation of physical beings, modern and contemporary "science" falsely-so-called have fostered within contemporary culture intellectual principles that naturally incline human beings to think and behave like fools and slaves, to be intellectually bewildered about the true nature of science, philosophy, or whether these have a nature; about why real science is most worth studying for human beings, or worth studying at all.

No surprise, then, that contemporary, utopian, socialist regimes have arisen to lead such intellectual herds to their promised land of destroying the world around us to force the physical universe to give up its secrets. Divorced from legitimate philosophical metaphysics to which it must be essentially connected to be science, as Plato well recognized, no science worthy of the name can exist. Hence, what masquerades as "science," "philosophy," today is often the foolishness of "philosophical and scientific bastards" serving the aims of despots to undermine individual perfection and happiness.

As the great modern physicist, Albert Einstein, has observed about contemporary "science," "the man of science has slipped so much that he accepts the slavery inflicted upon him by national states as his inevitable fate. He even degrades himself to such an extent that he helps obediently in the perfection of the means for the general destruction of mankind."[75] Such is the fate of any bastardized imitation of "science" that chooses to divorce itself from essential connection to philosophical metaphysics, human virtue, and happiness as a whole.

In opposition to this contemporary, enslaved and bastardized understanding of "science," St. Thomas claims that science investigates a genus by studying its principles because "science is perfected only through knowledge of principles."[76]

Thomas adds that two kinds of principles exist. Some are complete natures in themselves. Others are not.

In his *Commentary on the* de Trinitate, he refers to God as such a complete nature that metaphysics includes *as part of* its chief subject (being in general) because God is the principle of everything. In this sense of "principle," St. Thomas is thinking about a numerically-one substance.

Distinct from complete natures, other kinds of principles are incomplete substances in themselves, are principles of natures; as unity, he says, is the principle of number, point the principle of a line and form and matter principles of natural body."[77]

St. Thomas asserts we only know things inasmuch as they are in act. So, for instance, we can only know a principle like potency or matter by relating these to act or form. We can only know principles that are too weak to be complete natures in relation to acts of those complete natures of which they are principles, through existing signs and effects, and negations. Because some natures are too weak for us to grasp directly, we can only apprehend them through reference to acts of their substance through external signs, negations, and negative relations.

The same situation holds with respect to metaphysical beings, but for a different reason. In the case of immaterial forms, because they are too strong, too intensely actual for our intellects to apprehend, St. Thomas says we start knowing them like we start knowing anything else, by apprehending *that* they are; but "instead of knowing *what* they are we have knowledge of them by negation, by way of causality, and by way of transcendence."[78]

This situation presents what appears to be a contradiction. St. Thomas repeatedly claims that all our knowledge starts in the senses. He says that our intellectual apprehension originates in the imagination because "images are like objects to the intellectual soul." Further, he states:

> An image is the starting point of our knowledge, for it is that from which the operation of the intellect begins; not that it passes away, but it remains as the foundation of intellectual activity, just as principles of demonstration must remain throughout the whole process of science. This is because images are related to the intellect as objects in which it sees whatever it sees, either through a perfect representation or through a negation. Consequently, when our knowledge of images is impeded, we must be completely incapable of knowing anything with our intellect even about divine

things. Clearly, we cannot know that God causes bodies or transcends all bodies, or is not a body, if we do not form an image of bodies.[79]

Yet, according to St. Thomas, "we cannot know *that* a thing is without knowing in some way *what* it is, either perfectly or confusedly." The reason for this is that, "if a person knows that a man exists and wants to find out what a man is by definition, he must know the meaning of the term 'man.'" But this is possible only if the person can form a concept of a man even if he does not know the precise definition of a man. According to Thomas, we can do this "by knowing a proximate or remote genus and accidental characteristics which reveal him externally."[80]

In relation to God, then, and immaterial forms in general, in some way, we must know what they are in order to know that they are, that they exist.[81] Even in the case of material substances, Thomas claims we do not know their essential differences; "hence we have to signify them by the accidental differences which arise from the essential, as we designate a cause by its effect."[82]

At best, St. Thomas says, we apprehend the nature of immaterial forms that metaphysics studies obscurely by substituting negations for their genus and observable accidents. "The more negations we know of them the less vaguely we understand them, for subsequent negations limit and determine a previous negation as differences do a remote genus." He adds that this is the way knowledge of the heavenly bodies in his time was, for the most part, attained; but instead of apprehending them through accidental characteristics, they were known "with regard to the relationship of cause to effect or to the relationship of transcendence."[83]

Contemporary physics appears to operate in much the same way, absent the notion of transcendence. *In every science adequate image- and concept-formation often requires lengthy prior judgment and argumentation, often positive and negative debate.* Such debate can extend over wide periods of time, sometimes covering years, decades, and even centuries. Be this as it may, the crucial point to note about what St. Thomas maintains about metaphysical reasoning is that, even the metaphysician must start metaphysical reasoning through use of a knowledge of existing natures, using an image adequate to form a concept capable of suitably revealing the nature of the subject metaphysics studies: forms that do not, or need not, depend upon matter for their existence.

Since, on its own, the human imagination cannot provide an adequate image of such forms to the human intellect so as provide the intellect with a concept adequate to reveal the nature of the metaphysical subject, the human intellect must work with the imagination to provide its own image, by exercising negative judgment about the existential nature of the images the imagination presents to it. Since no physical image produced solely by the human imagination can adequately reveal the nature and mode of existence of an immaterial being, and since metaphysical reasoning relies on such an image throughout the whole metaphysical reasoning process, the human intellect must provide its own evidence of such a nature. It does so by negating the nature and mode of existence of the images that the human imagination presents to it.

This is a chief reason metaphysical reasoning must start with a negative existential judgment, and must continue to rely on it. The chief reason is not that we can only grasp existence through negative judgments or through metaphysics; or because the human intellect can, somehow, immediately grasp the existence of something with no dependence of its knowing upon sense images. Most, if not all, metaphysical reasoning must proceed through negation because metaphysicians necessarily must use negations (1) to form images, concepts, and definitions capable of adequately revealing to them the essences of immaterial beings and (2) adequately to judge their ways of existing.

3. What the being known contributes to forming the subject, formal object, of a science

While praising St. Thomas for moving science to a more dynamic plane by recognizing that the dematerialized way we know, not simply what we know, constitutes an essential element of the subject, formal object, of a science, Maurer calls our attention to a crucial element in understanding Aristotle's three-fold division of the speculative sciences, and, in so doing, Maurer notices something Crowley had missed.

At the same time, by calling our attention to the fact that the formal object, subject, of a science is not simply an existing form related to, activating, a human faculty, that this form does something within the being known to constitute it as proper object of being known scientifically, Crowley forcefully drives home that point that the formal object of a science must have precise qualities that enable it to relate to a knowing faculty as properly suitable for being known by a scientific habit. That is, *a formal object of a being known must, as an external sign, display the formal difference of intrinsic necessity as a mode of unity essentially flowing from its subject as from a first principle: a one and unchangeable principle upon which the being known proximately and necessarily depends for its being and scientific intelligibility.*

From the side of the thing known, a main reason, then, that Aristotle divided the speculative sciences into three classes is clear. He recognized the existence of three pairs of specifically distinct, kinds of unity, plurality, and opposition (similarity/dissimilarity, equality/inequality, and sameness/difference) *as the primary first principles of* per se *accidents, contrariety, opposition, and modes of necessary relation that exist within real substances that make these substances properly relatable and knowable to scientific habits as suitable subjects of study.*

Using these primary sets of opposition, or contrariety, as first principles, he reasoned, since we know scientifically through first principles, we are able scientifically to understand the different sorts of *necessary relations* that exist between *per se* subjects and their *per se* accidents, or properties. He thought of these *per se* subjects as proximate subjects constituted by distinctive kinds of common matter involving distinctive kinds of contrary opposites. Hence, the actions performed through their properties *reflect as signs, are signs of*, the same sort of opposition existing in their common matters.

Aristotle said we are able directly to sense two of these common matters. He claimed the third is "immovable and imperceptible."[84] Following much of what Plato said in Book Seven of the *Republic* about mathematics, music, and geometry, Aristotle limited the two classes of sensible substance to corruptible substances like animals and plants, and incorruptible substances, like movers of the celestial bodies, which ancient physics claimed to investigate.

Whether their matter is corruptible or not, scientifically or philosophically considered, as *per se* subjects of science or philosophy, as Maurer notes, according to St. Thomas, as scientists or philosophers, we study both classes of bodies *through distinctive modes of abstract consideration* of sensible effects they produce through their qualified matter (a surface body acting as the subject of qualities). The third class consists of objects (mathematical objects, abstractly considered quantified bodies), and separate substances (beings that can, do, or can be considered to exist apart from any and all matter).[85] Hence, Aquinas maintained, "as many parts of philosophy" exist "as there are parts of substance, of which being and unity are predicated and of which it is the principle intention or aim of this science to treat."[86]

A chief reason St. Thomas said this is because proper subjects of science, or philosophy, contain a specific principle of unity and permanence, determinacy (a nature), that necessarily generates the *per se* differences and principles of opposition and contrariety within the limits of a proximate-subject genus (related to a chief, common aim). *The different common matters* (proximate natures) *of the different sciences contain within their essence, or nature, different principles of contrariety and different first principles of scientific judging and reasoning.* And, through acts of intellectual abstraction, *these first principles of evidence* can essentially relate to, activate, our scientific habits of mind.

For this reason St. Thomas said, "geometry *speculates* about a triangle being a figure having 'two right angles,' i.e., having its three angles equal to two right angles; but it does not speculate about anything else, such as wood or something of the sort because these things pertain to a triangle accidentally." Geometry speculates about its subject genus in this limited way, through the quantitative principle of equality, and does not speculate about other sorts of likenesses or differences because, strictly speaking, as a speculative, scientific habit of intellect, these other objects do not relate to geometry's *per se* subject: "science studies those things which are beings in a real sense, . . . and each thing is a being insofar as it is one."[87]

The habit of geometry's proximate subject, its common matter, formal object, is not material substance or body. It is *quantified* material substance, *surface* body, a body with quantified, dimensively spatial, unity and permanence. Geometry speculates about a quantitative, not a political, medical, or any other, way of being one. The intrinsic, accidental property of quantity makes a substantial body a geometrical body by giving it surface unity and permanence.

Since *equality* is the principle of unity by which we grasp all the samenesses and differences that essentially relate to a body as a continuum body, such as having three angles quantitatively the same as two right angles, since, that is, equality (and, in a way, inequality, which depends upon equality for its intelligibility), considered *per se*, are quantitative principles of knowing a geometrical body in a geometrical way, the surface body that quantity unifies and makes somewhat permanent through the equality of its parts is the proper subject for the habit of geometrical study, or what we call, in a contracted way, "geometry."

For this reason, mathematical equations, the definitions mathematicians use that express the principles of the natures they study, are expressed in terms of equality. All the rules of geometry are principles that express true ways of theoretically understanding all the modes of opposition and principles of being one and many (equal and unequal) that can exist among figured bodies and practically constructing geometrical figures. *And, as Crowley understood, all the laws of the practical science of contemporary mathematical physics are directives to mathematical physicists about true ways of mathematically measuring different qualitative changes of different substances in terms of principles of unity (the equal).*[88]

Following Aristotle, recall that St. Thomas asserted that the proximate subject, or generic substance, about which the geometrician wonders is the surface body. This body is the immediate, chief, proximate, and principle subject of all plane figures, its intrinsic and necessary, or *per se*, accidents. Because these accidents intrinsically and necessarily flow from, and are intrinsically subjectified in, this geometrical body, these plane figures comprise a multitude of species (a many), *of hierarchically ordered opposites*, subjectified in, and caused by, a surface body, their generic body or substance. *They are its many necessary effects and signs.* The geometrician considers this subject analogously, that is, according to the same formal aspect and, also, according to unequal relationships, "just," as St. Thomas said, "it is clear that one science, medicine, considers all health-giving things."[89]

Hence, this multitude of species essentially flows from this generic body as from a principle (a one, because principles are starting points and points are unit measures, indivisibles, or ones). Since this concrete body (intellectually dematerialized and abstractly considered as the one generic body of all the members of its many species) proximately gives rise to these necessary and intrinsic accidents whose properties and behavior the philosopher, scientist, causally seeks to understand, this generic body is their *per se*, or proper, subject; and they are its *per se*, or proper, accidents. The philosopher, scientist, chiefly seeks to understand the first causes of these properties through reference to their proper and *per se*, not incidental, subject, body, or matter.[90]

The geometrical body (subject, matter, subject-matter, genus, or generic substance), not the sentient body, living body, or political body (all incidental bodies in reference to a geometrical body), is the body upon which the geometrician as geometrician chiefly, primarily, reflects, for the purpose of considering how the principles of this subject give rise to its different species, or *per se* accidents, and their ways of behaving through their properties.[91] Hence, this is the body about which the geometrician chiefly talks, or predicates his terms *per se*. As a result, Aristotle stated that science involves *per se* predication and that philosophy starts in wonder, not in universal methodic doubt or impossible dreams of pure reason.

Simply put, sameness (substantial unity), equality (quantitative unity), and similarity (qualitative unity and) are the formal objects through which we conceive all the different sciences because these per se accidents of unity are necessarily principles of their common matters that adequately express the contrariety "that exists" *within these matters.* Hence, it is through these formal objects, these modes of unity, *and only these modes of unity*, that our scientific habits of mind can be activated.

To put all this in another way, Aristotle's notion of philosophy, or science, like Socrates and Plato before him, rests upon his understandings of proximate material substance and *per se* predication. And his understanding of proximate material substance and *per se* predication rest upon his teaching about unity. He maintained that beings that belong to the same genus share a common matter and a common unit measure: the properties of sameness, equality, and similarity. For he claimed that "to be a measure" is a property of unity.[92] And he held that sameness, equality, and similarity are unity's primary accidents or properties. Through these common unit measures we know a subject's common matter in a permanent and unified way and can predicate their proximate effects *per se* of their proximate and *per se* subjects.[93]

Aristotle maintained, further, that unity measures "all things."[94] St. Thomas said that Aristotle made this claim because unity stops division. The undivided terminates division, is that beyond which no further division exists.[95]

Aristotle explained that we know those principles that constitute each thing's substance by analysis, by dividing or resolving a whole into its component parts, be the parts quantitative or specific (like matter, form, or elements). "Thus," he said, "the one is the measure of all things, because we come to know the elements in the substance by dividing the things either in respect of quantity or in respect of kind."[96] In short, indivisible intelligibles, as these relate to and activate distinctive habits of mind, are the extrinsic first principles of all science.

Analogously, Aristotle claimed we can call knowledge and perception "measures" of things because we know something by knowledge and perception. "[A]s a matter of fact," he said (specifically criticizing Protagoras for saying nothing while pretending to say something remarkable in his dictum, "man is the measure of all things"), human knowledge and perception "are measured," they do not "measure other things."[97]

According to Aristotle, a measure is the means by which we know a thing's quantity. That is, a measure is a unit, number, or limit.[98] Like Plato, Aristotle, recognized that we first derive the notion of measure from the genus of quantity. But, unlike Plato, Aristotle did not confound mathematical and all philosophical unity. He recognized that the proper opposite of unity is plurality, not number. Hence, he criticized Plato for conflating the notion of unity that is convertible with being with the unity that is the principle of number.[99]

Aristotle maintained that, once we arrive at the notion of unity negatively from association with it as a principle and measure of quantity, we can analogously transfer this notion and the idea of being a measure to other genera. Hence, in a way, Aristotle asserted, unity and quantity are the means by which we even know substance, knowledge, and quality:

Evidently, then, unity in the strictest sense, if we define it according to the meaning of the word, is a measure, and most properly of quantity, and secondly of quality. And some things will be one if they are indivisible in quantity, and others if they are indivisible in quality; and so that which is one is indivisible, either absolutely or *qua* one.[100]

Aquinas later commented on this passage that we find indivisibility in things in different, not the same, ways. Some things, like a natural unit, the principle of number, or a natural length, the principle of measured length, are definite and totally indivisible. Other things, like an artificial and arbitrary measure, "are not altogether indivisible but only to the senses, according to the authority of those who instituted such a measure wished to consider something as a measure."[101]

Aristotle thought that a natural body has *per se* unifying and formal principles, a *per se* formal object (or aim, end), intrinsic principles of indivisibility, that differentiate it from a quantified body, and a quantified body has *per se* unifying and formal principles, a *per se* formal object, intrinsic principles of individibility, that differentiate it from a qualified body. Each of these bodies differs from the other according to a distinctive kind of unity, intrinsic principle of indivisibility, that acts as the chief principle and measure of its distinctive kinds of contrariety and opposition based upon its distinctive kind of common matter. Each of these bodies reflects this respective kind of unity in acts that necessarily flow from it and act as signs of said unity.

A natural body's unity is composed of opposites, of matter and form. These opposites constitute it as a material nature and as a substantial nature in the genus of substance. This body is not the same as a quantitative body, the body in the genus of quantity, or as a qualified body. The natural body is the subject (proximate principle) of, the quantitative body, and the quantitative body is the subject (proximate principle) of the qualified body. Hence, in a way, the qualitative body, and its activities and modes of opposition, act as signs of its underlying qualitative body; and a quantitative body, and its activities and modes of opposition, act as signs of its substantial body.

Because of the distinctive kind of unity that the scientist, philosopher, studies, in his treatise *On the Unity of the Intellect against the Averroists*, while commenting upon a passage from Aristotle's *Physics*, St. Thomas states that the knowledge a scientist must have of a nature he studies must extend as far as understanding the essential relation the nature has to the chief end of the science.[102] So, for example, since the chief aim of medicine is health (that is, since the medical doctor chiefly studies the "health-generating body" as his scientific subject), a medical doctor must study the nature of a nerve as "health-related" (or generated) while, since the chief aim of a biologist is to study life (the "life-generating body"), the biologist must study the same nerve as "life-related" (or generated).

In both cases, both scientists must understand the nature of a nerve (its distinctive kind of unity, the unity of opposing principles that make it distinctively one, or what it is), but from a different formal perspective that is mainly determined in relation to the chief end (unity) of the science. Hence, while the "health-generating body (or nature)" is the scientific subject of study for the medical doctor, the "life-generating body" is the subject of study for the biologist.

Three properties of unity (sameness, equality, and likeness [or similarity]) allow us to conceive of a natural body as a scientific genus. And, relative to their respective intellectual habits, these properties give us the threefold division of speculative science, philosophy, based upon unity's properties.

Consequently, following Aristotle, St. Thomas said that we distinguish the parts of philosophy "in reference to the parts of being and unity." And he added that, according to Aristotle, "there are as many parts of philosophy as there are parts of substance, of which being and unity chiefly are predicated, and of which it is the principle intention or aim of this science [that is, metaphysics] to treat."

Aquinas identified these "parts of being" as "substance, quantity, quality, and so on."

> The parts of unity are sameness, equality and likeness. For things are the same when they are one in substance, equal when they are one in quantity, and like when they are one in quality. And the other parts of unity could be taken from the other parts of being, if they were given names.[103]

According to St. Thomas, in short, we divide philosophy, or science, according to the order of proximate natural subjects and the respective properties of unity that constitute the necessary and sufficient conditions for a proximate subject's ability to be the sort of subject it is (have the sort of unity it has) and activate our respective knowing habits as extrinsic necessary first principles, or formal objects.

As Crowley has rightly observed, Aristotle maintained that, as a natural body, a substantial body emanates in three magnitudinal directions from its substantial matter. These dimensions are extensions, divisions, and arrangements of the natural body within terminal parts in different directions in place.[104] They divide the natural body into parts that have a positional relation to each other and to bodies around them because position is contained within the notion of quantity.[105] These emanations quantify a natural body as a magnitudinal, extended, quantitative, or continuum body. *"This extension occurs both intrinsically to a body inasmuch as it places limits upon it within terminal parts internal to its substantial matter and externally inasmuch as it places limits upon the substantial body in the way it relates to its surrounding place."*[106]

When a material substance extends in one direction, Aristotle maintained it becomes a magnitudinal body terminated by a point. It becomes a linear body reaching from one point to another point. When it extends in two directions (from one point to another and one line to another), the substantial body becomes a surface, or wide, body stretching from one line to another. When the substantial body stretches from one surface to another surface, it becomes a solid, or deep, body and has depth. In this way, a quantified bodily substance acquires three natural intrinsic unit measures and termini (a point, line, and surface) that constitute it as a quantitative subject, a substance with quantity, the extended spatial unity and measure of which we call a quantitative "equal," the formal object of the speculative science of geometry.

As Aristotle noted, three kinds of magnitude exist: (1) a linear body, (2) a surface body; and (3) a solid body, all of which St. Thomas maintained, are essentially measurable and limited:

> if magnitude is divisible into continuous parts in one dimension only, it will be length; if into two, width; and if into three, depth. Again, when plurality or multitude is limited, it is called number. And a limited length is called a line; a limited width, surface; and a limited depth, body. For if multitude were unlimited, number would not exist, because what is unlimited cannot be numbered. Similarly, if length were unlimited, a line would not exist, because a line is a measurable length (and this is why it is stated in the definition of a line that its extremities are two points). The same things hold true of surface and of body.[107]

Aristotle thought that we initially derive our idea of measure from sensation, primarily from our sense awareness of a numbered length that arises from cutting a continuum body (from which we also derive such ideas as before and after, principle, and order).[108]

By cutting a continuum body, we divide it into a plurality of unit lengths. The unit that terminates the division is the limit of the division, an indivisible. Hence, it formally constitutes the division as a one and a number, an ordered and limited plurality. A number is an ordered and limited plurality, a one, and a measure. It is a measure precisely because it is a one, an indivisible, and a limit. Hence, as I have already noted, Aristotle said, "the one is the measure of all things."[109]

Since a measure is a one, just as we can predicate unity analogously, along with its accidental properties, which include being a measure, so we can analogously predicate continuous and discrete quantity and their accidental properties. So predicated, all these properties become analogous unit measures, ways we can use to comprehend an extended or qualified substance as limited and one, and, hence, knowable (because we cannot know anything totally indeterminate).

Aristotle maintained that these common properties are (1) of continuous quantity, large, or big, and small; (2) of number, much, many, large and little, few, small, and less; (3) of one-dimensional magnitude (length, or of a long body), long and short; of two-dimensional magnitude (a surface, or wide body), narrow and wide; of three-dimensional magnitude (a solid, or deep, body), high or deep, and low or shallow; (4) and of quality, heavy and light, hot and cold.[110]

Of all these analogously-predicated accidents, Aquinas said that "quantity is the closest to substance."[111] Of all the accidents, that is, quantity is most *per se*. Quantity is a *per se* accident of a material body because it necessarily inheres in, and emanates from, the body's natural matter. A quantitative body can thus be the proper subject of philosophical speculation for the geometrician as a proximate subject of accidents proper, or essential, to a point, line, and surface.

Similarly to the way in which dimensive quantity causes a material body to emanate extensively through its matter to natural intrinsic unit measures and limits, Aristotle claimed that a body emanates intensively through its form to natural intensive magnitudinal unit measures and limits of ability, positionally related to each other. By so doing, form constitutes a natural body as qualified, or a body with qualities, with limited and ordered abilities to act with more or less completeness or perfection, the proximate subject about

which the ancient physicist, metaphysician, and ethician can speculate, depending upon, Aristotle held, whether the matter in question
is corruptible or incorruptible, or human possessed of the faculty of
free choice.

Following Aristotle, St. Thomas said that we can understand
the term "perfect" in many senses. For example, (1) a thing is internally perfect when it "lacks no part of the dimensive quantity which
it is naturally determined to have." (2) We can understand the term
internally to refer to "the fact that a thing lacks no part of the quantity of power which it is naturally determined to have." (3) Or we can
use the term teleologically to refer to external perfection. For example, we can say that "those things are said to be perfect 'which have
attained their end, but only if the end is 'worth seeking' or good."[112]

St. Thomas maintained that we can call a thing perfect in relation to this or that ability because:

> [E]ach thing is perfect when no part of the natural magnitude
> which belongs to it according to the form of its proper ability
> is missing. Moreover, just as each natural being has a definite
> measure of natural magnitude in continuous quantity, as is
> stated in Book II of *The Soul*, so too each thing has a definite
> amount of its own natural ability. For example, a horse has by
> nature a definite dimensive quantity, within certain limits; for
> there is both a maximum quantity and minimum quantity be-
> yond which no horse can go in size. And in a similar way the
> quantity of active power in a horse which is not in fact sur-
> passed in any horse; and similarly there is some minimum
> which never fails to be attained.[113]

Hence, we can analogously transpose and predicate all the
concepts of measure that we derive from our awareness of being as
dimensively quantified and one to measure and comprehend quality
and all the other accidents, like place and time.[114] In this way, we

can talk about a color's magnitude because of the intensity of its brightness, the strength of heat because of the greatness of its effects, the greatness of a sin because of the magnitude of its offense to God, the quantity of perfection of an animal's ability to see, hear, or run, or the extent of perfection of someone's happiness, or an animal being higher or lower in its genus or species. Moreover, we can analogously extend the principle of unity and its parts to become principles and measures of sciences, philosophical disciplines, like ethics and politics.

To grasp Aristotle's view of philosophy and science more completely, we need to recognize a basic distinction he makes metaphysically between two types of quantity. Many philosophers familiar with Aristotle are aware that he distinguished between continuous and discrete quantity, continuous quantity being the proper, or *per se*, subject of the geometrician and discrete quantity being the proper, or *per se*, subject of the arithmetician. Few philosophers, even Aristotelians, appear to be aware that, metaphysically considered, he made a more basic distinction between dimensive (*molis*) quantity and virtual (*virtutis*) quantity.

Aristotle said that continuous and discrete quantity are species of dimensive, or bulk, quantity. They result in a substantial body from the emanation of a natural substance's matter to become a body divisible in one, two, or three magnitudinal limits, directions, or dimension: a long body, wide body, or deep body; or, more simply, as we say today, length, width, and depth.

He also maintained, however, that virtual quantity is a species of quantity. He said it emanates intensively from a natural substance's form, not extensively from its matter. And he claimed that the accidental form "quality," not dimensive "quantity," produces it.

Commenting on this distinction, St. Thomas reported: "Quantity is twofold. One is called bulk (*molis*) quantity or dimensive (*dimensiva*) quantity, which is the only kind of quantity in bodily thing . . ... The other is virtual (*virtutis*) quantity, which occurs according to the perfection of some nature or form." He added that we may also call this sort of quantity "spiritual greatness just as heat is called great because of its intensity and perfection."[115]

Aristotle, in short, thought that forms and qualities have their own kind of quantity and magnitudinal limit of natural or supernatural power, one that consists in the greater or less intrinsic perfection, completeness, or quantity of form, not in the extension of matter throughout parts within a spatial continuum. This virtual quantitative property of form permits to exist within a subject and a genus the opposition between privation and possession that is the principle of all contrariety. *Privation is the crucial addition that enables otherness, negation, or difference to involve contrariety.*

St. Thomas maintains that the differences of possession and privation that divide a genus into species are contrary to one another. Every change happens within a species, within a genus. And all such change involves movement between privation and possession of a specific form. For this reason, because the opposition between privation and possession is the first principle of all contrariety, he compares contraries, considered as *virtual quantities*, to be opposed "as the perfect to the imperfect."[116]

St. Thomas sees qualities as receptive intensities for action, the grounds of relation, and the principles through which substance acts. He thinks that relation occurs in things as a result of the intrinsic accident of quantity causing division of a body into potential parts. For St. Thomas, matter is the principle of numerical diversity only because intensive or dimensive quantity divide it into parts, which establish position and division according to before and after.[117] Division according to before and after, in turn, makes motion and time possible by making them actual.

Privation is a resistance to receptivity to action that exists within a potency within an existing subject. Potency devoid of privation is wholly indeterminate potency. Determinate potency is qualified potency. Privation is the ground of quality. Qualities exist within potential privations of a subject.

Privative potency is potency that resists receiving action in some way. Quality determines a subject's intensity, intensive quantity, or limit of receptivity to action by limiting its privation, making its potency receptive to action with determinate limits (this is the source of the medieval metaphysical principle that "whatever is received into a receiver is received according to the capacity of the receiver").

While existence (*esse*) precedes essence in the order of principles as a first principle, first act, of being in every finite being, it is only so as the act of numerically-one being, of this or that substance. Numerical unity, however, is consequent upon relation. Absent the total unity that the form of relation contributes to a substance, like the last piece needed to constitute a whole, no action (not even of *esse*) can happen.

While it coincides with relation and determinate potency in time, because it is consequent upon unity (which results from actual relation), action of a substance, or *ens*, presupposes relation and determinate potency in the order of proximate cause. Devoid of the proper qualities in acting and receiving subjects capable of actually relating, uniting, one thing (or principle) to another, no agent can exercise any action on any thing (for example, to lift something a person has to have properly *suitable* [qualified, relatable] strength and the thing lifted has to have properly *suitable* [qualified, relatable] size and weight).

Relation presupposes quality as the ground of the way one thing can exist and act toward another. Things relate to each other through their qualities. No real privations, no real qualities; no real qualities, no real relations. Since modern and contemporary "scientists," "philosophers" tend to by incapable of explaining real relations other than quantitative ones, this helps explain why the personal lives of such people so often tend to be irrational, a mess.

Qualities, moreover, like forms, are intensive quantities, intrinsic limits of opposition and complementarity that exist within a subject. They determine whether one subject can act or be acted on by another, and the extent, limits, to which this can occur. They are the proximate grounds of contrariety.

Dispositions are inchoate, incipient, incompletely-formed qualities. Habits, in turn, are completely-formed, maturely-developed, qualities. Dispositions are the source of human experience. Habits are the source of human art and science.

As sources, principles, of receptivity and inclination to human action, dispositions and habits relate numerically-one human faculty to its many acts. *As such, dispositions and habits establish the grounds for universal relation among the human subject, its faculties, and its action and passivities.*

Hence, dispositions, inclinations, numerically-one habits of human judgment and choice (human experience, art, and science) are the grounds of universality in human action. Such universality exists in the relation that exists between the subject and its acts through the subject's dispositions, inclinations, habits. This means that the person of experience, art, and science is the rightly-related ground of universality with regard to specific and individual human acts. Simply put, this properly-habituated person is the experiential, artistic, scientific, moral or ethical universal.

Contrariety, which includes contradiction, is total or partial privative negation. Total privative negation is contradictory opposition, total privation of some being, the complete subject, upon the being of another. Partial privative negation is limited negation of within a genus that extracts from a being some magnitude of its completeness of form.

Privation, in short, requires the disposition to have a form and the absence, in a definite subject at a definite time, of the form to which something is disposed.[118] For this reason, Aristotle maintained that opposition between privation and possession is the basis of opposition and contrariety.[119] Consequently, quality, or intensive quantity, as the foundation of all opposition and contrariety, (1) accounts for the limited possession of a finite being's existence; (2) in a way, is a principle of all science and philosophy; and (3) is an essential principle of all wonder! And so, too, is privation.

Moreover, Aristotle, maintained that basically two kinds of qualities exist: (1) essential differences and (2) differences, or alterations, of mobile bodies, like cold and hot, heavy and light, white and black. This second kind refers to the way we generally talk about "quality," "virtue and vice, and, in general, of evil and good."[120] Aristotle considered this sense of quality to be an accident related to motion, an intensive quantitative change of something moved as moved. Consequently, about virtue and vice, he said:

> Virtue and vice fall among these modifications; for they indicate *differentiae* of the movement or activity, according to which the things in motion act or are acted upon well or badly; for that which can be moved or act in one way is good and that which can do so in another—the contrary—way is vicious. Good and evil indicate quality especially in living things, and among these especially in those which have purpose.[121]

Regarding Aristotle's assertion that virtues and vices enable something to move well or badly, St. Thomas said that the terms "well" and "badly" chiefly relate to living things and "especially" to things having "choice." The reason Thomas gave for saying this is that living things, especially, act for an end and "rational beings, in whom alone choice exists know both the end and the proportion of the means to the end."[122]

Part of Aquinas's reasoning in his above commentary was that quality limits a motion or action, places it within bounds, and, in a way, gives it order and proportion (properties that, strictly speaking, belong to, and it receives from, continuous quantity), especially in connection to acting for an end. *This point is crucial to understand regarding any science involved in study of qualities because every science must study a genus in relation to opposition be-*

tween contrary members of a species. Like all oppositions, such opposition is grounded in the principles of possession, privation, and limits rooted in a subject's common matter. Hence, *this notion should be especially helpful for modern and contemporary physics and could easily be used to reintegrate philosophy, "science-truly-so called," and this physics because it appears to underlie all modern and contemporary physics.*

Aristotle thought that science, philosophy, studies one thing *chiefly,* a primary, or main, subject to which it analogously relates other subjects. Analogous predication, however, essentially involves predication of a term according to opposition of a many to a one. By this statement I mean that analogous predication involves predicating unequal relationships of existential possession and privation that different subjects have in reference to some one intelligible content that the predicate term conveys.

Hence, the medical doctor chiefly studies the subject of human health and its contrary opposite, disease, plus other unequally-health-related subjects and their opposites, like good and bad diet, exercise, operating procedures, medical instruments, and so on. Medical science chiefly studies human health because, strictly speaking, health exists chiefly and maximally, or in its main and maximum possession, in human bodies. Human health does not mainly and maximally exist in health-related subjects of study like human diet, exercise, operating procedures, or medical instruments.

Analogous predication involves predicating unequal reference of a common predicate, meaning, or term to different subjects according to different kinds of opposing relation, of greater and less (unequal, and, hence, not the same, or one) possession or privation by the subjects of the intelligible content the predicate term conveys, and that maximally exists in a main subject. No science, then, can proceed without considering proportionate and unequal relationship of possession and privation. Hence, all science uses the language of analogy to express the kinds of opposition that a multiplicity of unequally related subjects have to a chief proximate subject (the maximum species in a genus), *to a one* to which other *many* subjects of study are related as numerically-*one* end.[123]

One reason this last claim is true is that, as Aristotle rightly understood, substance is the chief subject of every science, or division of philosophy, not just of metaphysics. He criticized the ancient philosophers who made contraries their first principles because contraries cannot exist without, and are attributes of, a common subject: "All contraries, then, are always predicable of a subject, and none can exist apart, but just as appearances suggest that there is nothing contrary to substance, argument confirms this. No contrary, then, is the first principle of all things in the full sense; the first principle is something different."[124]

As Aristotle correctly noted, all science, philosophy, and knowledge chiefly concern a main subject, something about which the science, philosophical division, or knowledge *chiefly* talks and predicates relation of terms. The first principle of no science, philosophical division, or knowledge can be an unconnected multitude, an indeterminate many. It must be some one being, or our talk is meaningless.

Aristotle stated, further, that (1) quantity is the means by which we know substance; (2) a measure is the means by which we know a thing's quantity; (3) we first find unity as a measure in discrete quantity, number; and, (4), from this category, we analogously transfer the idea of a measure to other categories, like quality, time, place, and so on.[125]

In the case of quality, Aristotle maintained that we first perceive the notion of measure by comparing one thing to another and by noticing that one thing *exceeds* another in a specific quality, by noticing the inequalities of larger and smaller, or more and less, properties and pluralities of unity. We notice, for instance, that one thing has more weight or heat than another.[126] First and foremost, Aristotle considered equality and inequality to be quantitative divisions of numeral proportions.[127] He said that inequality is of two kinds: larger and smaller (or excessive and defective) and more and less. As inequalities, pluralizations of unity, we cannot understand excessive and defective, larger and smaller, and more and less apart from reference to equality. Equality, however, as a kind of unity (a one) is the measure of inequality, the means by which we know it.[128]

In the case of quality, Aquinas asserted that we cannot directly compare any two qualities. Quality as quality only directly refers to the subject in which it exists. Its being is a referential being to its subject. St. Thomas claimed that we can only relate one quality to another quality (1) by referring the one quality to the other as an active or passive potency of the other, as being a principle or source of acting or being acted upon (like cause and effect, heating and being heated) or (2) by referring one quality to another through reference to quantity or something related quantity; for example, when we state that one thing is hotter than another because its quality of heat is more intense.[129]

4. Why all science, philosophy, must formally be a study of the problem of the one and the many

Aristotle's teaching on contraries makes intelligible how we can indirectly compare two qualities quantitatively, the way contemporary physicists often do. For Aristotle contrariety is one of four kinds of opposition: (1) contradiction, (2) contrariety, (3) possession and privation, and (4) relation.[130] As partial, privative negations (not as contradictory opposites), contraries are forms, extreme differences, or specific extremes or limits of possession and privation, within the same genus between which a mean, middle, or intermediary can exist. When contraries have a mean or middle we can relate it to both extremes as a one, intermediate, or midpoint between possession and privation. In this situation, it is neither extreme, relates to both, and is opposed to both by an opposition of privative negation, not of contrariety, just as, for example, the midpoint between the extremely hot and extremely cold is not hot nor cold, and can become both, or a morally neutral person is not morally good or bad, and can become both.[131]

Moreover, Aristotle said that, when contraries have a mean, passage from one extreme to another involves an order of change, a necessary passage through the midpoint. Such being the case, the midpoint (a one) stands in a condition of equality in relation to both extremes, just as passage from the great to the small and the fast to the slow must be through what is equidistant from both (an equal, or one). Because the equal stands as a mean or midpoint between extremes of possession and privation of a form within a genus, and is, consequently a one, we can use it as a measure to know both extremes.[132]

In relationship to the equal, a one, two opposites exist, comprising the unequal (in this case, excess and defect of some form). Analogously speaking, we may refer to these inequalities as multiplicities or pluralities. This being so, we can measure qualitative differences, or difference of intensity in possession or privation of a quality, by comparing excessive and deprived possession to possession of equal intensity as pluralities measurable by a homogeneous unit. We can compare one quality to another by relating both qualities to a third, standing midway between them in intensity, much like we can compare the heaviness of two different bodies by using a balance scale that compares their weight relative to a state of equilibrium (a one). This one qualitative state becomes the measure of the other two (a many) and the principle by which we know them.[133]

According to Aristotle, (1) all science seeks to understand its subject-matter in terms of its principles, ways of being one and (2) causes and effects are opposite terms of relational opposition. Consequently, by studying causes, all science, all philosophy, must study (1) opposition and (2) dependence and partial and total negation because partial or total negation of a subject are the causes of all opposition. This explains why a science like medicine must study causes of health and disease, like diet and exercise, medical operations, and

medical instruments. All relate, as causes, to partial or total possession of health or disease in a human being.

For scientific purposes, according to Aristotle and St. Thomas, only three scientific subjects exist: substance as substance, quantified substance, and qualified substance. Sameness, equality, and
similarity are modes of unity that externally reflect, are signs of, effects of, the way substance acts through its substantial unity, quantitative unity, and qualitative unity.

Hence, Aristotle and St. Thomas use these three modes of
unity and the way they measure their opposites to understand the
intrinsic nature of substance and the necessary relation of the substance to its properties. Because all three modes of unity exist in a
substance, they necessarily reflect, reveal, different ways that a substance is intrinsically united and divided, the constitution of its parts,
and they way they relate to the whole substance and the way it be-
haves.

Because the human intellect is both an active and passive
power, and because science is an act of the intellect, St. Thomas
thinks that the intellect gets part of its formal object (subject matter)
from the thing known acting on it as a passive power (the mode of
necessity that the thing known has through its mode of unity that the
intellect abstractly apprehends through the intensive quantity of its
dematerializing power).

The more scientific the intellect the more intense is its dematerializing way of operating. The more intense its dematerializing
way of acting, the more abstract must be the being known (form)
that activates it. The more intensely abstract the ability of the intellect as a receiving power, the more highly scientific the intellect is
and the form that activates it must be.

The more a form exists without depending upon connection
with matter to exist, *from the side of the thing known*, the more immaterial and necessary is that form. From the side of the thing
known, the more a science studies such forms, the more "scientific"
is the science. For this reason, from the side of the thing known, *qua*

science, mathematics is more scientific than physics and metaphysics is more scientific than mathematics.

From the side of the knower, knowledge is formally more scientific due to the intensity of immateriality involved in its act of receiving a scientific form, reasoning about it, and judging it. A scientific form is one having a mode of unity, necessity, that can activate a scientific mode of intellectual conceptualization and judgment. The less such reception, reasoning, and judging involve dependence upon matter and motion for their operation the more scientific they are. *Being scientific involves more than what we know: a being that is necessary and more or less dependent upon matter for its existence and being known. It involves the way we know,* our *method* of knowing, of conceptually abstracting (dematerializing an essence from the material conditions that obscure its knowability), reasoning about, and abstractly judging such a being. For this reason, becoming scientific, philosophical, is hard work!

From the side of the intellect as an active power, the intellect completes the formal object of a science by comprehending the immaterialized nature of the thing known in a judgment that involves a dematerialized mode of verification, a mode of verification somewhat separate from matter and motion. The less the verification process depends upon relation to matter and motion, the more highly intellectual, immaterial, and scientific it is. *The scientific judgment is more intensely immaterial depending upon the initial degree of existential separation from matter and motion of the thing known and the intensity of the act of dematerialization the intellect has to use in conceiving and judging it.*

From the side of the knower, then, mathematics is more scientific than physics because the mathematical mode of intellectually conceiving and judging quantified being is more intensely immaterial, less dependent upon matter and motion, than is that of qualified being. Hence, to repeat some things already said, forming intellectual images that adequately reveal the natures of quantified beings (mathematical evidence), requires help from the imagination For this reason, the science of mathematics terminates its judgment in the human imagination (where its evidence is fully revealed), not in the external senses.

Similarly, from the side of the knower, metaphysics is more scientific than mathematics and physics because its proper mode of intellectually conceiving and judging substantial being *is more intensely immaterial*, less dependent upon matter and motion, than is that of quantified and qualified being. Hence, forming intellectual images that adequately reveal the natures of metaphysical beings (metaphysical evidence), requires over and above help from the imagination, help from the intellect. For this reason, the science of metaphysics terminates its judgment in the human intellect (where this evidence is fully revealed), not in the imagination or in the external senses.

The formal object of a science as speculative, practical, or productive comes from the chief aim of the intellect for considering its scientific subject. If a scientist wants to think about this subject for a chiefly speculative aim, the science is speculative. If he or she wants to do so for a chiefly practical or productive aim, the science is practical or productive. Whatever the case, as essentially a relation existing within the intellectual soul activated by a nature that it has helped dematerialize, an intellectual habit of science essentially unites the formal object of a specific science to the generic aim of the intellectual soul to think speculatively, practically, or productively for the human soul's chief natural aim: to make a person happy.

From the formal aspect of the thing known, the subject matter of a practical science is always a qualified body. In medicine this is a health-generating (medical) body. In economics, it is a wealth-generating (economic) body. In ethics, it is a freedom-generating (moral, or ethical, body: free human choice). In politics, it is a socially-unified, freedom-generating (political) body.

The science of medicine studies the opposites of health and disease (the many) with the chief aim of maintaining or improving bodily health, bodily unity. The science of economics studies the opposites of wealth and poverty (the many) for the chief aim of maintaining or improving economic wealth, economic unity. The science of ethics studies the opposites of virtue and vice (the many) for the chief aim of maintaining or improving ethical unity (perfection in use of freedom). The science of politics studies the opposites of war and peace (the many) for the chief aim of maintaining or improving the unity of the political body (social unity of a freedom-generating body).

By observing the effects that qualities and movements have on dimensive bodies, a mixed practical or productive science like mathematical physics uses mathematics to study opposing physical movements, forces, qualities (the many, like hot, cold, acceleration, deceleration, and so on) with the chief aim of understanding how mathematically to measure qualitative changes from a state of prior uniformity (equality) so as to be able to predict and regulate such changes, give them mathematical unity and productive intelligibility and regulation.

Hence, no science, no division of philosophy, can study its subject-matter without, simultaneously, studying the problems of the one and the many and opposition. This is because, strictly speaking, (1) as the major philosophers of ancient Greece clearly understood, philosophy and science are identical; (2) philosophy, or science, chiefly studies substance in terms of contrary opposites; (3) contrariety and opposition always involve the problem of the one and the many; (4) all philosophical and scientific study for all time essentially involves the problem of the one and the many.[134]

Our job as philosophers, scientists, then, is *chiefly* to wonder about the behavior of individually-existing things in terms of this proximate, *per se* subject (a one) and its intrinsic and necessary, *per se*, accidents (a many), a hierarchical order of species, contrary opposites, that a generically-considered, substantial body causes to flow from its existence, matter, and form. These species are contrary opposites because contraries of higher and lower species are extreme differences that exist within a genus, and Aristotle asserted that contraries are extreme differences sharing a common genus.

St. Thomas maintained that wonder is a species of fear that results from ignorance of a cause. Because the object of fear calls to mind a difficulty of some magnitude and a sense of personal weakness, an immediate sense of opposition, dependency, and privation, our desire to philosophize must arise within all of us as the product of a natural desire to escape from the natural fear we have of the real difficulty, danger, and damage ignorance can cause us. Hence, strictly speaking, we are not born philosophers; and, as Plato and Socrates emphasized, people cannot pour philosophy into us like water into an empty jug. Only those who have some knowledge and experience of this initial sort of fear, accompanied by the appropriate desire to put it to rest, can become philosophers, scientists.[135]

St. Thomas explained that this initial sense of fear grips us in two stages: (1) Recognition of our weakness and fear of failure causes us to refrain immediately from passing judgment. Then (2) hope of possibility of understanding an effect's cause prompts us intellectually to seek the cause.

Thomas added that, since philosophical investigation starts with wonder, "it must end in the contrary of this." We do not wonder about the answer to questions we already know, or about what is evident. And, strictly speaking, when working as philosophers, scientists, we do not seek to remain in a state of wonder. We seek to put wonder to rest by discovering the causes of the occurrences of things.

Since wonder is the first principle of all theoretical, practical, or productive philosophy, science, for everyone and all time, initially all philosophical first principles arise from our human senses, emotions, intellect, and something that causes in us the awareness of real opposition, possession and privation, not simply difference. Hence, for the ancient Greeks, philosophy, science, involved a study of opposites and relations, and, more precisely, of contrary opposites, because cause and effect are a species of relation and contrary opposites (precisely speaking, because relation is, as Aristotle claimed, one of the four kinds of opposition). But because, as Aristotle said, opposition between the one and the many is basic and the principle of all other opposition, because all other opposites are analogous transpositions of this sort of opposition, fundamentally, all philosophy, science, for all time, involves reflection upon the problem of the one and the many.[136]

That this should be the case should not cause us to wonder because all science, philosophy, chiefly aims at improving human possession of truth, uses truth, or its analogoues (like beauty and goodness) to measure all human scientific, philosophical, knowledge. No wonder, then, that when he helped design *The Great Conversation: A Reader's Guide to the Great Books of the Western World*, in a section entitled, "The Great Conversation Revisited," Mortimer J. Adler could not help but make this brilliant observation:

> On any subject being considered, the relation between truth and error is always that of a one to a many. The truth is always singular, while the errors it corrects are manifold. This fact should not be thought as invidious to the worth of reading the great books. On the contrary, it is of greatest positive importance. No truth is well understood until and unless all the errors it corrects are also understood and all the contradictions found are resolved. It is in the context of a plurality of errors to be corrected and of contradictions to be resolved that the brilliance of truth shines and illumines the scene.[137]

Michelangelo di Lodovico Buonarotti Simoni (1475–1546) needed repeated failures to perfect his paintings and sculptures. Galileo Galilei (b. 1564; d. 1612), needed repeated failures to perfect his principles of astronomy. Great military leaders need to experience repeated failures to become great military leaders. And the same is true of leaders in all other fields.

The chief reason for this is that we cannot progress in learning without making our thinking more precise. Disagreements, objections, failures are the essential enabling means for making our thinking more precise because *they are the essential enabling means for discovering the generic and specific differences* that help us refine the images, concepts, and definitions we use as principles of discovery and judgment in all divisions of learning.

To solve a problem or answer a difficult question, we must first narrow down our quest by generically and specifically defining the problem, or precisely framing the question we are seeking to answer. But we cannot generically and specifically define a problem or question without, in some way, recognizing some difference or common object of pursuit we are seeking that only a more precise definition can provide. Asking precisely the right question at precisely the right time helps solve this problem by putting investigators in the same genus as the subject they are seeking fully to comprehend.

We cannot discover the solution to any problem, especially a difficult one, without first discovering some specific difference that makes this problem unique, that separates it from other problems that closely resemble it. Without the help of failure, objections from others, hitting a brick wall in our thinking, difficult arguments to answer, crises, extreme hardships, political persecution, or some form of suffering, few human beings can make great discoveries. In some respect, all great artists, philosophers, scientists, theologians must suffer for their discipline. Without such help, at times, we might not even know we have a problem we need to answer.

And, even once we precisely frame a problem or question that is difficult to solve, except through luck, native genius, or miraculous intervention, without the help of further failure, arguments, objections, most of us can never hope to answer it.

The reason for this is that we answer difficult problems and questions by means of precise arguments. We can never arrive at precise arguments without using precise definitions. Since we can never arrive at precise definitions without understanding precise differences that exist among a group of beings that share something in common, without the help of failure, objections from others, difficult arguments to answer, or crises, we can never find that precise difference that separates a smaller class of beings from a larger one and arrive at a precise definition.

This is the reason why great physical scientists must in engage in so many experiments, great philosophers have to be able to answer many major objections, and why dealing with repeated failures is an essential enabling means for producing great leaders in any field.

The way we go about discovering these differences differs in different areas of learning. Mathematical physicists and medical researchers discover this difference chiefly by means of experiment. Athletes discover it mainly by means of athletic competition. Philosophers and theologians tend to discover it by means of verbal argument. Saints find it by successfully enduring great sufferings; and people in business, politicians, and cultural leaders tend to discover it by economic failure, political conflicts, and cultural crises.

Whatever the case, no sane human being engages in this kind of quest for no reason. We all do this as a result of the natual human quest to become happy.

Since we cannot achieve human happiness without knowing in what happiness consists, human nature has a natural inclination to generate sciences of diverse levels of intellectual perfection until, eventually, human beings arrive at first philosophy, human science in its most perfect form: wisdom.

To become happy we have to live wisely. To do so, we must generate sciences that help us live wisely. Sciences do this by putting us in contact with first principles, causes of the natures of things that exist around us in the physical universe in which we live.

As St. Thomas tells us, such principles consists in two kinds of natures: (1) incomplete, like the form and matter of a substance, its intrinsic quantity, and quality, its intrinsic and extrinsic relations, action, potentiality, time, and so on; and (2) complete, like material and immaterial substances.

Incomplete natures, the incomplete principles of a complete nature, are not the chief principles about which science, philosophy, mainly wonder; and they are not the whole about which scientific, philosophical, wonder chiefly aims to give us knowledge. Science, philosophy, wonder about, chiefly aim at enabling human beings to come to know about, the existence of higher substances, of immaterial beings, like angelic natures, gods, or a God: about whether or not such beings exist and, if they do, of what kind of nature they are.

The reason for this is simple to understand. No human being can become, or be, completely wise (and, hence, completely happy) in this life without knowing whether or not such beings exist. If such beings do exist, since all human beings are naturally inclined to listen to, and follow the advice of, human beings that know more than we do, we have an even greater natural inclination to listen to and follow the advice of beings of a higher intellectual nature. So, in this life, without knowing whether or not such beings exist, we can never be absolutely convinced we have come to possess happiness in its highest form.

Furthermore, if, in this life, some human beings (like religious leaders, revealed theologians) make claims that such higher intellectual beings exist and that evidence exists they have communicated with us, and continue to do so, given our natural inclination to listen to, and follow, the advice of intellects that know more than we do, without some measure of thoroughly-natural human science with which to judge such claims to be true or false, vis-à-vis achievement of human happiness, we put ourselves at a dangerous disadvantage.

Because contemporary "philosophers" falsely-so-called tend to identify philosophy with logic and philosophical principles with logical premises, if they ever think about metaphysics, they tend to gloss over the fact that desire to understand the nature of the highest of intellectual substances was the chief aim that motivated Aristotle to write his famous *Metaphysics*, which he identified as "theology." And even if they do recognize that Aristotle used the term "principle" to refer to incomplete natures, like form and matter, potency, act, quality, and quantity, they tend to be baffled about the connection of his study of these principles with that of the nature of a highest metaphysical and philosophical principle, "pure thought thinking thought." They tend not to comprehend how the study of this highest first cause unifies Aristotle's metaphysics and philosophy as a whole.

Unlike modern thinkers, ancient Greek philosophers did not chiefly conflate philosophical principles with logical premises. Like St. Thomas after them, they tended to identify philosophical principles with complete or incomplete natures, and, in the most complete sense, with complete natures: substances. Analogously, as they developed logic, they extended the use of the term to logical premises. Hence, the reason Aristotle considered metaphysics chiefly to be a study that sought to understand the first cause of everything was mainly because this was the first motivating cause of Greek philosophy and mythology since their inception.

What I am saying is so true that, in the *Phaedo*, Socrates tells us that, even though he would later find Anaxagoras' method wanting, as soon as he heard about Anaxzgoras' explanation for cause and order it pleased him. He said, "Somehow it seemed right that mind should be the cause of everything, and I reflected that if this is so, mind arranges each individual thing in a way that is best for it. Therefore, if anyone wished to discover the reason why any given thing came or ceased or continued to be, he must find out how it was best for a thing to be or to act or be acted upon in any other way."[138]

Because, since its inception, classical Greek science sought to understand how one principle could cause a multitude, could cause all the genera, species, and individuals that exist in this physical universe, by the time Christianity and St. Paul came on the scene, much of the ancient Greek intelligentsia would be highly receptive to the Christian message. This phenomenon also explains why the last of the major Greek philosophers, Plotinus, who saw in Christianity a competitor he did not like, so completely sought to explain the whole universe as an architectonically-ordered emanation of the many from the one.

In short, failure to understand the centrality of the problem of the one and the many in classical philosophy (and, with it, the architectonic nature of all human science, philosophy, and the reason for this nature, especially in relationship to first philosophy, the science of metaphysics) is (1) one of the greatest weaknesses of modern "science," "philosophy," falsely-so-called, and (2) a chief reason this mode of knowing became divorced from wisdom and caused modern modern "philosophers" and "scientists" to degenerate into fools and sophists (or, as Plato called them, "philosophical" or "scientific" bastards) who tend, in our time, to pander to utopian, socialist despots.

By this point, with the help of Aristotle and St. Thomas, the preceding pages of this work provide a blueprint for how fully to recover from this modern condition of degeneracy and restore Lady Philosophy to the position, by nature, that she inclines to occupy. In the next chapter, I will attempt to add some more details to this blueprint that will help me prepeare to build upon it in subsequent volumes of this work.

NOTES

1. St. Thomas Aquinas, *Summa theologiae*, ed. Piana (Ottawa: Collège Dominicain d'Ottawa, 1941), 1–2, proem., q. 90; see, also, Peter A. Redpath, "Why Double Effect and Proportionality are not Moral Principles for St. Thomas," in *Vera Lex* (Winter, 2004).

2. Aristotle, *Metaphysics*, trans. W.D. Ross, in *The Basic Works of Aristotle*, ed. Richard McKeon (New York: Random House, 1968), Bk. 14, 1, 1087b29–1087b31; my explanation appears in parenthesis.

3. Id., 1087a36–1087b3.

4. Id., 1087b34–1088b14; my explanation appears in brackets.

5. Aristotle, *Physics*, trans. R. P. Hardie and R. K. Gaye, in *The Basic Works of Aristotle*, ed. Richard McKeon (New York: Random House, 1968), Bk.1, ch. 1, 184a–192.

6. Aristotle, *Metaphysics*, Bk.1, 990b1–4.

7.   Id., Bk. 4, ch. 5, 1010a1–1011a1; see, also, Joseph Owens, "The Grounds of Universality in Aristotle," in John R. Catan (ed.), *Aristotle: The Collected Papers of Joseph Owens* (Albany, N,Y.: State University of New York Press), pp. 49–50; see further analysis of Aristotle's teaching about science in Peter A. Redpath "Post-Postmodern Science and Religion: A Critique," in *International Journal of World Peace*, 18, n. 1 (March, 2001), pp. 61–90.

8.   Aristotle, *Posterior Analytics*, Bk.1, ch. 1, 71b8–30.

9.   Id., Bk.1, ch. 27, 87a37–87b4.

10.   Aristotle, *Metaphysics*, Bk. 5, ch. 1, 1012b34–1013a23.

11.   Id., Bk. 3, ch. 4, 1001b1–1002b10, Bk. 5, 6, 1016b18–32.

12.   Id., Bk. 4, ch. 1,1003b22–34, Bk. 10, 1, 1052a15–1053b8, and 1053b23–24.

13.   Aristotle, *Posterior Analytics*, trans. G.R.G. Mure, in *The Basic Works of Aristotle*, ed. Richard McKeon (New York: Random House, 1968), Bk. 1, ch. 11, 77a5–9; see, also, Joseph Owens, "The Aristotelian Conception of the Sciences," in *Aristotle: The Collected Papers of Joseph Owens*, p. 24.

14.   Aristotle, *Posterior Analytics*, Bk. 1, 11, 77a5–9; see, also, St. Thomas Aquinas, *Commentary on the Posterior Analytics of Aristotle*, trans. F. R. Lacher, O.P. , based on the Leonine text (Albany, N.Y.: Magi Books, Inc., 1970), Bk. 1, l. 19.

15.   Aristotle, *Posterior Analytics*, Bk. 1, ch. 11, 75a18–37. See Aquinas, *Commentary on the Posterior Analytics of Aristotle*, Bk. 1, l. 14.

16.   Aristotle, *Metaphysics*, Bk. 11, ch. 8, 1064b30–1065b4.

17.   Plato, *Republic*, Bk. 1, 339D–347A.

18.   Aristotle, *Metaphysics*, Bk. 12, ch. 1, 1069a18–1069b32, *Posterior Analytics*, Bk. 2, ch. 2, 90b14–16.

19.   Id., Bk. 4, ch. 2, 1004a2–3.

20.   Aquinas, *Commentary on the Posterior Analytics of Aristotle*, Bk. 2, l. 2.

21.   Aristotle, *Posterior Analytics*, Bk. 2, ch. 2, 90b14–16.

22.   Aristotle, *Metaphysics*, Bk. 6, ch. 1, 1026b1–25; for a brilliant defense of the claim that the whole of the science of physics depends upon the certainty of the existence of a supreme intelligence of a non-material first cause, see Benedict M. Ashley and John N. Deely, *How Science Enriches Theology* (South Bend, Ind.: St. Augustine's Press, 2011), pp. 3–5.

23.   Id., Bk. 4, 3, 1003b36–37, Bk. 10, 1, 1053b23–104a19.

24.   Id.

25.   St. Thomas Aquinas, *Commentary on the Metaphysics of Aristotle*, 2 vols, trans John P. Rowan (Chicago: Henry Regnery, Co., Inc., 1961), vol. 1, Bk. 4, l. 2, n. 561.

26.   Aristotle, *Metaphysics*, Bk. 5, ch. 24, 1023a26-32, and ch. 26, 1024a29–1024b4.

27.   Aquinas, *Commentary on the Metaphysics of Aristotle*, Bk. 5, l. 22, n. 1121.

28.   St. Thomas Aquinas *Commentary on the* de Trinitate *of Boethius*, q.5, a. 4, reply, pp. 42–43.

29.   Aristotle, *Metaphysics*, Bk. 5, ch. 28, 1024b10–13.

30.   Aquinas, *Commentary on the Metaphysics of Aristotle*, Bk. 5, l. 22, n. 1125.

31.   For further explanation about the difference between these ways of predicating, see St. Thomas Aquinas, *The Division and Methods of the Sciences: Commentary on the* de

Trinitate *of Boethius, Questions V and VI*, ed. and trans., Armand A. Maurer (Toronto: Pontifical Institute of Mediaeval Studies, 3rd rev. ed., 1963), q. 6, a. 3, c., p. 75, fn. 15.

32. Aquinas, *Commentary on the Metaphysics of Aristotle*, Bk. 4, l. 2, n. 553.
33. Id., Bk. 4, l. 3, nn. 564–566.
34. Aristotle, *Metaphysics*, Bk. 12, ch. 1, 1069a18-1069b32; Bk. 5, 5, 1015b10–15.
35. Id., Bk. 9, ch. 10, 1052b19–22.
36. Aristotle, *Physics*, Bk. 1, ch. 1, 184a17–21.
37. Aristotle, *Metaphysics*, Bk. 9, ch. 10, 1052b19–22; Aquinas, *Commentary on the Metaphysics of Aristotle*, Bk. 4, l. 2, n. 553.
38. Aristotle, *Metaphysics*, Bk. 4, ch. 2, 1005a3–5.
39. Id., 1004b27-1005a13b, Bk 10, ch. 3, 1055a32–39; Aquinas, *Commentary on the Metaphysics of Aristotle*, Bk. 4, l. 4, nn. 582–587.
40. Aristotle, *Metaphysics*, Bk. 4, ch. 1, 1004a34–1005a18; Aquinas, *Commentary on the Metaphysics of Aristotle*, Bk. 4, l. 4, nn. 582–587.
41. Aristotle, *Metaphysics*, Bk. 10, ch. 3, 1055a33–1055b39; Aquinas, *Commentary on the Metaphysics of Aristotle*, vol. 2, Bk. 10, l. 6, n. 2058.
42. Aristotle, *Metaphysics*, Bk. 10, ch. 3, 1054a20–1055b39; Aquinas, *Commentary on the Metaphysics of Aristotle*, Bk. 10, l. 4, nn.1998-2022, 2035.
43. Maurer, "Introduction," *Commentary on the* de Trinitate *of Boethius, Questions V and VI. St. Thomas Aquinas: Division and Methods of the Sciences*, p. XV.
44. Id.
45. Id.
46. Id., XVI.
47. Aquinas, *Commentary on the* de Trinitate *of Boethius*, q. 5, a. 1, reply.
48. Id., reply to 4.
49. Id., q. 6, a. 2, reply, p. 45.
50. Id., q. 5, a. 3, reply, pp. 31–33; reply to 1, p. 34; reply to 3, p. 35; and a. 4, reply, p. 45.
51. Maurer, "Introduction, "*Commentary on the* de Trinitate *of Boethius, Questions V and VI. St. Thomas Aquinas: The Division and Methods of the Sciences*, p. XXIV.
52. Id.
53. Id., p. 27.
54. Étienne Gilson, *Thomist Realism and the Critique of Knowledge*, trans. Mark A. Wauck (San Francisco: Ignatius Press, 1986), pp. 172–173.
55. Maurer, "Introduction," *Commentary on the* de Trinitate *of Boethius, Questions V and VI. St. Thomas Aquinas: Division and Methods of the Sciences*, p. XIX.
56. Id., p. XXXIV.
57. Aquinas, *Commentary on the* de Trinitate *of Boethius*, q. 6 a. 3, reply, p. 77.
58. Maurer, "Introduction," *Commentary on the* de Trinitate *of Boethius, Questions V and VI. St. Thomas Aquinas: Division and Methods of the Sciences*, p. 75, n. 15.
59. Aquinas, *Commentary on the* de Trinitate *of Boethius*, q. 5, a.4, pp. 39–49..
60. St. Thomas Aquinas, *Commentary on the Metaphysics of Aristotle*, proem, ed. Cathala-Spiazzi, pp. 1–2; cited after Maurer, *Commentary on the* de Trinitate *of Boethius*,

Questions V and VI. St. Thomas Aquinas: Division and Methods of the Sciences, "Appendix II," p. 85.

61.   St. Thomas Aquinas, *Commentary on the* de Trinitate *of Boethius*, q. 5 a. 1, reply, pp. 12–13.

62.   Id.

63.   St. Thomas Aquinas, *Commentary on the Nicomachean Ethics of Aristotle, In I Eth.*, lect. 1, ed. Pirotta, nn. 1–2; cited after Maurer, *Commentary on the* de Trinitate *of Boethius, Questions V and VI. St. Thomas Aquinas: Division and Methods of the Sciences*, "Appendix I," p. 86.

64.   See Piotr Jaroszyński's excellent work on the essential connection between science and culture, *Science in Culture*, trans. Hugh McDonald (Amsterdam and New York: Editions Rodopi, B.V., 2008).

65.   Aristotle, *Metaphysics*, Bk. 1, 980a–983a; Aquinas, *Commentary on the Metaphysics of Aristotle*, vol. 1, Bk. 1, l. 1, n. 35.

66.   St. Thomas Aquinas, *Commentary on the* de Trinitate *of Boethius*, q. 6 a. 4, reply, p. 85.

67.   St. Thomas Aquinas, *Summa contra gentiles*, proem. Bk. 1; Aristotle, *Metaphysics*, Bk. 1, ch. 2, 982a18, and Bk. 12, ch. 10, 1075a14–16.

68.   St. Thomas Aquinas, St. Thomas Aquinas, *Commentary on the Nicomachean Ethics of Aristotle, In I Eth.*, lect. 1, ed. Pirotta, nn. 1–2; cited after Maurer, *Commentary on the* de Trinitate *of Boethius, Questions V and VI. St. Thomas Aquinas: Division and Methods of the Sciences*, "Appendix I," p. 85; Aristotle, *Metaphysics*, Bk. 1, ch. 2, 982a18.

69.   See Sir Francis Bacon, *New Atlantis* and *Novum organum*.

70.   St. Thomas Aquinas, *Commentary on the* de Trinitate *of Boethius*, q. 6 a. 4, reply, p. 85.

71.   St. Thomas Aquinas, *Commentary on the Nicomachean Ethics of Aristotle*; cited after Maurer, *Commentary on the* de Trinitate *of Boethius, Questions V and VI. St. Thomas Aquinas: Division and Methods of the Sciences, In I th. Lect. 1*, ed. Pirotta, nn. 1–2, "Appendix I," pp.. 85–86.

72.   Id.

73.   Id.

74.   Aristotle, *Metaphysics*, Bk. 10, ch. 1, 1052a19–1053b8; Aquinas, *Commentary on the Metaphysics of Aristotle*, vol. 2, Bk. 10, l. 2, nn. 1920–1960; Charles B. Crowley, *Aristotelian-Thomistic Philosophy of Measure and the International System of Units (SI)*, ed. with a prescript by Peter A. Redpath (Lanham, Md.: University Press of America, 1996), pp. 25–47, 249–260.

75.   Albert Einstein, "The Scientist's Responsibilities," in Donald H. Whitfield with James L. Hicks, science consultant (eds.), *What's the Matter?* (Chicago: The Great Books Foundation with support from Harrison Middleton University, 2007), p. 501. I thank David Curd, president of Harrison Middleton University, for providing me with a copy of this text and article.

76.   St. Thomas Aquinas, *Commentary on the* de Trinitate *of Boethius*, q. 5, a. 4, reply, p. 42.

77.   Id., pp. 42–43.

78. Id., q. 5, a. 3, reply, p. 78.

79. Id., q. 6, a. 2, reply to 5, pp. 71–72.

80. Id., q. 6, a. 3, reply, pp. 75–77.

81. Id., q. 6, a. 1, reply, p. 74.

82. Armand A. Maurer, *On Being and Essence*, 5, p. 52; "Introduction," *Commentary on the* de Trinitate *of Boethius, Questions V and VI. St. Thomas Aquinas: Division and Methods of the Sciences*, p. XXXV, n. 50.

83. Aquinas, *Commentary on the* de Trinitate *of Boethius*, q. 5 a. 4, reply, p. 78.

84. Aristotle, *Metaphysics*, Bk. 12, ch. 1, 1069a30–1069b3.

85. Aquinas, *Commentary on the* de Trinitate *of Boethius*, q. 5, a. 1, reply, PP. 6–9.

86. Aquinas, *Commentary on the Metaphysics of Aristotle*, vol. 1, Bk. 4, l. 2, n. 563.

87. Id., Bk. 6, l. 2, nn. 1175–1176.

88. Crowley, *Aristotelian-Thomistic Philosophy of Measure and the International System of Units (SI)*, pp. 25–47, 249–260.

89. Aquinas, *Commentary on the Metaphysics of Aristotle*, vol. 2, Bk. 6, l. 2, nn. 1172–1189.; see, also, Armand A. Maurer, "The Unity of a Science: St. Thomas and the Nominalists," *St. Thomas Aquinas*, 1274–1974, *Commemorative Studies*, 2 vols. (Toronto: Pontifical Institute of Mediaeval Studies, 1974), vol. 2, pp. 269 and 271.

90. Aristotle, *Metaphysics*, Bk. 5, ch. 6, 1016b44–1019a; Bk. 10, ch. 4, 1055a4–1055a32; Aquinas, *Commentary on the Metaphysics of Aristotle*, vol. 1, Bk. 3, l. 8, n. 432 and Bk. 5, l. 10, n. 898 to l. 12, n. 935.

91. Aquinas, *Commentary on the Metaphysics of Aristotle*, Bk. 6, l. 2, nn. 1175–1176.

92. Aristotle, *Metaphysics*, Bk. 10, ch. 1, 1052a1–1053b,; ch. 4, 1055a4–1055a32; Aquinas, *Commentary on the Metaphysics of Aristotle*, Bk. 5, l. 2 and l. 3; Bk. 10, l. 2, nn. 1920–1960; Bk. 10, l. 5, nn. 2024–2026.

93. Aristotle, *Metaphysics*, Bk. 10, ch. 4, 1054a1–1055a. Aquinas, *Commentary on the Metaphysics of Aristotle*, Bk. 4, l. 1, n. 561; Bk. 10, l. 4, nn. 1999–2000.

94. Aristotle, *Metaphysics*, Bk. 10, ch. 1, 1052b15–19.

95. Aquinas, *Commentary on the Metaphysics of Aristotle*, vol. 2, Bk. 10, l. 2, n. 1952.

96. Aristotle, *Metaphysics*, Bk. 10, ch. 1, 1053a24–27.

97. Id., 1053a32–1053b3.

98. Id., 1052b20–27.

99. Id., Bk. 14, ch. 2, 1088a15–1093b30.

100. Id., Bk. 10, ch. 1, 1053b4–9.

101. Aquinas, *Commentary on the Metaphysics of Aristotle*, vol. 2, Bk. 10, l. 2, n. 1953.

102. St. Thomas Aquinas, *On the Unity of the Intellect against the Averroists*, trans. Beatrice H. Zedler (Marquette: Marquette University Press, Medieval Philosophical Texts in Translation No. 19, 1968), Ch. 1, # 29, p. 34; see Aristotle, *Physics*, 194b11–12.

103. Id., Bk. 4, l. 2, nn. 561–563.

104. Charles B. Crowley, *Aristotelian-Thomistic Philosophy of Measure and the International System of Units (SI)*, pp. 25–47, 249–260.

105. Aquinas, *Commentary on the* de Trinitate *of Boethius*, q. 5, a. 3, reply to 3, p. 35.

106.   Redpath, "Presecipt," in Crowley, *Aristotelian-Thomistic Philosophy of Measure and the International System of Units (SI)*, p. xiii.

107.   Aquinas, *Commentary on the Metaphysics of Aristotle*, vol. 1, Bk. 5, l. 15, n. 978.

108.   Aristotle, *Metaphysics*, Bk. 5, ch. 1, 1013a1–24.

109.   Id., Bk. 10, ch. 1, 1052b32–1053a23; Aquinas, *Commentary on the Metaphysics of Aristotle*, Bk. 5, l. 1, n. 749.

110.   Aristotle, *Metaphysics*, Bk. 5, ch. 12, 1020a18–1020b12; Aquinas, *Commentary on the Metaphysics of Aristotle*, Bk. 5, l. 15, n. 981, and l.16, n. 998.

111.   Aquinas, *Commentary on the Metaphysics of Aristotle*, Bk. 5, l. 15, n. 982.

112.   Id., l. 18, nn. 1038-1039; Aristotle, *Metaphysics*, Bk. 5, 16, 10212b12–1022a3.

113.   Aquinas, *Commentary on the Metaphysics of Aristotle*, Bk. 5, l. 18, n. 1037.

114.   Aristotle, *Metaphysics*, Bk. 10, ch. 1, 1020a25–33; Aquinas, *Commentary on the Metaphysics of Aristotle*, Bk. 5, l. 15, n. 984.

115.   St. Thomas Aquinas, *Summa theologiae*, q. 1, a. 42, ad 1. See also, *Summa theologiae*, 1–2, q. 52, a. 1, c. For a more extensive treatment of the notion of virtual quantity in Aristotle and Aquinas, see Crowley, *Aristotelian-Thomistic Philosophy of Measure and the International System of Units (SI)*, pp. 25–47, 249–260.

116.   St. Thomas Aquinas, *Summa theologiae*, 1, q. 1, a. 7, respondeo.

117.   Aquinas, *Commentary on the* de Trinitate *of Boethius*, q. 5, a. 3, reply to 3.

118.   Aquinas, *Commentary on the Metaphysics of Aristotle*, vol. 1, Bk. 5, l. 14 nn. 962–965.

119.   Aristotle, *Metaphysics*, Bk. 10, ch. 14, 1055a33–1055b18.

120.   Id., Bk. 5, ch. 14 1020a33-1020b25; Aquinas, *Commentary on the Metaphysics of Aristotle*, vol. 1, Bk. 5, l. 16, nn. 987–999.

121.   Aristotle, *Metaphysics*, Bk. 5, ch. 14, 1020b18–25.

122.   Aquinas, *Commentary on the Metaphysics of Aristotle*, vol. 1, Bk. 5, l. 16, n. 998.

123.   Aristotle, *Metaphysics*, Bk. 4, ch. 1, 1003b11–19; Aquinas, *Commentary on the Metaphysics of Aristotle*, Bk. 5, l. 1, nn. 534–544.

124.   Aristotle, *Metaphysics*, Bk. 14, ch. 1, 1087b38–42.

125.   Id., Bk. 10, 1, 1052b19–1053b8; Aquinas, *Commentary on the Metaphysics of Aristotle*, vol. 2, Bk. 10, l. 2, nn. 1937–1960.

126.   Id.

127.   Aristotle, *Metaphysics*, Bk. 5, ch. 14, 1020b26–1021a14; Aquinas, *Commentary on the Metaphysics of Aristotle*, Bk. 10, l. 2, n. 1008.

128.   Id.

129.   Aquinas, *Commentary on the Metaphysics of Aristotle*, Bk. 10, l. 2, n. 1008.

130.   Aristotle, *Metaphysics*, Bk. 10, ch. 4, 1055a33–1055b3.

131.   Id., 1056a10–30.

132.   Aquinas, *Commentary on the Metaphysics of Aristotle*, vol. 2, Bk. 10, l. 7, nn. 2059–2074. For extensive analysis of the way contemporary physical scientists use the equal as a measure, see Crowley, *Aristotelian-Thomistic Philosophy of Measure and the International System of Units (SI)*, pp. 27–28.

133.   Aristotle, *Metaphysics*, Bk. 10, 1, 1052b19–1053b8; Aquinas, *Commentary on the Metaphysics of Aristotle*, vol. 2, Bk. 10, l. 2, nn. 1937–1960;; Bk. 10, l. 2, n. 1008; Crow-

ley, *Aristotelian-Thomistic Philosophy of Measure and the International System of Units (SI)*, p. 28.

134.   Aristotle, *Metaphysics*, Bk. 5, ch. 10, 1018a9–1019b9.

135.   Aquinas, *Commentary on the Metaphysics of Aristotle*, vol. 1, Bk. 1, l. 3, nn. 53–68; see, also, *Summa theologiae*, 1–2, q. 42, a.4, ad 5.

136.   Aristotle, *Metaphysics*, Bk. 10, ch. 1. 1052b32–1053a23; ch. 4, 1055a33–1055b3; 1056a10–30; 1056b5–30.

137.   Plato, *Phaedo*, trans. Hugh Tredennick, in Edith Hamilton and Huntington Cairns (eds.), *The Collected DialoguesIncluding the Letters* (New York: Pantheon Books, Bollingen Series 71, 1966), 79C.

138.   Mortimer J. Adler, "The Great Conversation Revisited," in Robert McHenry (ed. in chief)), *The Great Conversation: A Reader's Guide to the Great Books of the Western World* (Chicago, fifth printing, Encyclopaedia Britannica, Inc., 1994), p. 27.

Seven

CONCLUSION

1. What I did in the previous six chapters of this book, and why

I devoted the previous six chapters of Volume One of this study chiefly to recovering our understanding of the nature and Western history of philosophy and science from the ancient Greeks up to St. Thomas. I did so because, without a proper grasp of the nature of philosophy and science, and their history in the West up to, and subsequent to, Aquinas, ending the separation between wisdom and science is not possible.

The separation between wisdom and science that started centuries ago is a root cause of the subsequent separation among wisdom, philosophy, and science that presently exists in the West. This separation, however, first started with attempts made by early medieval Jewish and Christian thinkers *to separate wisdom from philosophy and to reduce the whole of wisdom to revealed theology.* The separation was facilitated by the fact that the understanding of philosophy's nature that had prevailed among leading thinkers of antiquity like Socrates, Plato, Aristotle, and Plotinus did not take a foothold during the Christian middle ages. Instead, a distorted understanding of philosophy that confounded this subject with one or more of the liberal arts and revealed theology tended to dominate the middle ages up until the time of St. Thomas.

Within the preceding chapters of this book, I think I have been able, more or less, to restore the proper understanding of philosophy's, science's, nature as the ancient Greeks and St. Thomas conceived this study. What remains for me to do now in this book is to show how, after the death of St. Thomas, by (1) depersonalizing philosophy and (2) reducing philosophical activity to systematic logic, Western intellectuals increasingly attempted to dismantle the unity of philosophy, science, and wisdom that St. Thomas had restored. By doing these things, they prepared the ground for René Descartes to reduce all truth, science, philosophy, and wisdom to an act of will-power, Jean-Jacques Rousseau to reduce metaphysics to a utopian-socialist hermeneutic for reading history, and later thinkers to identify all science with mathematical physics. The last thing I must do is to give a summary of what more needs to be done completely to reunite wisdom to science, philosophy, in the West.

2. The separation of philosophy, science, and wisdom after the death of St. Thomas

While the separation between philosophy and science proximately started with René Descartes in the seventeenth century, the remote intellectual foundation for this separation happened at the tail end of the middle ages in the work of William of Ockham (b. 1287; d. 1347). More remotely it goes back to the teaching of double truth held by Latin Averroists, not Averroes, within the faculty of Liberal Arts at the University of Paris during the thirteenth century.

As Armand A. Maurer has noted, the understanding of philosophy as a "body or system of knowledge" originated in the thought of the nominalists of the late thirteenth and early fourteenth centuries. "Its chief theoretician and popularizer," Maurer said, "was William of Ockham."[1]

Crucial to notice about this event is that, initially, nominalists did not do this by getting rid of the notion that science is a habit of mind or by relocating science in the human will. They did so by eliminating intellectually-independent forms as part of the formal object of the habit of a science, by eliminating intelligible natures or essences from reality. Hence, Maurer added:

> Once the nominalists eliminated intelligible natures or essences from reality a new explanation for the unity of a science had to be found. For Ockham, the object of science is no longer the real world but the propositions we form about

it. Corresponding to each demonstrated proposition there is a scientific habit in the intellect. There are 'partial sciences' which can be integrated into a 'total science,' such as physics or metaphysics, by the logical interconnection of the terms of the scientific propositions.[2]

To distinguish Ockham's teaching from that of Aquinas, and to set the record straight about precisely what St. Thomas had taught about science's nature, Maurer claimed that, during the thirteenth century, Thomas had gotten from Aristotle a quite different understanding of philosophy or "science as a stable *habitus* . . . of the intellect. As such it is an intellectual virtue, a perfection of the mind acquired by repeated acts enabling its possessor to demonstrate truths through their causes or principles."[3]

Maurer said that, for St. Thomas, "each science has its own formal object, whose unity gives unity to the science."[4] By this, Maurer did not mean that the formal object is something that gives unity to science by being passively viewed by a habit. In a complete sense, the formal object of a science is a being produced in and through the intellectual habits of conceiving and judging as a result of the intellectual act of abstraction (dematerialization) completely assimilating the being known, through the senses and imagination, to immaterial conditions of intellectual knowability.

As a result, strictly speaking, *the habit as essentially related to what necessarily activates it as an active intellectual power of the intellectual soul accounts for the unity of a science.* A formal object is only a formal object through an essential relation to a faculty or habit that it activates. Hence, as Maurer rightly noted, "The habit is the principle by which (*principium quo*) the scientist demonstrates all his conclusions and establishes an order among them. Without this one *habitus* there would be no systematic unity in the activities and conclusions of the scientist."[5] The unity of a science, he maintained, chiefly comes from the unity of the habit, not from the multitude that is considered through the habit.

Strictly speaking, while what Maurer said is close to being "on the money," more than anything else, the unity of the relation of a multitude to numerically-one habit established by the chief aim of the habit essentially related to the chief aim of the human intellect, not the unity of the habit, is the chief cause of the unity of science and of a science. For the chief aim of the habit as related to the chief aim of the intellect is what generates the consequent relation that establishes the habit's generic and specific unity.

Essentially a habit is the principle of a relation that arises from a habit's nature as a quality of the intellectual soul. A quality is a principle of relation through which a substance generates modes of unity and opposition through which a substance acts and is acted upon. While the members of the multitude that relate to the numerically-one habit do so unequally, the common and necessary relation of the many to one and the same habit (the necessary relation of a many to a one) transforms them from being members of a disconnected multitude into parts (terms, limits) of a whole (order, relation). *This also explains why the language of science, philosophy, must be analogy, not univocity, like that of the logician.*

While the terms of the relation (the numerically-one habit and the multitude) are essential elements of the resulting order, like the general who is the head of an army, the chief aim of the habit in uniting the chief aim of the whole to the chief subject of the habit establishes a common, and unequal, relation among the multitude to the habit from which the generic and specific unity of the whole in relation to parts arises. This common, universal relation, which transforms the multitude into parts of a generic and specific whole and the generic and specific whole into a general and specific order of parts, is the chief cause of the unity of any science or of science considered as a whole. Prior to the existence of this common relation, no generic or specific part/whole unity exists. And this is the chief unity upon which scientific unity depends.

For example, since the chief aim of the habit of firefighting and of its highest fire chief is the practical aim of the whole fire department (extinguishing fires), as a genus, firefighting is practical. Without this chief aim of its highest habit of organization distributed throughout all its members, no individuals can become part of a firefighting organization, and none of their acts can be specifically those of fire-fighters.

Be this at it may, by the end of the middle ages, scholars had not assimilated St. Thomas's teachings about the proper way to unify sciences. To some extent, this was because, on the third anniversary of St. Thomas's death (07 March 1277), at the encouragement of the Pope John XXI (Peter of Spain, b. ca. 1215; d. 1277), Bishop of Paris Stephen Tempier (d. 1279) condemned 219 propositions related to teachings by faculty members at the University of Paris. While this famous Condemnation of 1277 was chiefly aimed at the Latin Averroist movement in the undergraduate faculty of the University, which had sought radically to separate truths of revelation from those of reason (radically to separate revealed faith and natural reason), one of what Ralph M. McInerny has called the "great ironies" of the Condemnation was that it condemned several propositions held by St. Thomas (who had taught in the graduate faculty of theology). [6]

As Étienne Gilson has said, an effect of this irony was that, if animosity had not been the chief cause of the dispute, it was one of its consequences. "Theologians became increasingly suspect of the activities of philosophers, and there was subsequently a tendency for the theologian to pursue his proper effort in growing independence from philosophical speculation. The reverse side of the coin, of course, was the tendency of philosophers who were also believers to ignore the relevance of their faith to their philosophizing."

The attacks on St. Thomas were mainly spearheaded by "a large group of conservative and Augustinian theologians, who triumphed in 1277, but could not suppress the reading of Aristotle or any other pagan philosopher." Pope John XXI was one of them. He largely interpreted the universe in an Augustinian way and considered dialectics (logic) to be the first of all the arts. His book *Summu-*

lae logicales was on the list of university readings for more than three centuries.[7]

Not being able to suppress reading Aristotle's works, some Augustinian theologians, even some Dominicans, worked to reinterpret St. Thomas and Aristotle in such a way as to create what Gilson has called an Aristotle "not contrary to faith." Gilson saw this Condemnation of 1277 as the historical point that brought the golden age of medieval scholasticism to an end. In so doing, it helped generate the humanist movement of the Italian renaissance.[8]

Teachers of the liberal arts and theologians opposed to the Arabized Aristotle of Averroes saw this Condemnation as a clarion call to unseat from Christian culture Aristotle and Averroes, and any vestige of Greek or Arabic necessitarianism that might limit the freedom and power of God. The Franciscans John Duns Scotus and Ockham were early leaders of this movement.

Later they would be joined by Italian humanists like Francesco Petrarcha, who attempted to neutralize the influence of Aristotle by studying other pagan authors, like Plato. Eventually these humanist thinkers came to recognize that the ancient Greek philosophical notion of "form" was a depersonalized metamorphism of a pagan god. Hence, following Ockham's lead, but in their own way, they increasingly sought to remove every vestige of form, secondary cause, from the physical world. *God and only God was to become from their time on the only agent in the created universe.*

Once we recognize precisely what constitutes the unity of the sciences, precisely understanding how to destroy this unity becomes simple. While St. Thomas Aquinas appears to have been the only thinker during the middle ages who understood in a highly-developed way in what the unity of the sciences, philosophy, consists, theologians who wanted to destroy that unity, even without understanding St. Thomas's teaching, easily grasped how it could be wrecked: break or change the real foundation of the terms of the relation between the scientific habit and the extra-intellectual ground of its scientific subject.

By the start of the Italian renaissance in the fourteenth century, by eliminating the necessary relation of a numerically-one habit to a multitude of facultatively-independent acts that generate the habit, nominalism destroyed the real foundation of human and scientific relations between the individual knower and intellectually-independent beings. In the process, it eliminated the real scientific universal, the scientific genus: the habit's common relation to the multitude of beings that cause it to know them and to the chief aim of the human intellect: human happiness.

A formal object of a science is only the scientific formal object of a scientific habit through an essential relation of the formal object to an intellectual faculty and habit of an intellectual soul that it activates. The nominalists broke this relation by moving the form of the scientific object, the known essence, from being intellectually-independent to becoming intellectually-dependent being. They replaced real natures, real principles (sensible substances and their intrinsic accidents, properties) with intellectual propositions (logical premises). In so doing, they reduced philosophy, which popularly went by the pejorative name "scholasticism" at the time, to a nominalistic logic, something it has, more or less, remained until this day.

The new unity of the sciences dominated by nominalistic Aristotelian logicians promoted by the Augustinians (a kind of systematic habit of logic) was only able to remain in ascendancy for a short time, until petty academic jealousies once again generated a new Battle of the Arts among Italian humanists. Poets and rhetoricians would now fight this battle against Aristotelian logicians (another member of the classical trivium) and Latin Averroists.

To help in this effort some Italian rhetoricians and poets (humanists) revived the fight among members of the liberal arts that had started in the ninth century about which of these arts was truly philosophy. In so doing, they were reviving the ancient Greek fight among poetry, rhetoric, and philosophy (that had put Socrates to death and had driven Aristotle out of Athens) regarding which one of these three disciplines was true science, true philosophy.

To assist in this effort, as I showed in the first chapter of this book, humanists deconstructed philosophy's history so that the poet, not the nominalist logician, would become the true, philosopher, scientist. This ideological history interpreted philosophy, science, to be a hidden teaching, an esoteric body of knowledge, that ancient poets had sought to preserve and protect from being falsified and destroyed by "the vulgar" by supposedly burying it in poetic works and hermetic writings. As a result, only the hermeneutical reading ability of poets could properly decipher its message. Properly speaking, only poets could be real philosophers, real scientists.

For a couple of centuries during the Italian renaissance, poetry and rhetoric would unseat the neutered Aristotelian logic of the nominalists as the queen of the sciences, replacing it with poetic theology. By the tail end of the Italian renaissance, however, the wondrous work of Galileo Galilei, which, among other things, combined nominalistic, Aristotelian logic and mathematics, would replace poetry with mathematics as the queen of the sciences and the sole measure of natual wisdom.

By fundamentally altering the understanding of human nature that, from the time of the ancient Greek philosophers until the sixteenth century, had dominated Western culture, a century before Galileo, through his attack on the trustworthiness of human reason, the Augustinian monk Martin Luther (b. 1483; d. 1546) had laid foundations for a new attack against the notion of philosophy being a mental habit and for diminishing the stature of any kind of philosophical wisdom. In its place, Luther had put the view of the person held by ancient sophists like Thrasymachos and the "might makes right" teaching of ancient Greek demagogues like Callicles. Unwittingly, the work of Galileo contributed to this diminishment of subsequent trust in natural reason and natural human wisdom.

This relation between Luther and the ancient Greek sophists is no accident. It arose within him as a result of his fascination with nominalism. Like Poryphry before him, and all human beings, Luther could only think the way he could, not the way he wished. As a result, he allowed the metaphysical problem of universals to help him misunderstand human nature and knowledge.

As Gottfried Wilhelm von Leibniz (b. 1646; d. 1716) has told us, in agreement with Gregory of Rimini (b. ca. 1300; d. 1359), Gabriel Biel (d. 1495), and "the majority of the Augustinian Order," Luther's early writings "reveal an affection for nominalism." Leibniz added that almost all the modern philosophical reformers of his time "were nominalists" and that, with the passage of time, nominalism started "to influence all the monks." Leibniz claimed that reports of the origin of "the sect of nominalists" attribute that origin to Roscelin, who, together with his followers, supposedly maintained that individuals alone are real, rejected the reality of universals, and considered universals simply to be names (*nomina*).[9]

Like Leibniz, contemporary "philosophers" falsely-so-called tend to tie nominalism's origin to Roscelin (b. ca. 1045; d. ca. 1120). They also tend to claim that nominalism was a medieval "philosophy." Both claims are false.

Nominalism arose with the ancient Greek sophists, with thinkers who, like Protagoras, claimed that "man is the measure of all things." Like Protagoras before them, those coming after these sophists think they say something intellectually lofty when they claim that universals originate in the mind.

Nominalism is not a philosophical teaching, or claim. It has never been one. It is, and always has been, a sophistic claim. It is a sophistic fallacy, apologetic, about the nature of human knowing that its proponents mistakenly pose in the form of ideas. It claims that universal ideas that exist in the mind have no principle from which the human mind derives these ideas in reality. Its proponents propose it in an attempt to justify their intellectually meaningless claim that "man is the measure of all things."

The contemporary prevailing understanding of the problem of universals is not correct because, strictly speaking, this problem is chiefly about judgments, not ideas. Considered simply as such, ideas have no universality or non-universality. Considered simply as an idea (as John N. Deely, faithfully following St. Thomas, well says), an idea is a psychological quality that has the ontological status of a sign vehicle, a term within a sign relation. In and of itself, a sign has no universality or non-universality.[10]

Centuries ago, St. Thomas Aquinas solved the problem of universals by recognizing that universality arises in the human intellect and outside the human intellect as a result of relations, not as a result of universal ideas in the mind or universal forms or essences in things. In the mind universality arises from universal predication, from judging a multitude of predicates to be predicable of (relatable to) numerically one subject. Outside the intellect, universality arises from the relation of a numerically-one subject (like the Sun) or a habit of soul (like the art of music) unequally distributing its operation (the heat of the Sun, or the act of music) to a multitude, or in a multitude of ways.

The problem of universals as sophists propose it in their defense is meaningless because it makes all opinions, including contradictory ones, equally true. If this is the case, nothing any human being says can be definite. Nothing can be definitely true or false. If that is the case, then the claim that "nothing we say is definite" says nothing definite, is meaningless.

The whole of modern and contemporary philosophy, science, rests upon this principle of sophistry. By so doing, the whole of modern and contemporary philosophy, science, is meaningless.

If human reason is totally depraved, no possibility exists for it to possess science through its own natural faculty or acquired habits. If science exists anywhere in a human being, it could only do so in the human imagination as a gift of grace. In a Lutheran *qua* Luther interpretation of human knowing, naturally-acquired, intellectual habits are useless for the acquisition and exercise of science.

Worse, they are pernicious. Hence, in his 1520 "Appeal to the Nobility of the German Nation," Luther railed against Aristotle, declaring, "any potter has more knowledge than . . . these books [of Aristotle, which] . . . I can only believe . . . the devil has introduced .

. ... His book on Ethics is the worst of all books. It flatly opposes divine grace and all Christian virtue."[11]

Luther could accept the infused virtues of faith, hope, and love entering and leaving the human soul in an instant through possession or loss of the grace of the Holy Spirit. He could not tolerate naturally-acquired virtues of the soul that were generated, maintained, and lost over time through habitual practice. Hence, the propensity of modern thinkers who have been influenced by Luther to replace the notion of habit with "spirit" or regulated spiritual train (intellectually blind train of feelings): "system."

Because Aristotle was the chief source of the philosophical teaching about natural virtues and habits, Aristotle haunted Luther like the ghost of Banquo haunted Macbeth. These natural habits, virtues, simply had to go. While Luther could not drive Aristotle out of Athens, he did the next best thing. He tried to drive his ghost out of Western culture.

Following Luther's lead, as I have shown in detail in my book, *Cartesian Nightmare: An Introduction to Transcendental Sophistry*, in the seventeenth century, Descartes would reduce all science, philosophy, wisdom and truth to will-power and almost entirely destroy Western confidence in the notion of science as a habit of soul.[12] As this attack to remove philosophy, science, as a habit of the soul was growing, under the new aegis of mathematics, the *quadrivium* would solidify its capture of the throne of queen of the sciences. Descartes contributed to Luther's project and to the destruction of the unity of the sciences by going beyond eliminating habits of the soul. He removed faculties of soul, too. More, he removed the traditional notion of soul from the human person, deconstructing the soul into mind, which he conceived as a nominalistic system of ideas, or revelations.

Not long after he had done this, a new movement, spearheaded by Cartesian Augustinians like Nicolas Malebranche (b. 1638; d. 1715) initiated a fight aimed at totally purging the human mind of remaining connection between the mind and extra-mental forms. In the mind of these thinkers, Descartes had not gone far enough. While he had removed habits from the human mind, through clear and distinct ideas, he had still left some direct access of the human mind to some external forms. He had still left a trace of form in the physical universe directly knowable to a trace of capacity in the human mind to know form.[13]

Since Descartes had not totally destroyed direct communication between the substance called the human mind and the substance called physical forms, Malebranche decided to make this move for him by placing God between the human mind and physical forms. God would become the great communicator between mind and matter and, therefore, the only being that could, strictly speaking, unify the sciences.

Unhappily for Malebranche, as Étienne Gilson told the story, the Anglican priest George Berkeley (b. 1685; d. 1753) happened to be waiting on Malebranche while the Frenchman was ill. Inadvertently, apparently, Berkeley wound up increasing the poor man's illness and precipitating his death via metaphysics by indicating to Malebranche an implication quite unattractive to the French priest. What need exists for a material world if the direct object of the human mind, including that of matter, is an idea? God can put an idea of a physical being into the human mind whether or not a physical being actually exists independently of the human mind.[14]

Berkeley, however, had not counted on secularized Augustinians like Jean-Jacques Rousseau, David Hume (b. 1711; d. 1776), and Thomas Hobbes (b. 1588; d. 1679) coming along and conceiving of disconnected multitudes of ideas or feelings, with or without God, building themselves into a scientific social system unified by a social mind or general will-to-power. Nor could he envision the grandiose idealist architectonic of Immanuel Kant, the neo-gnostic spiritualism of Georg Hegel, or the system of necessary historical and economic relations of Karl Marx.

In short, having lost all the principles of science within an individual human knower, the secularized Augustinians of modernity made some slight modifications within the traditional Augustinian model of knowing to accommodate uniting the sciences by means of a collectivist human knower, a historical social system. In the teaching of St. Augustine human knowledge, "philosophy," "science," is chiefly faith seeking understanding. Within Augustine's noetic, after introductory prayer, human reason moves immediately from experience of intellectual conflict with an external sense object to interior memory and intellect, from consideration of lower kinds of forms to higher ones, until illumination from God (Eternal and Immutable Being) helps resolve the conflict being experienced by restless reason.

In the modern Enlightenment model, no external forms exist. Neither does any hierarchy of forms, any mystery, or even an individual human intellect or soul. Hence the natural order of perfection of human minds cannot be one of an individual mind from lower forms to higher ones. Modern and contemporary, secularized Augustinians solve this problem by reducing all scientific human reason to social reason, to a social system, and all human knowing, philosophy, to a historical movement of opposites from recollection of the past to projection into the future.

In such a secularized version of Augustine (what I call "Augustine in Drag"), Sir Francis Bacon's utopian City of Man replaces God. And philosophy becomes a historical narrative and project in which the social system comes to progress in scientific self – awareness through increasingly Enlightened attacks on essentially backward religions, especially on Catholicism, Evangelical Protestantism, and Judaism.[15]

A great benefit that accrues to contemporary "philosophers" falsely-so-called in this understanding of "philosophy" is that, as essentially secularized Augustinian theologians, secularized Catholics, Protestants, and even Jews, can continue to fight the centuries-old Battle of the Arts under the pretext of being philosophers, scientists. That is, they can hide the theological roots of these disputes as they pretend to be "above" and "beyond," too Enlightened to engage in, such debates.

Moreover, being largely ignorant of Western intellectual history, many of these poor secular, fundamentalist souls unwittingly fabricate history in terms of a utopian political project. Then, in light of this fantasy, they sincerely fight intellectual battles without realizing that they are simply repeating theological conflicts that have been going on for centuries, many of which were resolved long ago. In so doing, they resemble Don Quixote attacking windmills.

Centuries ago, in the desire to be left alone from the intrusion of people who called themselves "metaphysicians" and "theologians" into their attempts to do independent research, mathematicians and physicists lost their understanding of the essentially architectonic nature of human science, philosophy. In the attempt to liberate themselves, they made the egregious mistake of identifying their habits of study with the whole of science. Worse, not wanting to subordinate their disciplines to any higher intellectual authority, they unwittingly became philosophical bastards who generated the socialist state to which they subsequently became slaves.

3. What work still needs to be done to solidify the reunion of wisdom and science, and science and philosophy, that this book has initially established

Over centuries, dating back to the start of Christianity, some Western intellectuals began a move to separate wisdom from philosophy, science. Presently, the West is reaping the fruits of that successful separation and is near civilizational collapse. In the preceding pages I have detailed how this separation arose. In brief, this happened in the following way:

(1) Before the start of Christianity ancient Greek thinkers had largely lost their understanding that philosophy, sci-

ence, is chiefly a philosophical habit involving the study of the problem of the one and the many.

(2) What passed over into the Christian middle ages under the rubric of philosophy was a distorted understanding of philosophy that generally conflated philosophy, science, with the liberal arts mixed with revealed theology: faith seeking understanding through the practice chiefly of the *trivium*.

(3) Before the start of the middle ages, some Jewish and Christian thinkers had sought to separate wisdom from philosophy, science.

(4) By the tail end of the middle ages, St. Thomas Aquinas had started to realize precisely Aristotle's teaching about the nature of philosophy, science, and that the prevailing medieval understanding of philosophy's nature was wrong.

(5) In studying Aristotle, among the things Aquinas discovered were that philosophy's unity and scientific nature essentially depend upon (a) pursuit of wisdom as the highest human science; (b) accepting the existence of God, the human soul, and human habits; (c) accepting philosophy to be chiefly the act of a habit of the intellectual soul that starts in sense wonder and ultimately terminates in first philosophy, the science of metaphysics.

(6) After the death of Aquinas and the 1277 condemnation of Latin Averroism, Ockhamistic nominalism, renaissance humanism, Galileo, Luther, and Descartes, and their Enlightenment followers (especially Rousseau) contributed to separating the classical understanding of the human person and substances known by a person from being essential principles upon which the unity of philosophy, science, and their connection to wisdom essentially depend.

(7) While, by attacking human reason as essentially depraved, Luther contributed to the West's subsequent distrust of natural human reason, science, philosophy, and
wisdom, by replacing human faculties and the human
soul with a mind and relocating all truth, science, philosophy, and wisdom in the human will, Descartes conflated philosophy, science, with systematic logic and located all truth, science, philosophy, and wisdom within
will-power

(8) Under the influence of Rousseau and his progeny, over
the past several centuries, the West has: (a) progressively
separated science and philosophy and, during the twentieth century, reduced philosophy to the realm of opinion,
not science; (b) identified science with the Enlightened,
utopian, socialist will-to-power (a neo-Averroistic, socialist intellect attempting to generate scientific unity
through class unity supposedly generated through the
historical emergence of progressively-Enlightened utopian projects and the hermeneutic of tolerance); (c) attempted *metaphysically* to account for the nature and
unity of science by means of propagandistic intellectual
history (social science: the history of the human spirit's
exercise of its will-to-power, freedom, progress); (d) reduced the whole of science of the universe (the hand-
maiden to contemporary utopian, socialist metaphysics
[social science]) to mathematical physics (natural history: mathematical reading of the physical universe).

Having explained precisely the nature of "philosophy," "science," truly-so-called, and its essential connection, to natural human
wisdom in its highest form (philosophical metaphysics, first philosophy), in the preceding chapters of this book I think I have, beyond
reasonable doubt, re-established the essential connection between
science and philosophy, and of both of these with wisdom. Having

done so, we are now in a position to provide a general outline of how to reverse the decline in Western civilization that these have produced and give a blueprint to solidify the reunion of science, philosophy, and wisdom that this book has established. To do so, as Gilson has told us, we must find God and ourselves again by once again getting in touch with sense reality without the help of technology, mathematical physics, and the utopian, socialist state.

Since the separation of philosophy and science, science and wisdom, was chiefly effected by destroying the classical, philosophical, unity of the person as a psychosomatic whole naturally possessed of faculties capable of acquiring natural habits, restoring the unity of the sciences essentially involves reestablishing the classical philosophical unity of the person. This involves doing three things: (1) Making sensible being the facultatively-independent starting point of human knowing; (2) reintegrating the human soul, knowing faculties, and human habits into subjective starting points, principles, of the bodily knower; and (3) relating the knowing subject and the intellectually-independent content of this knower in such a way as to able to generate a formal object for a numerically-one habit of science that essentially contributes to the chief natural aim of an intellectual soul: human happiness.

In short, we need to re-personalize science, philosophy, by showing, at least in general, how, even today, in all divisions of science, philosophy, the (1) individual knower that naturally aims at becoming happy, the soul/body composite, is a first principle of science, philosophy, wisdom and (2) that the physical content the individual knower understands is an intellectually-independent nature.

Since St. Thomas Aquinas already did all these things in detail in his own time, the way completely to end the continued separation between philosophy and science, science and wisdom, is simply to (1) revive, in a way suitable to our time, St. Thomas's teachings about the nature of the human person, human knowing, and the unity of the sciences and (2) show how, by so doing, we can help practitioners of contemporary "philosophy, "science" falsely-so-called improve their understanding of precisely what they do and why they do it.

The time has come for contemporary mathematicians and physicists, and other individuals who pride themselves in assuming the title "scientist" and "philosopher" to liberate themselves from servitude to utopian socialism and the cultural destruction it is currently producing. The contemporary world is too dangerous for serious intellectuals to tolerate such intellectual slavery to continue. It is time for such "intellectuals" completely to end the depersonalization of science and separation of mathematics and physics from true science and wisdom and end the unnecessary separation between "philosophy" falsely-so-called and "science" falsely-so-called that continues to this day. In Volume One of this project, I have initiated the end of this separation. In Volume Two, with the help of St. Thomas, I hope to be able to strengthen the unity this work has initiated.

NOTES

1.   Armand A. Maurer, "The Unity of a Science: St. Thomas and the Nominalists," in Armand A. Maurer (ed.-in-chief), *St. Thomas Aquinas, 1274–1974, Commemorative Studies*, 2 vols. (Toronto: Pontifical Institute of Mediaeval Studies, 1974), vol. 2, pp. 269 and 271.

2.   Id., p. 291.

3.   Id., p. 271.

4.   Id., p. 272.

5.   Id., p. 273

6.   Ralph M. McInerny, *A History of Western Philosophy*, Volume 1. *From the Beginnings of Philosophy to Plotinus* (Notre Dame, Ind. and London, England: University of Notre Dame Press, 1963), p. 346.

7.   Etienne Gilson, *History of Christian Philosophy in the Middle Ages* (New York: Random House, 1955), pp. 246–247.

8.   Id., p. 471.

9.   Id.

10.   John N. Deely, *Four Ages of Understanding: The First Postmodern Survey of Philosophy from Ancient Times to the Turn of the Twenty-first Century* (Toronto, Buffalo, London: University of Toronto Press, 2001), p. 463.

11.   Brian P. Copenhaver and Charles B. Schmitt, *Renaissance Philosophy* (Oxford and New York: Oxford University Press, 1992), pp. 38–39.

12.   Peter A. Redpath, *Cartesian Nightmare: An Introduction to Transcendental Sophistry* (Amsterdam and Atlanta: Editions Rodopi, B.V., 1998).

13.   For a detailed analysis of the Western "philosophy" falsely-so-called from the Cartesians to Hegel, see Peter A. Redpath, *Masquerade of the Dream Walkers: Prophetic Theology from the Cartesians to Hegel* (Amsterdam and Atlanta: Editions Rodopi, B.V., 1998).

14.   Etienne Gilson, *Unity of Philosophical Experience* (New York: Charles Scribner's Sons, 1965), pp. 194–195

15.   For a detailed critique of Enligtenment "philosophy" as secularized Auguttinian theology see Peter A. Redpath, *Masquerade of the Dream Walkers: Prophetic Theology from the Cartesians to Hegel* (Amsterdam and Atlanta: Editions Rodopi, B.V., 1998). For Bacon's specific role is transforming "philosophy" into a kind of secular utopianism see Piotr Jaroszyński, *Science in Culture* (Amsterdam and New York: Editions Rodopi, B.V., 2007).

ABOUT THE AUTHOR

Peter A. Redpath is a presently Rector of the Adler-Aquinas Institute (www.adler-aquinasinstitute.org), tutor at Harrison Middleton University, Tempe, Arizona, managing editor of the Philosophical Book Series and executive editor of the Adler-Aquinas Institute Special Series in Philosophy for the Socratic Press. Former Full Professor of Philosophy at St. John's University, Staten Island, New York, Redpath has taught philosophy on the college and university level for over forty-four years, plus courses at the Staten Island, Arthur Kill Correctional Facility and New York City's Riker's Island. He is author/editor of 11 philosophical books and dozens of articles and book reviews; has given over 200 invited guest lectures nationally and internationally; is president and co-founder of the International Étienne Gilson Society; co-founder and vice president of The Gilson Society, former vice-president of the American Maritain Association, Chairman of the Board of the Universities of Western Civilization and the Angelicum Academy home school program; a member of the Board of Directors of the Great Books Academy home school program; a member of Board of Trustees of the Institute for Advanced Philosophic Research; a member of Board of Directors and Executive Committee of the Catholic Education Foundation; Academician of The Catholic Academy of Sciences in the United States of America; former executive editor of Value Inquiry Book Series (VIBS) for the Dutch publisher Editions Rodopi, B. V.; former editor of the Studies in the History of Western Philosophy special series for Editions Rodopi and current editor of the Gilson Studies special series for the same publisher; former associate editor, and current advisor of the journal *Contemporary Philosophy*; a recipient of St. John's University's Outstanding Achievement Award; a distinguished alumnus of Xaverian High School; a Fellow of the Priority Thinking Institute; and former Graduate Fellow at the SUNY at Buffalo. He currently resides with his wife, Lorraine, in Cave Creek, Arizona.

INDEX